Storytelling and Education in the Digital Age

Matteo Stocchetti (ed.)

Storytelling and Education in the Digital Age

Experiences and Criticisms

PL ACADEMIC RESEARCH

Bibliographic Information published by the Deutsche Nationalbibliothek
The Deutsche Nationalbibliothek lists this publication in
the Deutsche Nationalbibliografie; detailed bibliographic
data is available in the internet at http://dnb.d-nb.de.

Library of Congress Cataloging-in-Publication Data
Names: Stocchetti, Matteo, editor.
Title: Storytelling and education in the digital age : experiences and criticisms / edited by Matteo Stocchetti.
Description: Peter Lang : Frankfurt am Main, 2016.
Identifiers: LCCN 2016027466| ISBN 9783631675441 | ISBN 9783653069761 (E-Book)
Subjects: LCSH: Digital storytelling. | Education--Effect of technological innovations on.
Classification: LCC LB1042 .S817 2016 | DDC 372.67/7--dc23 LC record available at https://lccn.loc.gov/2016027466

ISBN (Print) 978-3-631-67544-1
E-ISBN (E-PDF) 978-3-653-06976-1
E-ISBN (EPUB) 978-3-631-70126-3
E-ISBN (MOBI) 978-3-631-70127-0
DOI 10.3726/978-3-653-06976-1

PL Academic Research is an Imprint of Peter Lang GmbH.

Peter Lang – Frankfurt am Main · Bern · Bruxelles · New York ·
Oxford · Warszawa · Wien

This publication has been peer reviewed.

www.peterlang.com

Preface

This volume is the second book-length publication of the research programme Media and Education in the Digital Age – MEDA.

MEDA is an interdisciplinary programme whose main goal is to support the circulation of critical knowledge about the educational role of digital technology. It should be clear that MEDA does not promote the use or the rejection of digital technology. Rather, it promotes a critical attitude towards the values, goals and, ultimately, pedagogical projects that inspire its usages in education. In this endeavour, MEDA shares many of the assumptions, interests, intellectual goals and conceptual tools of the critical traditions that pay attention to the changes affecting education as part of a larger reflection on the nature and direction of social change.

The notion of 'critical' that inspires the work and ambitions of MEDA includes at least three features: First, an explicit attention to the relations of power implied, reproduced, challenged or otherwise associated with the uses of digital technologies in education. Second, sensitivity towards the idea that the study of social phenomena is not detached from but very much part of and actually influential upon the phenomena investigated. Finally, the normative commitment to the idea that improvement in education should be defined in relation to a notion of the 'individual' as a value in herself and independently from other configurations instrumentally associated with this notion in the economic, political or religious domains.

In this volume the focus is on the impact of the digitalisation of education (the 'digital turn') on the educational role of storytelling. While the importance of this role can hardly be overestimated, the impact of digitalisation is more ambivalent. The contributors take a critical stance towards the alleged emancipative affordances of digital storytelling in education. The collection is inspired by the effort of making professional educators aware of the risks of the digital turn in educational storytelling but also of the opportunities and the conditions for critical engagements. Based on research and field experience, fifteen scholars discuss in nine chapters these risks and opportunities, providing ideas, evidence, references and inspiration to educators and researchers.

Also this project has been supported by the following friends and colleagues towards whom I gladly acknowledge a debt of gratitude: Belinha De Abreu (UNESCO Communication & Information Section), Ana Bermejillo Ibanez, (Universidad CEU San Pablo), Emiliano Blasco Doñamayor (Universidad CEU San Pablo), Claudio Franco (University of Bedfordshire), Kjetil Sandvik (University of Copenhagen), Sultana A. Shabazz (University of Tennessee), Karen Ferreira-Meyer (University of

Swaziland), Raine Koskimaa (University of Jyväskylä), Paul Mihailidis (Emerson College and Salzburg Academy on Media & Global Change), Rebecca Renatus (Technische Universität Dresden). Thanks also to Sami Rouhento for his precious help. Last but not least, the publication of this volume has been made possible also thanks to funding provided by the Fonden för Teknisk Undervisning & Forskning.

Notes on the Contributors

Cristina Aliagas-Marín (PhD) is a Postdoctoral Researcher in the Faculty of Education at Universitat Autònoma de Barcelona. Her interests in research encompass Ethnography and Digital Literacies. She researches on matters of literacy, youth culture, identity and digital reading/writing practices. Within this broad area, her publications cover a variety of topics: digital literacies in children's and youth life, the interface between digital literacies and the curriculum, and the role of digital literacies in curriculum innovation and change. Among her publications, she has recently published, with her colleague Ana María Margallo, the study "iPads, Emergent Readers and Families" in M. Manresa and N. Real (Eds.), *Digital Literature for Children* (2015, Peter Lang).

Greg Curran (PhD) is an English as an Additional Language (EAL) Teacher, and a Lecturer in Education at Victoria University, in Melbourne, Australia. His academic expertise encompasses literacy, EAL methods, health promotion, e-learning and education philosophy. His most recent academic publication is 'Are you Married: Exploring the Boundaries of Sexual Taboos in the ESL Classroom' in the publication, *Disrupting Pedagogies in the Knowledge Society: Countering Conservative Norms with Creative Approaches*, edited by Julie Faulkner (2012). Greg's teaching interests include media production to build literacy skills, e-learning, and student voice and agency especially as it relates to social justice related issues. Greg regularly writes for his education-related blog at PushingTheEdge.org. He also hosts and produces a podcast titled 'Pushing The Edge with Greg Curran' that focuses on innovation and social justice in education. Greg can be contacted at gcurran@iname.com.

Vincenzo De Masi (vdemas@gmail.com) is currently a Lecturer and Assistant Professor in Art and Media Technology at New York Institute of Technology (Beijing Campus at Communication University of China). He obtained his PhD at the University of Zurich and Lugano with a dissertation on creative industries focused on Chinese animation. His interests focus on three areas of inquiry: analysis of creative industries policy and strategy in creative economy in Asia, Culture and Media Studies, and Conceptual Art and its relation to New Media. He has written several articles and papers about that, and a book focusing on the Chinese animation industries is going to be released. www.vincenzodemasi.com

Tracey Leigh Dowdeswell is an attorney and a PhD candidate at Osgoode Hall Law School. She studies the applicability of the laws of war to counter-terrorism and counterinsurgency operations, focusing mainly on the Middle East region. She has recently published a critique of American and British reconstruction efforts in Iraq with her colleague Patricia Hania, as "Regulating Water and War in Iraq: A Dangerous Dark Side of New Governance" (2014)21:2 Indiana Journal of Global Legal Studies, Vol. 21, No. 2: 453–482.

Esin-Orhun Simge, is continuing her academic career as an Assistant Professor in the Communication Design Program at Özyeğine University. She obtained her Bachelor's Degree in 1995, Master's Degree in 1998 and PhD in 2007 in Architecture. She is running research projects, courses and publications relating to spatial communication, information architecture and design education. Her research interests focus on interactive exhibiting, design education, spatial communication in public spaces and interaction design ergonomics. Her academic work and achievements can be accessed at http://simgeesin.com

Julie Faulkner is a senior lecturer in the Faculty of Education at Monash University, Melbourne. She writes on matters of literacy, popular culture, identity, and digital reading and writing practices. Her research supervision includes intercultural communication pedagogies, critical reading practices, curriculum design and video games, such as *Minecraft*, as powerful learning environments. She has edited *Disrupting Pedagogies in the Knowledge Society: Countering Conservative Norms with Creative Approaches* (IGI Global), and has jointly authored *Learning to Teach: New Time, New Practices* (Oxford University Press), currently in second edition.

Nachshon Goltz is an academic, entrepreneur and lawyer. Nachshon teaches law at York University, he is the co-founder and editor in chief of Global-Regulation.com, the world's largest search engine of legislation and related regulatory documents, and is licensed to practise law in Israel and Canada. Nachshon is completing his PhD at Osgoode Hall Law School, York University (Canada), and earned his LLM in law and technology from Haifa University (Israel), LLB from the Academic Center (Israel) and a BA (Psyc.) from Haifa University (Israel). With Tracey Dowdeswell, he is currently writing a book, "The Imaginationless Generation" (forthcoming).

Gloria Gomez-Diago (PhD) has a postgraduate degree in Pedagogy from the University of Vigo. Her research combines theoretical and practical perspectives on research methodologies in communication research, virtual communication, and the uses and applications of online platforms such as virtual worlds. Among her latest publications are "Communication in crowdfunding online platforms" (2015) in Nelson Zagalo and Pedro Branco (eds.): *Creative Technologies: Create and Engage Using Art and Play.* London: Springer Verlag, and "The role of shared emotions in the construction of the cyberculture. From cultural industries to cultural actions. The case of crowdfunding" (2016) in Sharon Tettegah (ed.): Emotions, *Technology and Social Media*. Elsevier.

Yan Han is currently a PhD candidate in Animation and Digital Arts at the Communication University of China. She holds a Master in Animatronics from the Communication University of China. She published *The Key Points of Developing Innovative Talent in Animation Education* in China Animation Yearbook 2013 and *The Study on Creativity Loss of Chinese Cartoon Industry Basing on the History of Shanghai Animation Film Studio* in an essay collection of China Doctoral Forum of Digital Innovation Art in the New International Media Age in 2014. Her research interest is in original Chinese animation films. She has developed a great passion for animation and also made an animated short film.

Ana M. Margallo (PhD) is a lecturer in the Faculty of Education at Universitat Autònoma de Barcelona. Her research focuses on the teaching/learning of literature. Her publications follow several lines of inquiry: the ways through which the school project approach affords children and young people to become competent readers, how to choose literary works for pedagogic purposes and the integration of literature in classrooms for supporting the learning of new-coming immigrant students. More recently, she has been interested in media literacy, social practices and school practices in digital environments, resulting in publications such as the following one, co-authored with her colleague Cristina Aliagas, currently in press in the Wiley journal *Literacy*: "Children's responses to the interactivity of storybook apps in family shared reading events involving the iPad".

Nathalie Hyde-Clarke (PhD) is Head of the Department of Culture and Communication at Arcada University of Applied Sciences, and a Docent in Media and Communication at the University of Helsinki. She has a strong interest in representation in news media, particularly as it pertains to African communities in the global media. She has also published a number of academic articles based on her teaching and learning experiences at the tertiary level. Her most recent publication on this topic is: Hyde-Clarke, N. 2013. Facebook and Public Debate: an Informal Learning Tool for the Youth. *Journal of African Media Studies 5(2):* 131–148.

Anne Katrine Nørgaard Isholdt is employed at VUC Storstroem, an adult educational centre in Denmark. She works as a pedagogical IT consultant, supporting the teachers' use of ICT and working with strategic development involving ICT. Her areas of special interest are learning games, game development for students, video-based teaching and virtual learning environments. She is collaborating with a researcher in the areas of blended learning, innovative teacher development and game-based learning, but personally, she is not currently conducting research. Furthermore, she participates in networks and projects involving scenario-based e-learning and game-based learning in the adult educational sector.

Susana Tosca is Associate Professor of Digital Aesthetics at the IT University of Copenhagen. Her PhD dissertation, a poetics of hypertext literature, was awarded the summa cum laude distinction in 2001. She has worked on electronic literature for many years, the storytelling potential of computer games, and complex reception processes, with a side interest in fan activity and the distributed aesthetic formats of the Web 2 era. She is the author of Understanding Videogames, third edition (Routledge, 2016).

Matteo Stocchetti is a Docent in Political Communication at Åbo Academy, Docent in Media and Communication at the University of Helsinki and Principal Lecturer in Critical Media Analysis at Arcada University of Applied Sciences in Helsinki, Finland. He is the main coordinator of the programme Media and Education in the Digital Age – MEDA. His research and teaching work is inspired by critical approaches to communication, education and media. Among his recent publications is Stocchetti Matteo, (2015) 'Making Futures: The Politics of Media Education'. In Kotilainen S. and Kupiainen R. (eds.): *Media Education Futures.* Nordicom: Clearing House Göteborg, pp. 183–193.

Niklas Tarp-Petzke is a graduate from the IT University of Copenhagen and Goldsmiths University London. He is currently employed as a communications consultant at HOFOR (Greater Copenhagen Utility), working with strategic communications and social media. His areas of special interest are digital network structures, surveillance society, remediation as a translator within critical media studies, and social media. He is part of a research network called Open System Association (http://opensystem.org.uk/about/).

Table of Contents

Matteo Stocchetti

The Politics of Education and the Digital Turn in Storytelling: A Critical Introduction

Abstract Storytelling is an activity with important social and political functions. The digital turn in education affects the educational functions of storytelling in ambivalent ways. While the emancipative affordances of this turn are given much visibility in academic and corporate discourse, the risks are neglected. Education and storytelling are influential practices in the social construction of reality. The uncritical endorsement of the digital turn in storytelling, however, makes education vulnerable to the influence of technocentrism and its myths. The ideas that images "have power", that digital community can compensate for the isolation of the individual and that the digital "revolution" brings about the "end of history" and politics are influential manifestations of these myths. The possibility for the digital turn in education and storytelling to open up emancipative opportunities depends on the extent to which educators are aware of and able to develop countermeasures against the oppressive tendencies associated with technocentrism and its myth. The chapters in this collection aim at supporting the efforts in this direction.

1. The Politics of Education, the Functions of Storytelling and the Problem of Control

The politics of education is a key dimension in the competition for control over the future of society. For the actors participating in this competition, mastering the functions of storytelling is both crucial and elusive. It is crucial because storytelling is the activity through which the meaning of the world and the social world itself are created. It is elusive because storytelling is everywhere, present in numerous forms and shapes, public and private, and mediated and non-mediated communication.

The dual and perhaps contradicting nature of storytelling functions poses a very practical problem for those forces in society that are in apprehension of the intrinsic capacity of storytelling's meaning-generation ability to subvert existing relations of power. The political ambivalence of this capacity reflects the broader ambivalence of education: necessary but dangerous. The question of control is rooted in this ambivalence and in the efforts to resolve the uncertainty it generates in one direction or another.

In much of the relevant literature, digital storytelling is credited with all the functions of traditional storytelling in addition to the alleged virtues of digital technology. The potential of this combination seems to exceed the mere sum of its parts. In this chapter I discuss the power of storytelling and the implications of the "digital turn" separately, in order to avoid confusing the two. Clarifying this confusion is especially important because it helps to avoid the intrinsic attribution of the emancipative properties of storytelling to digital technology while disclosing the ideological implications of the digital turn in the politics of education.

By changing the rituals associated with the practices of storytelling, *the digital turn frames the role of storytelling in education within the myths associated with digital technology and, in doing so, enforces the performative control of digital institutions on the subversive potential of the culture, if not the content, of storytelling itself.*

It may be a good idea to start by discussing the power of storytelling, its fundamental ambivalence and the problem of control that it implies. Among the most effective and, in a sense, most radical cases for the power of storytelling is still that made by Jerome Bruner when he claimed that reality itself is constituted through narrative form (Bruner, 1991: 5). All other functions commonly attributed to storytelling, including its pedagogical functions, are in fact included in the idea that narratives are the tools through which reality itself, as accessible to humans, is constructed.

If the idea of the "narrative construction of reality" sounds too generic to underscore the problem of control, one should consider that most of the relevant practices to establish, reproduce or subvert relations of power are based on and are intelligible through storytelling of some sort.

The broad notion that storytelling is essentially about sense-making points, for example, to a variety of communicative practices with important political implications such as the legitimisation of political power, the construction and manipulation of the symbols of collective identity, the interpretation of history and collective memory, the social construction of truth etc.

Justification, for example, is a particular form of sense-making through storytelling: an explanation with strong moral elements that perform important emotional and cognitive functions at individual and collective levels. Painful personal experiences need to be made sense of to deal with their emotional implications but also with the rational need to control the possibility of their occurrence in the future. At the collective level, events that can seriously undermine the integrity of the community also need justification. The best examples that come to my mind are the narratives of war casualties, especially in the Great War, and the narratives of economic "austerity" deployed in Western Europe since 2008. The justification of war casualties usually contains the idea that the sacrifice of so many young lives has not been in vain. This is obviously easier for the societies of those states that won the war. But the idea of sacrifice in these narratives also contains normative values that stretch into the future: from the sacrifice of the past into the lives of the present and the possibility of their sacrifice in the future (Mosse, 1990). More recently, the economic crisis triggered by the financial speculation in the US has been made sense of through narratives of sacrifice similar to those used in war, but ones in which democracy seems to be the first casualty: a luxury that the European citizen may not be able to afford anymore (Silva & Escorihuela, 2013: 1–8).

When wars or other dramatic events occur that may undermine social cohesion, institutions may engage in "authoritative sensemaking" through forms of storytelling that reduce public anxiety but also reassert the integrity of social institutions that the crisis may undermine, through myths that depoliticise the crisis (Brown, 2004: 95–112).

The concept of legitimisation usually describes the form of justification involved when political power is at stake. The legitimisation of the forms of authority described by Max Weber – traditional, charismatic and legal-rational – is grounded in narratives of one form or another. It is through these narratives that traditions, charisma and law itself become influential in the daily lives of people. In practice, to legitimise the power of some individuals, groups or institutions means to justify their power but also, and maybe this is the distinctive content of this concept, to issue an implicit claim about the rightfulness of the concrete manifestations of this power in the future.

In the critical tradition, Walter Benjamin's ideas about the importance of storytelling and the politics of truth are probably among the most influential in contemporary research. Narges Erami, for example, uses Benjamin's essay *The Storyteller* to deploy a metaphorical linkage between carpet making and storytelling in support of the case for the ethnographic and "experiential" significance of the latter (Erami, 2015).

Inspired by the same essay, in addition to the works of Kierkegaard, Jung, Heidegger, Bruner and others, Patrick J. Lewis juxtaposes research and storytelling in a passionate plaidoyer for the value of the latter in human life in general and teaching in particular (Lewis, 2011: 505–510).

Annabel Herzog argues that Hannah Arendt's ideas about political storytelling and the "redemptive power of narrative" (Benhabib, 1990) were inspired by Benjamin's notion of storytelling as interpretation and the relation that, through this notion, connects history to those who experience it (a collective) through storytelling (Herzog, 2002: 89). The emancipative function of storytelling emerges quite clearly in both Benjamin and Arendt's endorsement of the idea that the truth that can be passed on by the storytellers is the

> point of view of the defeated and the dead … the story told by those who have experienced the events and who, by virtue of this very fact, cannot tell and will never be able to tell any story. (Herzog, 2000: 15)

In this account the power of storytelling consists in the recovery of a "destructive standpoint" which "dissociates the linearity of the victors' commemoration and wrecks conformist historical narrative" (Herzog, 2000: 15).

If storytelling is the activity that can recover the truth of those who are denied the power of objectivity, one may appreciate with a certain dose of irony, the idea that even the authority of science needs narrative support.

Jean-Françoise Lyotard famously argued about the importance of narrative legitimisation of truth in the practices of scientific enquiry to ground its thesis about the "incredulity towards metanarratives" that, in his view, is the distinctive trait of the "postmodern condition" (Lyotard, [1979] 1982: xxiv). In relation to our discussion, I would argue that this "condition" is not one in which storytelling has lost its power but rather one in which performativity or "legitimization by power" (Lyotard, [1979] 1982: 45–48) signal a fundamental change in the nature of the dominant "grand narrative": a new story in which "truth" is replaced by "operativity" as the leading criterion inspiring the quest for reliable knowledge (Lyotard, [1979] 1982: xxv). From the perspective of Benjamin and Arendt's notion of political storytelling, one may therefore argue that, in the postmodern condition, storytelling may constitute the "destructive standpoint" from which modern science can resist performativity and legitimation by power – a point that unfortunately I cannot address in this chapter.

In sum, all forms of political power need the support of storytelling: the process through which the grounds, values and beliefs on which these forms are based are established and re-actualised in the community. There is no engagement with storytelling that is not directly or indirectly, explicitly or implicitly associated with relations of power. However, storytelling is also the activity through which all forms of power can be challenged, or delegitimised and the 'magic' of storytelling can work in different ways. Whether we like it or not, to deal with storytelling is to deal with an important process in the establishment, preservation, challenging and subversion of relations of power. And it is because of this intrinsic ambivalence that the discussion about the political functions of storytelling is always, in one way or another, a discussion about the *control* of these functions. The ambivalence intrinsic in the affordances of storytelling constitutes the problem of control as the fundamental problem associated with this activity because *it is the very power and ambivalence of storytelling that prompts the effort to control this form of communication.* If we restrict the discussion about the virtues of storytelling in education to the power of storytelling, without looking at the forces that inside and outside the educational arena are competing to control this power, we make ourselves, educators and learners vulnerable to these forces. If scientific research is incapable or unwilling to broaden the scope of its attention to capture this dimension and to make a credible case about the nature of the risks involved, it will fail its mission.

In a critical perspective, the main goal in educational storytelling is first of all to make people aware of the fact that the ambivalent nature of the power of storytelling supports influential efforts to control its subversive potential in education and elsewhere. Other critical competences, such as recognising the moral and social implications of alternative stories, assessing the impact of particular stories on particular relations of power, and even the capacity to create stories that can effectively support a more emancipative social order, depend on this awareness.

2. The Digital Turn

If the emancipative or subversive potential of storytelling is already, albeit ambivalently, embedded in storytelling, and this very potential is at stake in the politics of education and, more broadly, in the competition for the control over the distribution of values in society, what is the impact of the digital turn on this state of affairs? My suggestion here is that this 'turn' can be interpreted in relation to the problem of controlling the productive capacity of storytelling through the repression of its radical potential. This is where digital technology enters our story.

At least some of the important functions usually associated with storytelling pertain not only to the "story", for example, in Jonathan Gottschall when he discusses the role of story as "a counterforce to social disorder, the tendency of things to fall apart" or "the center without which the rest cannot hold" (Gottschall, 2012: 138), but also to the "telling". Intuitively, an "untold" or uncommunicated story is a non-story. What this means is that whatever storytelling can do depends not only on the features of the story but also on the conditions of the "telling": the nature of the relations in which storytelling occurs as a communicative event and that the event itself contributes to reproduce, or subvert. The case for the importance of this dimension was famously made by James W. Carey in his discussion of the "ritual view of communication" (Carey, 1988: 14–22). The importance of these rituals is discussed, for example, by Nick Couldry in relation to the symbolic power of television to keep alive the "myth of the centre" (Couldry, 2003: 36–54). Even more radically, Marshall McLuhan's renowned phrase "the medium is the message", which lends the opening chapter of *Understanding Media* (McLuhan, 1964) its title, expressed the idea that the main story in the media is always, albeit implicitly, about the media themselves. In this way he argued convincingly for the kind of shift in attention from issues of content to the capacity of new media to change the nature of relations in society. Neil Postman made a similar point even more explicitly, in relation to the educational role of computers:

> What we need to consider about the computer has nothing to do with its efficiency as a teaching tool. We need to know in what ways it is altering our conception of learning, and how, in conjunction with television, it undermines the old idea of school … New technologies alter the structure of our interests: the things we think about. They alter the character of our symbols: the things we think with. And they alter the nature of community: the arena in which thoughts develop. (Postman, 1993: 19–20)

From this point of view, the movement from traditional to digital storytelling implies a movement from one set of rituals to another. The problem I am discussing here is to understand the implications associated with the rituals enforced by the digital turn. To ask this question is important because the idea that digital storytelling has all the goodies of storytelling plus the bonuses of digital technology is a philistine simplification. To neglect the changes brought about by the digital turn in the rituals, relationships and ultimately "power" of storytelling is a form of reductionism that endangers the critical assessment of this "turn" in education.

To put it otherwise, the problem is not only to assess the impact of more or less dramatic changes in the quantity or quality of information that can effectively be embedded in digital stories, but also that of understanding the implications, changes and continuities in the relationships involved. Particularly significant among these is the relation between storytelling and its legitimising functions and the forms of power associated with the "digital turn". The idea that digital storytelling makes it easier to produce and circulate "immersive" stories, thereby increasing the "power" of the Author, hides the enormous complexity of the digital infrastructure, the variety of political conditions, actors, negotiations, interests, struggles etc. supporting it, and ultimately the magnitude of the social change associated with its effects.

In traditional storytelling, the relationship between the "teller" and her audience is probably the most salient one. In the digital age, however, an equally if not even more salient relation is that between the human and the digital interface or, more precisely, between the human motives that establish the narrative relation and the infrastructural constraints (ideology, interests, conditions of use etc.) that transform storytelling into a productive activity and stories in textual objects that can be produced, promoted, circulated, consumed etc. In these circumstances, it seems to me, issues relating to the possibility of emancipative changes in content may be no more relevant than issues pertaining to changes in the rituals associated with the digital turn in storytelling.

Among its supporters, digital storytelling seems to be considered a new educational tool and one that is useful for emancipative purposes. Enthusiasts are fascinated by the attributes of appeal and "circulability" of digital storytelling and seem to believe that, because of these, digital storytelling can credibly perform as critical pedagogy: one that could enable the excluded and marginalised voices to be heard and, consequently, to support political inclusion. Sceptics, however, point to problems that have more to do with access and implementation than with the ideological and pedagogical implications of the digital turn in storytelling.

According to Gregori-Signes, for example, "digital story is a genre that allows students to work both individually and in group to produce a critical opinion about a conflicting social issue" and "multimodality should receive the same attention that we give to reading and writing" (Gregori-Signes, 2014: 247).

Rina Benmayor acclaims digital storytelling as "a signature pedagogy for the New Humanities in the 21st century" (Benmayor, 2008: 201) for its formidable pedagogical, political and even theoretical power enabling students to

> bring their own cultural knowledge and experience to the fore … to transform their thinking and empower themselves …[to] encourage historically marginalized subjects, especially younger generations, to inscribe emerging social and cultural identities and challenge unified cultural discourses in a new and exciting way …To demystify theory and … to become theorizers of their own historical and cultural experiences. (Benmayor, 2008: 200)

More critical formulations point to a variety of problems. For Robert Clarke and Andrea Adam, for example, the actual assimilation of digital storytelling into students' curriculum may be more complicated than some of the enthusiastic supporters are ready to acknowledge. Problems include

> the time required to undertake such projects, the necessity of training for teachers; the importance of alignment with curricula goals; the need for clearly articulated goals and structures; the importance of awareness of the emotional sensitivities of students; the problems associated with access to digital hardware and software; and the challenges of appropriately assessing individual digital storytelling projects. (Clarke & Adam, 2010: 173)

This kind of criticism, however, underestimates the performative power of the technological infrastructure and the "complex underweave of power at play in the digital mundane" (Beer, 2009: 999), especially when this all applies to storytelling in education.

For example, recent research suggests that, in the digital environment of social media, the practices of storytelling are vulnerable to the "capitalist regime of time" (Fuchs, 2014) and to self-representation strategies that ultimately reflect the sense-making role of technological platforms (De Ridder, 2013: 370).

A convincing argument in support of the emancipative potential of digital storytelling must first decouple the potential of storytelling from the changes associated with the digital turn. As I argued in this section, the political potential of storytelling is ambivalent, and an important question is to understand if the changes introduced by the digital turn can resolve this ambivalence in an emancipative or oppressive direction. The relevance of the educational functions of digital storytelling is a reflection of the functions of traditional storytelling. The digitalisation of these functions is a process with ideological and political implications that cannot be ignored. In the next section I will look into these implications from the point of view of the myths associated with digital technology.

3. Storytelling and Digital Mythologies: Images, Community and Revolution

My analysis of the digital myth here is inspired by Roland Barthes' *Mythologies* (Barthes, [1957] 2000) and Vincent Mosco's analysis of cyberspace as a mythic space (Mosco, 2004). Through this analysis I intend to offer a few propositions as a preliminary interpretative framework to understand how the digital turn may bring about the repression of the emancipative potential of storytelling in education.

First, myths are a special kind of story. The first proposition is that myths are stories but of a special kind. They appear as timeless and authorless, effectively hiding their origins as part of the charm which endows them with some sort of everlasting wisdom. While the significance of every story can be established in relation to particular events, spaces, time, authorship etc., a myth is a story whose significance resides in the indeterminacy of the same elements. This is one preliminary reason why, as Barthes suggested,

> myth does not deny things … it purifies them, it makes them innocent, it gives them a natural and eternal justification, it gives them a clarity which is not that of an explanation but that of a statement of fact. (Barthes, [1957] 2000: 143)

A myth is productive of other stories. A second and related proposition is that myth is a story of a special kind also because it establishes the symbolical grounds for the intelligibility of other stories that keep the myth itself alive. As such, a myth is the source of "magic" from which the "magic" of storytelling depends. In this capacity myths establish meanings that, albeit implicitly, support the intelligibility of other stories. The dependence of these stories from the story-myth however reproduces the fundamental symbolical elements of the latter whenever the former are communicated. From this perspective, myths are not "true or false" but "living or dead" (Mosco, 2004: 29) depending on their productivity: their capacity to generate, inspire, instigate and encourage new stories.

Myths have a special relation with truth. As sense-making devices, the social influence of myths does not depend on the correspondence between the mythic and the empirical event(s) since, in fact, "myths persist in the face of powerful evidence that they do not accurately embody an underlying reality" (Mosco, 2004: 49). Myths do not tell an empirical or verifiable truth. But they tell no lies either. Rather

> they give meaning to life, particularly by helping us to understand the seemingly incomprehensible, to cope with problems that are overwhelmingly intractable, and to create in vision or dream what cannot be realized in practice. (Mosco, 2004: 14)

In their capacity as interpretative framework, "attractive vision or template of perception" (Mosco, 2004: 49) supporting specific forms of engagement with problematic aspects of the world, a myth is a narrative device to preserve beliefs, together with the principles, values and the relations of power associated with them, from the erosive effects of time and social change. Mosco appropriates Barthes' notion of myth as "depoliticized speech" arguing that

> this conception of myth as living, meaningful story is particularly powerful because it suggests why people embrace it even in the face of otherwise compelling contrary evidence. Myth does not embody a truth, it shelters truth by giving it a natural, taken-for-granted quality. (Mosco, 2004: 29–30)

Myth in bourgeois society is depoliticised speech. While Mosco adopts Barthes' notion of myth as depoliticised speech, one should not forget that Barthes coined this notion as a "semiological definition of myth in a bourgeois society" (Barthes, [1957] 2000: 143) to describe the strategy of the bourgeoisie in the ideological competition with the revolutionary forces in society:

> The bourgeoisie hides the fact that it is the bourgeoisie and thereby produces myth; revolution announces itself openly as revolution and thereby abolishes myth. (Barthes, [1957] 2000: 146)

For Barthes, this myth performs identifiable ideological functions, and there is little doubt that

> statistically, myth is on the right. There, it is essential; well-fed, sleek, expansive, garrulous, it invents itself ceaselessly. It takes hold of everything, all aspects of law, of morality, of aesthetics, of diplomacy, of household equipment, of Literature, of entertainment. (Barthes, [1957] 2000: 148)

The bourgeoisie and capitalism rely on myth to present as eternal what is contingent and as natural what is social. Myths legitimise beliefs to be believed not because they are true but – especially when they are not true – because they are necessary to preserve the credibility of values, visions, identities, hermeneutic frameworks and the relations of power associated with them – e.g., a certain idea of France to justify French imperialism or, in our case, a certain idea of the digital to enforce technocentrism in education. Myths are therefore stories performing the legitimisation of relations of power by hiding the political dimension of these relations: the competition for power, the uncertainty of the struggle before it is won by one of the parties and ultimately the vulnerability of relations of power to the possibility of social change. In this perspective, the important contribution of Mosco consists in revealing how the myths of the "digital sublime" are the functional equivalent of that certain idea of France.

The analysis of myth performs the re-politicisation of speech. The political functions of myth that Barthes and Mosco synthesise with the formula of depoliticised speech result from the cultural productivity of myths and their peculiar relation with truth. This special relation with truth makes the analysis of myth useful to gain a deeper understanding of the aspects of reality that may otherwise be overlooked because they are taken for granted. Mosco suggests that "myths can be understood for what they reveal, for example, the desire for identity and community, but also for what they conceal" (Mosco, 2004: 154).

If myth performs the depoliticisation of speech by naturalising the capitalist order, the critical analysis of myth applied to cyberspace may bring about the re-politicisation of speech as a way "to loosen the powerful grip of myths of the future on the present" (Mosco, 2004: 15).

> If the telling and retelling of the mythic story shields cyberspace from the messiness of down-to-hearth politics, then the critique of the myth, told many times over in many different ways, gives new life to the view that cyberspace is indeed a deeply political space… It is here, on the intellectual border, where cultural and political economic understandings meet, that the analysis of myth becomes particularly productive. (Ibid. 31)

In his argument about the "cyberspace as a mythic space" and the political relevance of the "myths of our time" attached to it, Mosco described three central myths: the end of history, the end of geography and the end of politics (Mosco, 2004: 13–14). In my analysis I look at another set of myths that in my opinion is more relevant to understanding the political impact of the digital turn in educational storytelling: the myth of the "power" of images, the myth of the digital community, and the myth of the digital revolution. More precisely, I argue that the influence of the digital myth

- misconstrues the political role of digital visuality, misplacing the political from the process of interpretation and the user of images to the image itself;

- naturalises the digital community as a political community, neglecting to problematise the nature of the forces it depends on for its existence and of the constraints to its political role that are associated with this dependence; and
- enforces a deceptive, "revolutionary" representation of the changes associated with the digital turn, whereas notions such as the "end of history" and the "end of politics" have fundamentally conservative implications.

3.1 The "power" of images

The mythic relevance of the cyberspace extends to the technological affordances of this space absorbing and giving a new appeal to the myth of the "power" of images. The argument that digital storytelling has superior educational potential because of its visual affordances combines the myths of the digital turn with at least two beliefs associated with the so-called "visual turn". First is the idea that "one image is worth a thousand words" or, put more technically, that images are "living organisms" (Mitchell, 2005: 11) that can "speak to us" (Mitchell, 1980: 3). As I argued elsewhere, giving agency to inanimate objects is a pathetic fallacy with serious ideological implications (Stocchetti, 2011: 11–38). Claiming that images can "want" or "speak" is an apparently innocent figure of speech that legitimises the removal of human agency from the process of sense-making, which is then construed as depending on the image itself: the naturalisation Barthes describes so effectively in relation to the image of the "Negro giving the French salute" (Barthes, [1957] 2000: 116–117). Second is the belief that the power of digital visuality is a revolutionary power: a form of communication that supports democracy and participation by exposing and discrediting the practices of tyrannical regimes. This belief not only underestimates the capacity for resistance of these regimes but, most unfortunately, also simplifies the complexity associated with successful revolutionary efforts and the role of material and immaterial factors such organisation, ideology, leadership etc. (Stocchetti, 2014).

These interpretations of the 'power' of images depoliticise the process through which not only the meaning of images but the meaning of visuality is established. As Walter Benjamin, Guy Debord and, more recently, Jonathan Beller, among others, have argued, this is a most political domain: a place of struggle between competing forces. The recognition of this struggle and the forces involved is repressed because it exacerbates the problem of control resulting from the ambivalent power of storytelling. This is why the emancipative potential of digital storytelling cannot be taken for granted but has to be critically assessed. Neglecting to recognise what remains hidden in the naturalisation of visual meaning makes visual storytelling in education vulnerable to the same forces that Benjamin discussed in relation to the "capitalist exploitation of cinema" (Benjamin, 2008: 33–37), Guy Debord described in his analysis of "the society of the spectacle" (1967) and Jonathan Beller discussed in terms of the "industrialization of the visual" (Beller, 2006: 3–7).

3.2 The digital community

The idea that digital storytelling has (digital) community-building capacity seems to be the newer version of an older myth about the capacity of technological progress to conquer distance in the physical sense but also in the metaphorical one: erasing difference, bridging intellectual or emotional distances, making us "equals" in the fruition of technological opportunities (Mosco, 2004: 117–140). Digital storytelling promises to reconstitute the lost sense of community in the mythic space of cyberspace (Coskie, Trudel and Vohs, 2010: 2–9). This promise contains a moral appeal to democracy, egalitarianism, polyphony (plurality of voices), participation, empowerment of marginalised identities etc., which makes digital storytelling quite appealing especially in education. While this promise effectively voices the hope that a technological infrastructure could not only overcome spatial barriers and distance but most importantly diversity of identity and interests, it also hides the fear that feeds this hope. The appeal of this promise is all the more seductive in the conditions of late modernity, when the dissolution of traditional communities generates new form of precarity which transforms the experience of freedom into an experience of insecurity – a process that Zygmunt Bauman, Ulrich Beck, Anthony Giddens and others refer to as "individuation". The belief in the digital salvation of the community needs to be re-evaluated against the fact that digitalisation is one of the constitutive processes of late modernity. The fears, frustration and alienation associated with this condition feed the need to believe in the egalitarian, participatory and democratic virtues of storytelling. Construed within the coordinates of the digital myths and the end of history and politics, the same fears, frustration and alienation may easily turn to the power of digital narratives for the legitimisation of inequality, exclusion and authoritarianism. The question is then to see if utopia will prevail over dystopia: if the communities of late modernity will be inspired by their hopes more than their fears since, as we know, the power of storytelling is ambivalent.

3.3 Digital Revolution: End of History & Politics

The myths of the end of politics and the end of history converge in the myth of the digital revolution and the faith in the revolutionary potential of digital storytelling – in education and presumably elsewhere. The ideological implications of this myth were already clear in the early stage of this "revolution". Cees J. Hamelink for example, observed that

> in contemporary society – almost worldwide – a powerful myth is being persuasively told by numerous story-tellers. It is the myth of the information society … The tone of the myth is 'computopian': it expects that the application of computer-steered technologies will effectively terminate the social structure which is characterized by an endless struggle between winners and losers, between rulers and ruled. (Hamelink, 1986: 7–8)

The idea that the digital turn in educational storytelling has "revolutionary" capacities, participates in the digital myth evoking and betraying its political significance: it evokes the radical subversion of an established order but betrays the emancipative promise by hiding the conservative, if not reactionary implications of technological determinism. In fact,

> the development of information technology makes centralized control over decentralized activities simpler than ever before … Moreover, the link between information technology and democratization is guided by unwarranted expectations about what machines per se can do. (Hamelink, 1986: 13)

As Robert McChesney's observed in the case of American society, the idea of a revolution brought about almost automatically by technological progress is easily embraced by the "celebrants" of the digital that

> mostly tap into an untethered love of some combination of technology, gadgetry, markets, utopianism, progress, and individualism that is quintessentially American and downright intoxicating; you get the benefit of revolution without the messy of politics. This may explain why it is so widely embraced in the mainstream culture and can be regarded as the dominant mode of thought about the internet. (McChesney, 2013: 12)

The belief that education in digital storytelling is an emancipative practice for subjugated identities, one that makes the power of recognition suddenly available to everyone able to master digital technology reflects the mythical belief that

> the Information Age transcends politics because it makes power available to everyone and in great abundance. The defining characteristic of politics, the struggle over the scarce resource of power, is eliminated. In this respect, myths create a new history, a new time, by denying history. (Mosco, 2004: 35)

By performing a fundamental misconstruing of the nature and working of relations of political power, the myth of digital revolution gains egalitarian connotations that increase its appeal in education and strengthen the incitation to forget the past, embrace the future and challenge the authority of educational institutions and its representatives. The same notion, however, hides the power of the institutions ruling the digital space, the double processes of increased concentration and decreasing liability of corporate power in the digital industry, and ultimately the resilience of capitalist exploitation in late modern societies. In practice, as Mosco noted, "for all its revolutionary potential these myths tend to hide the continuities with the past" (Mosco, 2004: 49).

4. Steps Towards a Critical Engagement with the Role of Digital Storytelling in Education

The digital turn in storytelling is a process that contributes to the normalisation of education in the digital age. This process consists of the suppression of the radical potential of digital media, storytelling and education by framing them all within the coordinates of technocentric discourse. The credibility of this discourse is supported by the informal reproduction of the myths associated with technology in general and digital technology in particular.

The functions of storytelling are politically relevant, and the educational use of storytelling should introduce students to them: to the processes through which meanings, relations, values and indeed the whole reality is socially constructed.

What has changed in the nature and functions of story/storytelling in the movement from the analogue to digital world? Does digital technology introduce some significant difference in the functions of storytelling? And if digital storytelling is indeed a "powerful tool in the 21st century classroom" (Robin, 2008: 220–228), what is the nature or direction of the changes it can bring about? Do they support emancipation? The answer is yes to the important changes and not necessarily to emancipation.

Digital storytelling is not only about delivering stories with other means. Rather is it about changing the way meaning is created and changing the nature of the relationships based on those meanings. Educators need to question the nature and direction of the change brought about in the social creation of meaning by the digitalisation of storytelling.

Digital storytelling takes the functions of storytelling and wraps them up in the technocentric myth. This, like all myths, is a form of depoliticised speech in which storytelling loses its subversive potential. Digital storytelling thus becomes a form of communication that is supportive and reproductive of capitalism, of its cultural logic, of the functional identities, relations of power and transformative tendencies associated with it.

If one keeps in mind the fundamental importance of education in the construction of societal future, and the competition for the control of this future in the politics of education, one cannot disregard the impact of the ideological elements that accompany the digital turn in storytelling. My suggestion is that the digital turn in education may indeed perform the repression of the subversive potential of both storytelling and education by repositioning these activities within the performative reach of the myths associated with technology.

In these conditions it is crucial that critical educators become aware of the risks of the digital turn in educational storytelling. This is a preliminary step to developing forms of educational engagement with digital technology and storytelling that are endowed with credible emancipative potentialities.

The chapters in this collection are inspired by the effort to make educators aware of these risks but also of the opportunities for critical engagements as these emerge for the experience of researchers in this field.

In the next chapter, **Nachshon Goltz** and **Tracey Dowdeswell** discuss the risks associated with the growing use of virtual worlds for children, presenting evidence that this kind of digital storytelling lacks many of the positive aspects of non-digital storytelling, may inhibit the development of imagination in children, and appears to reproduce corporate and commercial narratives and values. While more research is needed in order to determine the long-term effects of virtual worlds on child development, the authors invite caution and suggest that virtual worlds may indeed be an inappropriate educational tool for developing children's storytelling abilities.

Even more radically, **Vincenzo De Masi** and **Han Yan's** report on the Chinese animation industry is an empirical falsification of the belief that the digital turn in storytelling is associated with or strengthens emancipative tendencies in society. At least in that society, the "digital turn" has transformed cultural repression into a productive process while at the same time thwarting dissent and marginalising whatever emancipative functions this 'turn' may have.

Bringing the focus back to Western education, **Nathalie Hyde-Clarke** argues for the educational productivity of storytelling and its usefulness, even without the support of digital technologies. Her experience confirms the idea that the educational potential of this practice is not dependent on the digital infrastructure but rather on the teacher's competence and, ultimately, commitment to creating an engaging learning experience for methodology courses usually "deemed to be boring or a 'necessary evil'"

In the other chapters of this collection, the attention shifts to experiences of more critical use of digital technology in support of practices involving storytelling as a tool or as an educational outcome.

Cristina Aliagas-Marin and **Ana M. Margallo** conduct a microanalysis of the implementation of digital storytelling in an Initial Teacher Education course on literary education. The study highlights the importance of appropriating digital storytelling in each particular educational context, rather than thinking of digital storytelling in education broadly and just applying it generally. This chapter discusses the complexities involved in the process of making sense of digital storytelling in a particular subject, and testifies to the need of empirical educational research analysing the process, challenges and effects of introducing digital storytelling in the classroom across the educational span.

Simge Esin Orhun discusses the effects of the digital turn in design education and argues for the need of revising the traditional approaches in this field. Her chapter describes the Communication Design Program, an educational initiative based on storytelling in which digital media are used to facilitate youth participation in the use of cultural knowledge in the transformation of meanings.

Julie Faulkner and **Greg Curran** report on their experience as educators not only aware of the risks associated with the uncritical introduction of digital technology in education, but also committed to developing its emancipative affordances. In their chapter, they give a closer look to the conditions in which these emancipative affordances may be actualised in the construction of meanings associated with personal identity.

Gloria Gómez-Diago suggests a conceptual shift from storytelling to storymaking, arguing that while the former is based on a linear mode of communication, storymaking describes a communicative environment resulting from a shift in emphasis from investigative and writing skills to new collaborative and participatory skills. In her chapter, the author describes the use of storymaking as an environment for learning in which students can become aware and gain control of conceptual, procedural and tacit knowledge.

Finally, the linkage between critical uses storytelling and critical pedagogy is explicit in the chapter of **Susana Tosca**, **Anne Katrine Nørgaard Isholdt** and **Niklas Tarp-Petzke**. Their chapter recounts an experiment, inspired by Paulo Freire's *Pedagogy of the Oppressed*, in which social media are used as a tool to teach literature in a Danish high school. The authors coined the notion of "social media storytelling" to describe the practice through which a social medium is used as technological infrastructure for role playing – and role playing itself as a participatory approach to a Danish medieval ballad.

References

Barthes, R. ([1957] 2000). *Mythologies* (Annette Lavers, Trans.). London: Vintage.

Beer, D. (2009). Power through the algorithm? Participatory web cultures and the technological unconscious. *New Media & Society 11(6)*: 985–1002.

Beller, J. (2006). *The Cinematic Mode of Production. Attention Economy and the Society of the Spectacle.* Lebanon, NH: University Press of New England.

Benhabib, S. (1990). Hannah Arendt and the Redemptive Power of Narrative. *Social Research Vol. 57, No. 1*, 167–196.

Benjamin, W. (2008). The Work of Art in the Age of Its technological Reproducibility. In Jennings, M., Doherty, B., and Levin, T. (2008). Walter Benjamin: The Work of Art in the Age of its Technological Reproducibility: Writings on Media. (pp. 19–55) Cambridge: Harvard University Press.

Benmayor, R. (2008). Digital Storytelling as a Signature Pedagogy for the New Humanities. *Arts & Humanities in Higher Education 7(2)*: 188–204.

Brown, A. D. (2004). Authoritative Sensemaking in a Public Inquiry Report. *Organization Studies 5(1)*: 95–112.

Bruner, J. (1991). The Narrative Construction of Reality. *Critical Inquiry*: 1–21.

Carey, J. W. (1988). *Communication as Culture. Essays on Media and Society.* Cambridge: Unwin Hyman.

Clarke, R. and Adam, A. (2010). Digital Storytelling in Australia. Academic perspectives and reflections. *Arts & Humanities in Higher Education 11(1–2)*: 157–176.

Coskie, T., Trudel, H. and Vohs, R. (2010). Creating Community through Storytelling. *Talking Points 22(1)*: 2–9.

Couldry, N. (2003). *Media Rituals: A Critical Approach.* Abingdon: Routledge.

De Ridder, S. (2013). Are digital media institutions shaping youth's intimate stories? Strategies and tactics in the social networking site Netlog. *New Media & Society 17(3)*: 356–374.

Debord, G. (1967) *La société du spectacle.* Paris: Buchet-Chastel.

Dush, L. (2012). The ethical complexities of sponsored digital storytelling. *International Journal of Cultural Studies 16(6)*: 627–640.

Erami, N. (2015). Of ladders and looms: Moving through Walter Benjamin's 'Storyteller'. *Anthropological Review 15(1)*: 92–105.

Fuchs, C. (2014). Digital prosumption labour on social media in the context of the capitalist regime of time. *Time & Society 23(1)*: 97–123.

Gottschall, J. (2012). *The Storytelling Animal: How Stories Make Us Human.* Boston: Houghton Mifflin.

Gregori-Signes, C. (2014). Digital Storytelling and Multimodal Literacy in Education. *Porta Linguarum*: 237–250.

Hamelink, C. J. (1986). Is there life after the information revolution? In M. Traber, *The Myth of the Information Revolution* (pp. 7–20). London: Sage.

Herzog, A. (2000). Illuminating inheritance. Benjamin's influence on Arendt's political storytelling. *Philosophy and Social Criticism 26(5)*: 1–27.

Herzog, A. (2002). Reporting and Storytelling: Eichman in Jerusalem as Political Testimony. *Thesis Eleven 69(1)*: 83–98.

Jameson, D. A. (2001). Narrative Discourse and Management Action. *Journal of Business Communication 38(4)*: 476–511.

Lambert, J. (2009). *Digital Storytelling: Capturing Lives, Creating Community 3rd edn.* Berkeley: Digital Diner Press.

Lewis, P. J. (2011). Storytelling as Research/Research as Storytelling. *Qualitative Inquiry 17(6)*: 505–510.

Lyotard, J.-F. ([1979] 1982). *The Postmodern Condition: A Report on Knowledge.* Minneapolis: University of Minnesota Press.

McChesney, R. (2013). *Digital Disconnect. How Capitalism is Turning the Internet Against Democracy.* New York: The New Press.

McLuhan, M. (1964). *Understanding Media: The Extensions of Man.* New York: Mentor.

Mitchell, T. W. (2005). *What do Pictures Want? The Lives and Loves of Images.* Chicago: University of Chicago.

Mitchell, W. J. (*Ed.*). (1980). *The Language of Images.* Chicago: The University Press of Chicago.

Mosco, V. (2004). *The Digital Sublime. Myth, Power, and Cyberspace.* Cambridge: The MIT Press.

Mosse, G. L. (1990). *Fallen Soldiers. Reshaping the Memory of the World Wars.* Oxford: Oxford University Press.

Postman, N. (1993). *Technopoly.* New York: Vintage.

Robin, B. (2008). Digital storytelling: a powerful technology tool for the 21st century classroom. *Theory into practice 47*: 202–228.

Silva, J. F. and Escorihuela, L. A. (2013). Introduction. In J. F. Silva & L. A. Escorihuela *(Eds.), Dictatorship of Failure. The Discourse of Democratic Failure in the Current European Crisis* (pp. 1–25). Helsinki: Helsinki Collegium for Advanced Studies.

Stocchetti, M. (2011). Images: Who gets what, when and how? In M. Stocchetti & K. Kukkonen (*Eds.), Images and Power in the Digital Age* (pp. 11–38). Amsterdam: Benjamins.

Stocchetti, M. (2014). Images and Power in the Digital Age: The Political Role of Digital Visuality. *Kome. An International Journal of Pure Communication Inquiry 2(2)*: 1–16.

Nachshon Goltz & Tracey Dowdeswell

Children's Storytelling in Virtual Worlds: A Critique

Abstract In this chapter, we offer a critique of the growing use of virtual worlds for children, particularly as tools to teach children the basic elements of storytelling: language, narrative, the creative imagination, and generativity in applying learned skills. We argue that virtual storytelling is not like other forms of storytelling, particularly for children, who are still developing these abilities. There is evidence that digital storytelling through virtual worlds lacks many of the positive aspects of non-digital storytelling, and may even inhibit the development of imagination in children. In this chapter, we review the literature on children and virtual worlds, focusing on the importance and development of the creative imagination in children. We discuss the visualization hypothesis – a theory that was developed to explain how television produces a reductive effect on the imagination because it presents the user with ready-made visual images – and generalize it to new media, including virtual worlds. We posit the 'displacement hypothesis', which states that when manufactured content is supplied ready-made to the individual, then it displaces the creative and imaginative processes that the individual would otherwise supply for him or herself. The more immersive the medium, the more psychological dimensions are captured by this displacement – such as sound, the visual, narrative content, time, space, physical presence – the more reductive are the effects on the individual's imagination. We conclude that further research is needed in order to determine the long-term effects of virtual worlds on child development, and that in the meantime virtual worlds are an inappropriate medium for children's storytelling.

Introduction

Virtual worlds – games in which the user interacts with a persistent digital environment through a self-representation known as an "avatar" (Hew and Cheung, 2010: 34) – are a unique form of digital storytelling. Unlike ordinary games, virtual worlds are highly immersive, and create the impression that the user has a good deal of control over their interactions with their virtual environment. Therefore, it might appear at first glance that virtual worlds can become an important tool for children's storytelling, for engaging and teaching children skills in language, constructing narratives, and developing imagination. Indeed, virtual worlds have begun to be used in this manner, even for pre- and primary school-aged children (ibid.). Some scholars, such as Bitarello (2008: 2), argue that virtual worlds have long existed in literature, art, and mythology, and they view virtual worlds as merely an extension of these non-digital forms of storytelling. In this chapter, we challenge this view of virtual worlds, focusing on the negative effects that virtual worlds can have on the development of the creative imagination in young children, and thus on their ability to learn the complexities of language and narrative – the essentials of storytelling. We argue that there is a fundamental difference between non-virtual storytelling that seeks to ignite the imagination, and virtual storytelling, which can limit and oppress the development of the imagination in young children.

The research on *non-digital* storytelling shows that it enhances children's imagination (Raines and Isbell, 1994: 264–265), supports and extends children's social lives (Britsch, 1992: 80), further develops their cognitive skills (such as "deferred imitation", speculation and knowledge) and contributes significantly to all aspects of language development (Cooper et al., 1992: 10–11). There may be a temptation, therefore, to assume that digital storytelling through virtual worlds can be similarly effective in teaching young children. While some authors argue to the contrary (Miller, 2008: 189–227; Lundby, 2008: 1–21), we argue that digital storytelling through virtual worlds not only lacks these positive aspects, especially with respect to the imagination, but may actually suppress them.

Many of the negative effects that virtual worlds have on the development of the imagination are caused precisely by the characteristic that makes their use in education seem attractive: their degree of immersion, which is a heightened sense of interactivity between the user and the virtual environment. We refer to this as a 'sense' or 'appearance' of interactivity, because it actually masks the fact that the user remains bound by the rules of the game, while it draws the user in to a greater degree than do ordinary games. As Sanchez-Vives & Slater (2005) remind us, "[t]he degree of immersion is an objective property of a system that, in principle, can be measured independently of the experience that it engenders" (p. 333). There are therefore possible avenues for testing the level of immersion that a virtual world engenders, and thereupon to also test for its effects upon the user. We posit that virtual worlds can harm the normal development of imagination in children by the fact that it displaces true make-believe play, while *pretending* to provide it. Not only does this displace the benefits of make-believe play, but it distorts children's developing sense perceptions and negatively impacts their ability to tell reality from fantasy; the imagination and the creativity it engenders is thus stunted, while rule-based and sensory-motor thinking predominate. Thus, storytelling through virtual worlds is in direct conflict with the main goals of storytelling itself. This heightened degree of immersion can also give rise to many of the ill effects produced by the use of virtual worlds, including Internet Addiction

Disorder (IAD) and Pathological Internet Use (PIU) (Hilarie et al., 2012: 292–298; Kuss et al., 2014: 27). Moreover, the context of storytelling emphasizes the fundamental difference between non-virtual storytelling that seeks to ignite and foster the imagination, and virtual storytelling, which can displace, distort, and limit children's developing imagination. This chapter will open with a discussion and review of the literature on virtual worlds, particularly those that target children, and will discuss potential harms to the development of children's imagination through their interactions with virtual worlds. Next, we review the literature on the development of imagination in children and the empirical research concerning the impact of artificial media on this development. We conclude that virtual worlds are an inappropriate medium for children's storytelling.

Virtual Worlds

A virtual world is an artificial environment created by computer software that enables users to interact with other users and with the software itself using self-representational figures called avatars (Hew and Cheung, 2010: 34). Communication can be performed through text, graphics, avatar movements, gestures and sounds (Wadley and Benda, 2007). The user logs onto the internet to a server hosting the software creating the virtual world. This software introduces the user to perceptive stimuli and the user can manipulate objects in the presented environment, thereby experiencing a certain degree of virtual presence. These virtual worlds can look similar to the real world or to a fantasy world – a world in which the rules of nature are different than the rules of the real world and the characters in it are not known in reality (Hunter, 2003: 443).

In her book, *Reality is Broken: Why Games Make Us Better and How They Can Change the World*, Jane McGonigal (2011) illustrates the staggering influence of virtual worlds on our lives:

> [I]f you add up all the hours that gamers across the globe have spent playing World of Warcraft since the massively multiplayer online (MMO) role-playing game (RPG) first launched in 2004, you get a grand total of just over 50 billion collective hours – or 5.93 million years. To put that number in perspective: 5.93 million years ago is almost exactly the moment in history that our earliest human ancestors first stood upright. (McGonigal 2011: 52)

McGonigal concludes that we have therefore spent as much time playing *World of Warcraft* (WoW) as we have spent *evolving as a species* (ibid.).

Virtual worlds, as a result of their high degree of immersion, are often very good at drawing players in for long periods of time, and this is an important source of the revenue they are able to generate. *World of Warcraft* reaps an estimated

$100 million every single month (Superdata, 2013). McGonigal points out that "no other computer game has ever made so much money keeping so many players occupied for so long. Each WoW player spends on average between seventeen and twenty-two hours per week in the virtual world, more time than any other computer game attracts" (ibid.).

Children's virtual worlds are not far behind in their abilities to generate large revenues. Research suggests that children are using electronic media at younger ages (Rideout et al., 2003), and news reports indicate that children as young as three are participating in virtual worlds (Chmielewski et al., 2008). There are over 400 virtual worlds designed and targeted specifically to children (Smolen, 2012; Kzero, 2013). According to some estimates, virtual worlds garnered over one billion users in 2010, roughly half of whom were under fifteen years old, with 219 million users being between the ages of 5 and 11 years old (Watters, 2010).

One popular virtual world for children is *Webkinz*. Dellinger-Pate and Conforti (2010) describe *Webkinz* as an all-encompassing experience, stating that

> [*Webkinz*] is not merely a mode of children's entertainment, a beloved stuffed toy, a profit-driven phenomenon, an educational tool, a source of family negotiation, an aggressive marketing device, a source of addiction, or a comment on cultural values. It is all of them. (Dellinger-Pate and Conforti 2010: 252)

This description illustrates the growing influence exerted by virtual worlds on children's early experiences. There is no standard definition or description for children's experience in virtual worlds. However, most of the major brands in the market are based around a mix of social interaction and casual game-play. One classic example is *Club Penguin*.

In *Club Penguin*, children sign up as registered users and take on the form of penguin avatars. They then go to a fantasy world called Penguin Island where they can play games, customize their characters and talk to other children's penguin avatars. Chat is moderated to ensure that there is no kind of anti-social behavior. Registered users of Club Penguin, typically aged 6–12 with a slight skew towards girls, can get a basic entertainment experience for free. If they want the complete experience, they have to pay a subscription fee of $6–8 per month (*Club Penguin*, 2015).

Club Penguin's headline statistics indicate that the site has 175 million registered users in 190 countries, up from around 12 million at the time of its 2007 purchase by Disney for $350 million (Eldon, 2007). This indicates strong growth, but perhaps more important is the number of children who choose to pay for premium access. Disney is coy, but analysts estimate this is around 5–10% of registered users (White, 2012). If these estimates are correct, then Disney may be generating as much as $122.5 million per month from subscription fees alone, which indicates the extremely large profits to be made from children's virtual worlds.

Two key differences that separate virtual worlds from other video games are that virtual worlds are both persistent and dynamic (Lastowka and Hunter, 2004: 5–6). This means that even when the player is not in the virtual world, the virtual environment continues to exist and change over time (Rogers 2008: 407; Castronova, 2005: 80). Virtual worlds' heightened sense of interactivity is another important difference between video games and virtual worlds. Jenkins (2009) states that "[v]ideo games like Zelda, Halo, or Harry Potter allow players to enter into an environment and interact with objects, but they don't allow the player to create an environment and that's what virtual worlds are all about." But it is precisely their persistence, dynamism, and heightened sense of interactivity that we argue lead to the ill effects of virtual worlds. Dellinger-Pate and Conforti (2010) illustrate the potential harmful influence on children through the following story:

> She [the author's colleague] and her family were traveling for Christmas and unable to get to a computer easily when her son wanted to play on Webkinz. When her son was finally able to log on he became instantly panicked and cried uncontrollably over the fear that his pet was dying. He saw that his beloved avatar was very ill and in the hospital due to malnutrition. The mother knew the pet was, indeed, not going to die; the website makes that clear to parents in its introduction. Yet her son was distraught over having neglected his poor pet during the Christmas season. He vowed never to let that many days go by without caring for the animal's needs. (Ibid: 267)

This story illustrates the child's inability to distinguish between the virtual nature of the *Webkinz* pet and reality. His perception of the virtual world's persistence is derived from his experience in the real world. He reacts normally to an abnormal environment. However, this is to the child's detriment, and to the website operator's financial benefit.

There are those who argue that the growing number of virtual worlds geared toward young children is a benefit, one that can "provide young learners with experiences that scaffold skills needed for community building and civic engagement" (Berson et al., 2009: 28), while interconnecting with people and issues they confront in real life (Wang, 2010: 32). One broad-based review of the literature showed that virtual worlds can have a positive impact in creating communicative spaces for remote users, as well as in assisting experiential skills learning, although this study focused on older children and adult learners (Hew and Cheung, 2010: 45–47). Another study found that virtual worlds had a positive impact on primary students' achievement and motivation in learning geography facts (Tüzün et al., 2009: 75–76).

Others disagree, citing evidence of the negative effects of virtual worlds on child development. Many of these critiques point to the narratives embedded in the virtual worlds themselves and demonstrate their harmful effects on children. For example, Marsh (2010: 30) states that while virtual worlds are a space in which children can engage in make-believe and narrative-related play, this is impeded by the ways in which virtual worlds restrict children's choices (ibid.: 35-6). Similarly, Hannaford (2012: 17) found that children engaged imaginatively with one another and the virtual environment, and that they took the narratives they learned there back with them into the outside world. Both Marsh and Hannaford discuss children's imagination and make-believe play in terms of identity practice, and so one might be tempted to conclude from their work that if we constructed better and more inclusive narratives for children in their virtual worlds, then this problem might be overcome.

However, the problems go deeper than the narrative content and are often embedded in the structure of the game itself. Dellinger-Pate and Conforti's (2010) study of *Webkinz* led them to conclude that the game harms children's developing communication skills and social connectivity. They state, "there is no scenario where cooperation between players takes place. There is no true community in this playground. Although the site visuals offer the illusion of community (a village with shops and friendly, furry characters waving to each other, with open, green fields to run and play in), they are fleeting images and never experienced by the player" (p. 264). Grimes (2015a: 120) has also found that the narratives in children's virtual worlds promote consumer culture. Children are instructed to acquire and display items and to construct social hierarchies based on acquisition (where restrictions based upon a lack of funds are taught as "fair play"). Respecting copyright and other corporate rules are embedded in the structure of the game itself (ibid.), as is the practice of "immersive advertising," which "enables interactive and deeply embedded forms of product placement" (ibid.: 122). Even more invisible are the ways in which children are co-opted into performing forms of immaterial labor, such as data mining and market research, but also less tangible forms of labor (ibid.: 126). After all, it is the participation of the children themselves in the game that actually constructs the virtual environment, and it is their interactions with and emotional connection to the game that lend it its meaning, its cultural value and, ultimately, its immense monetary value as well (ibid.).

Grimes (2015b: 136) concludes that virtual worlds provide very limited opportunities for children to exercise their imagination in make-believe play, since adults ultimately shape and impose an idealized play environment on the child. She states:

> By restricting opportunities for children to create their own UGC [user-generated content], reappropriate branded content, or even speak freely about the commercial content encountered, these worlds have excluded some of the most potentially valuable dimensions of children's play. (ibid.: 142)

Plowman (2004: 221) found that when their own imagination exceeded the functionality of a "smart" toy, children quickly became unhappy and preferred to play with the toy switched off. We conclude that, even if adults could design "suitable" narrative content into the virtual world, its use would continue to have harmful effects on children's developing imagination. The virtual worlds would continue to displace children's true imaginative interaction with adult-generated rules and constructs – ones whose weaknesses cannot easily be discerned or simply switched off.

The Imagination

The essence of imagination lies in its generativity, in the fact that through our imagination we can conjure up experiences and representations that are wholly novel to our lived experiences. Imagination is critical to children's mental development and abilities to learn, as we discuss further below. Despite its importance, it remains intangible and difficult to define. Cohen & MacKeith (1991) described psychologists' ambivalence towards it, stating that "on the one hand, it fascinates. Just as no other species can speak, no other species can imagine or invent. On the other hand, it is extremely hard to study imagination – especially experimentally" (ibid.: 11–14).

Despite this ambivalence, there have been numerous attempts to define and classify the imagination, none of which have yet received widespread consensus. Vygotsky (1978) defined imagination as "a new formation which is not present in the consciousness of the very young child, is totally absent in animals and represents a specifically human form of conscious activity. Like all functions of consciousness, it originally arises from action" (ibid.: 537). One can imagine, for example, a bird turning into a snake while flying over a lake without ever having seen such a transformation actually taking place. One can produce novel representations in the mind by generatively combining past perceived representations.

Elaborating on this definition, Singer & Singer (2005) define imagination as a

> form of human thought characterized by the ability of the individual to reproduce images or concepts originally derived from the basic senses, but now reflected in one's consciousness as memories, fantasies, or future plans. These sensory-derived images, 'pictures in the mind's eye', mental conversations, or remembered or anticipated smells,

> touches, tastes, or movements can be reshaped and recombined into new images or possible future dialogues. (Ibid.: 16)

The emphasis is on the "images or concepts originally derived from the basic senses" that are then "reshaped and recombined". But this raises the question of whether "images or concepts" that are artificially mediated – and which are usually the product of the imaginary process of a TV show or video game creator – will function in the same way as basic building blocks for the user's imagination.

Other authors have defined the imagination in the context of the human spirit. For Watkins (1990: 75), the imagination is "the intermediate universe – the universe between pure spirit and the physical, sensible world – which is the world of the symbol and of imagining". According to Latham (2003: 91), "[i]maginative capacity thus underpins our species' ability to make sense and guide us beyond ego-directed aims and conditions that life brings our way. Creative fantasy freely expressed is our key to balance and wholeness". Dubos (1965: 7) argued that "[m]an's propensity to imagine what does not yet exist, including what will never come to pass … most clearly differentiates him from animals. The more human he is, the more intensely do his anticipations of the future affect the character of his responses to the forces of the present". The imagination bridges the time from the present to the future.

Ulanov and Ulanov (1991) point out that there is no life of the spirit without imagination. "Properly understood and pursued," they state, "the imagination is perhaps our most reliable way of bringing the world of the unconscious into some degree of consciousness and our best means of corresponding with the graces offered us in the life of the spirit" (ibid.: 3). In our spiritual lives, the imagination enables paths that cannot be traveled in any other way, and its absence detaches us from the unconscious and the spirit. This is in stark contrast to the superficial and artificial representations of children's virtual worlds, with their flat and fleeting images, a world in which everything is offered, but nothing can truly be experienced.

A more prosaic definition of the imagination claims that imagination is an activity of the human brain, operating much like memory or logic or any other cognitive process (Misson, 2000). In this view, there is nothing mystical about the imagination: it is simply working on the material present in the brain (Feldman et al., 1994: 47). The critical character of the imagination lies in its generative and transformative abilities, to take existing ingredients and bring them together to generate something novel. It is perhaps for this reason that imagination is critical to learning. As Egan (1990: 166) states, "all learning that is to be of educational value seems necessarily to involve an imaginative-finite creative component. The imagination is the making, composing, vivifying power that is required if the student is to reconstitute codes into living knowledge".

Generally, imagination has not been studied as a single concept. Valkenburg and van der Voort (1994: 316–317), in a review of the research on the influence of TV on daydreaming and creative imagination, found three closely related but distinguishable imaginal processes, which they define as follows: imaginative play – play in which children transcend the constraints of reality by acting "as if"; daydreaming – a state of consciousness characterized by a shift of attention from external stimuli to internal thoughts and images; and creative imagination, which is defined as the capacity to generate many different novel or unusual ideas (Valkenburg and Calvert, 2012: 158). This chapter will not deal with daydreaming, being outside the scope of this discussion, but it will discuss below imaginative play, the creative imagination, and the negative effects of media on the imagination as expressed in dreams.

Virtual worlds differ in many ways from authentic imaginary experiences, and these differences may actually impede the development of imagination in young children. According to Cobb, the psychological distance between the self and the object of desire "is the locus in which the ecology of imagination in childhood has its origin" (ibid.: 56). In virtual worlds, the distance between "the self and the object of desire" is vague since the self is portrayed as a virtual avatar; the object of desire is always at hand in the virtual environment but cannot be reached in the real one.

Scholars have defined four key characteristics of children's imaginary worlds: first, the child must be able to distinguish between what they have imagined and what is real; second, the child's interest in the fantasy world persists for months or years; third, the child will be proud of the world and consistent about it; lastly, the child will feel that the world matters to him or her (these worlds usually disappear by the age of ten) (Cohen and MacKeith, 1988: 14; Silvey and MacKeith, 1988: 173–174). As with the tale of the child whose *Webkinz* pet fell ill from his disuse of the game, virtual worlds can mimic the last three characteristics. However, it is on the first characteristic that virtual worlds fall short: the child has not imagined the world, and is not in control. The child may, therefore, have significant difficulties distinguishing the virtual world from the real one.

Others contend that the development of the imagination is critical not only to our individual development but also to our collective development. Jung (1933), already cognizant of the pressures of our modern life, warns us not to abandon our species' hard-fought accomplishments in developing our spiritual life. "The wheel of history," he states, "must not be turned back, and man's advance toward a spiritual life, which began with the primitive rites of initiation, must not be denied" (ibid.: 125). The consequences of losing or not developing our imaginative capacities can have serious and as yet unforeseen repercussions and, as Jung warns us, our collective accomplishments can be turned back.

In summary, the imagination is unique to humans, and it is critical for our learning and for children's proper intellectual development. It is also a key part of what makes us *human*. In addition, the imagination is a learned ability, one which is not yet present in young children (we can conclude from Piaget's theory on make-believe play that the imagination develops along with make-believe play). It is originally derived from the basic senses, works on the material that is present in the brain and bridges the gap between the self and the object of desire, as well as the time from the present to the future. The development of the imagination also appears necessary in order to be able to distinguish between the imagined and the real. In children, the imagination develops and expresses in imaginative play and creative imagination. The emphasis is on the novel reshaping of already-familiar images and experiences. These skills are all essential for both understanding and creating stories. But the question that we wish to raise in this chapter is whether the images and concepts that children receive from playing in virtual worlds function as building blocks for the development of the child's imagination in the same way as images and concepts derived from less artificial media. To take a simple example, the images a child gets from having a book read to them come from his or her own mind's eye, but the images they get from watching a show on TV come from the creator and are imposed upon the child, crowding out the images in the mind's eye the child would otherwise create. Because a virtual world is an even more fully-immersive experience for the child than a television show, even more of the images and concepts that child users receive are imposed upon them, thus increasing the ill effects of the medium. Below, we describe good reasons why we think this is the case, and why further research needs to be done in this area.

The Development of the Imagination

Imagination is critical to children's learning and development. Vygotsky (2004: 11–12) states that "child's play is not simply a reproduction of what he has experienced, but a creative reworking of the impressions he has acquired. He combines them and uses them to construct a new reality, one that conforms to his own needs and desires". When the child is rehearsing a situation from his life with toys, he is not only duplicating the situation in reality but is creating a scenario that exceeds that reality and portrays what will or may happen, according to the child's fears, hopes and other internal drives. Winnicott (1971: 72–73) further states that "[i]t is in playing and only in playing that the individual child or adult is able to be creative and to use the whole personality, and it is only in being creative that the individual discovers the self". These two steps are essential. First, imaginative playing will enable creativity, and only in creativity will we discover ourselves.

While many animals engage in play, it lacks the generativity of children's play. Cobb (1977: 29) contends that "while other animals do play, the human child's play includes the effort to be something other than what he actually is, to 'act out' and to dramatize speculation". Wittgenstein (1949: 37e) pondered, "Could one imagine a world in which there could be no pretend?". Play is essential for the imagination, but it is pretend play that most deeply express and develops our creativity and imagination.

According to Piaget's (1962) influential developmental theory, there are three main types of children's play that direct and foster a child's mental development: practice games, symbolic games and games with rules. When a child jumps over a stream for the fun of jumping, she is engaging in a practice game. Games with rules are "games with sensory-motor combinations (races, marbles, ball games, etc.) or intellectual combinations (cards, chess, etc.), in which there is competition between individuals (otherwise rules would be useless) and which are regulated either by a code handed down from earlier generations, or by temporary agreement" (ibid.: 142). Symbolic games imply representation of an absent object, since there is a comparison between a given and an imagined element. For example, a child pushing a box and imagining it is a car. It is the symbolic, or pretend, games that are most important in the context of the development of imagination.

Piaget argues that "while mere practice play begins with the first months of life and symbolic play during the second year, games with rules rarely occur before stage II (age 4–7) and belong mainly to the third period (from 7–11)" (ibid.: 142). Piaget theorizes that from ages 4 to 7, symbolic games begin to lose their frequency, but continue to appear in the same intensity. From the age of 7 to 11 or 12, symbolic play declines and games with rules (social games) emerge. According to Piaget, symbolic play takes place mainly from about age 2 to 7. Singer and Singer (1990: 32) agree that "imaginative play emerges toward the end of the child's second post-partum year, struggles fitfully toward a flowering well into the third year, and in the fourth, fifth, and sixth years is a significant factor in the child's behavioral repertory". However, they claim that while "Piaget seemed to suggest that imaginative play fades by the early school years as 'operational' thought takes over, we shall suggest that it is merely submerged in the interest of the changing demands of school decorum and other social pressures" (ibid.). In their view, it is not an internal psychological force that propels the shift, but external ones. We posit that the use of virtual worlds may spur on this shift, making the symbolic play period shorter and thus impairing the process of imagination development.

Recognizing the developmental importance of the imagination, Singer & Singer propose that "our human stream of consciousness emerges gradually in childhood from children's play and from their pretend games" (ibid.). As explained by Grossman & Degaetano (1999: 58):

> The brain of the child is not a miniature version of the adult brain … the young brain is an organ that will change considerably as it matures over the course of childhood and adolescence. As it builds neural structures for optimal development, the young brain is very vulnerable to stimulus from its environment.

Without pretend play, the imagination will not properly develop in young children, and the literature suggests that some of the deficits created thereby may be life-long. We posit that another mechanism whereby virtual worlds may be harming this development by misleading the child's brain to think he is engaged in pretend play, while he is actually engaged in a combination of practice and rule games.

Cobb's (1977) findings seem to support this proposition. She writes:

> The sense of wonder is spontaneous, a prerogative of childhood. When it is maintained as an attitude, or a point of view, in later life, wonder permits a response of the nervous system to the universe that incites the mind to organize novelty of pattern and form out of incoming information. The ability of the adult to look upon the world with wonder is thus a technique and an essential instrument in the work of the poet, the artist or the creative thinker. (Ibid.: 27)

The artificial medium and the mediated stimulus it sends to the senses curtail this sense of wonder. Instead of experiencing the world in wonder, the child is experiencing the virtual world where the alleged wonder is mediated, misleading, and masks the 'true' imaginary universe with the ready-made and mediated one.

The Role of Play

The chief value of play in child development lies in the child's total control over their imaginary universe, free from external constraints – an accomplishment that is simply not possible in the mediated virtual world. Piaget (1962: 87) argued that "[u]nlike objective thought, which seeks to adapt itself to the requirements of external reality, imaginative play is a symbolic transposition which subjects things to the child's activity, without rules or limitations". Although Piaget and Vygotsky experienced a theoretical controversy about the nature of imagination, there was a mutual understanding between them that "the symbolic game as a whole is again a practice game, but a practice game which exercises (and more particularly 'pre-exercises') the specific form of thought which is imagination" (Piaget, 1962: 118). Symbolic games develop the imagination free from any external constrains, a freedom which is not possible in virtual worlds that are inherently bound to some rules.

Mitchell (2002: 4) explains that "pretense or make-believe is a mantel activity involving imagination that is intentionally projected onto something". More elaborately, make-believe is "the use of … props in imaginative activities," where props are "objects of imagining" (Walton, 1990: 25). Props include the pretenders themselves and the objects. Pretence in play is called "symbolic play", but pretending also occurs outside play, and need not be "playful"(Mitchell, 2002: 4). Pretence is essential for the imagination development either in play or outside it. But it is only possible when there are no external constraints forced on the child.

Adults and other children might force external constrains, the same as do virtual worlds. The difference is that external constrains in the real world are obvious and apparent, while virtual worlds actually enforce external constraints, while pretending to provide props for imaginative play. For example, a child can dress its penguin in *Club Penguin*, which is allegedly imaginative play, but *cannot use the penguin as a chair*, i.e., the child cannot stand the penguin as a symbol for some other object or idea, which constitutes true imaginative play.

Singer and Singer (1990) support the developmental value of symbolic games, stating that when "children engage in symbolic games they are practicing mental skills that will later stand them in good stead, just as practice in walking, balancing, or swimming aids the development of motor skills" (ibid.: 22). In a follow-up study of children from age eight to twelve, twenty years later, Shiner, et al. (2003: 1165–1166) found that those children who scored high in social skills, academic attainment, and work competence maintained these patterns as adults. These kinds of skills are the same as those found to emerge from imaginative play in the earlier years (Singer & Singer, 2001: 16–20; Smilansky, 1986: 926). Therefore, deficits in imagination in early years are correlated with long-term deficits in other pro-social skills.

Symbolic play enables children to have a clear sense of what is real and what is fantasy (Aronson and Golomb, 1999: 1424;). Russ conducted a study with 121 first and second graders, and then a follow up study with 31 of them in fifth and sixth grade. She found that "children who play imaginatively in their early years are more likely to think creatively … good early play skills predicted the ability to be creative and generate alternative solutions to everyday problems" (Adams, 2003: 3). Therefore, children who substitute their imaginative play with the rule-bound play in virtual worlds may not fully develop these skills.

Make-believe play produces other important outcomes. Spiegel (2008) argues that it develops the ability to self-regulate; Singer and Singer (1990: 10) posit that imaginative play is associated with more positive emotions in children. Other studies have shown how children engaging together in make-believe play demonstrate advances in recognizing others' thoughts, or in differentiating fantasy representations from reality (Rosen & Singer, 1997: 1133; Schwebel, Rosen and Singer, 1999: 334). Children engaged together in play in virtual worlds are not involved in make-believe play; rather, they are playing games with rules, but these are the rules set by the creators of the virtual world.

An illustration of the negative effects of the lack of pretend play was made by Wulff (1985: 141), who finds that autistic children have severe early deprivations in symbolic play. Harris (2000: 6) states that "the study of early pathology shows that it is the absence of early imagination, and not its presence, that is pathological". He continues, stating that "[o]ne of the major characteristics of the syndrome of early childhood autism is an absence or impoverishment of pretend play… The long term social and cognitive restriction of people with autism suggest that the capacity for pretence is an important foundation for lifelong normality" (ibid.). The imagination, the ability to think symbolically, and therefore the development of normal cognition are all closely linked. This can clearly be seen in children who have serious deficits in symbolic thinking and cannot engage in symbolic or pretend play, as occurs in children who are on the severe end of the autism spectrum.

Children playing in virtual worlds might, therefore, interact with the virtual world as though they are engaged in make-believe play, while they are really engaged in rule-bound play. We argue that this interaction with the game removes the benefits children would otherwise receive from their play. First, children are not receiving the benefits from symbolic play when they play in virtual worlds, and second, because they may acquire a learned deficit in the ability to distinguish the real world from the fantasy.

The Creative Imagination

It should be noted that this chapter deals with the *creative imagination* rather than *creativity* itself. The commonalities and differences between the two are beyond the scope of this chapter. Singer and Singer (1990) have noted some of the differences between the two concepts, stating that "[i]magination seems freer and broader, since our thoughts may remain as private and as fanciful as we may want them to be, with no constraints. Imagination may take the form of visual imagery with no obvious outcome other than the pleasure it affords us" (p. 268–269). It is the creative imagination in this sense that we discuss below.

Vygotsky saw creativity as a way of adapting to the challenges posed by our environment. "A creature that is perfectly adapted to its environment," he states, "would not want anything, would not have anything to strive for, and, of course, would not be able to create anything" (ibid.: 29). Rogers (1959: 69) points out that, with the kaleidoscope of changes that are occurring at a geometric rate, the development of genuine, creative adaptation may represent the only way forward to build a constructive continuity As Rogers (1959) states, "[u]nless man can make new and original adaptations to his environment as rapidly as his science can change the environment, our culture will perish. Not only individual maladjustment and group tensions but international annihilation will be the price we pay for a lack of creativity" (ibid. 70). There may be a heavy price to pay, therefore, if genuine creative adaptation cannot be fostered. At the same time as our real environment is changing rapidly, our virtual environment is changing in the opposite direction, becoming more and more convenient for us and adapting to our whims, rather than posing challenges to our creativity.

In this context, Winnicott (1971: 91) argues that "everything that happens is creative except in so far as the individual is ill, or is hampered by ongoing environmental factors which stifle his creative processes". When the child is spending time in the pre-designed environment of the virtual world, his creativity is stifled in this manner. Cobb (1977: 15) states that "a major clue to mental and psychosocial health lies in the spontaneous and innately creative imagination of childhood, both as form of learning and as a function of the organizing powers of the perceiving nervous system". As can be seen in children with severe autism, the lack of symbolic thinking and the creative imagination presents itself as a severe cognitive pathology.

Winnicott (1971: 87) further states that "many individuals have experienced just enough of creative living to recognize that for most of their time they are living uncreatively, as if caught up in the creativity of someone else, or of a machine". However, children have not yet experienced enough creative imagining of their own to realize they are "caught up in the creativity of someone else, or of a machine". Vygotsky (2004) concludes that "[t]he entire future of humanity will be attained through the creative imagination … The development of a creative individual, one who strives for the future, is enabled by creative imagination embodied in the present" (p. 88). But what if there is no "creative imagination embodied in the present" because of the influence of an all-encompassing virtual environment?

The Senses

The argument that technology alters our sensory perception is not new. McLuhan (1964) remarked on the changes in the senses as a result of the introduction of technology, stating that "[i]f technology is introduced from within or from without a culture, and if it gives new stress or ascendancy to one or another of our senses, the ratio among all our senses is altered. We no longer feel the same, nor do our eyes and ears and other senses remain the same" (ibid.: 24). Advanced technologies, such as virtual worlds, provide more powerful sensory output, like time and interaction, all of which were not present at the time of McLuhan's writing. We ought, therefore, to think carefully about how our sensory perceptions are being altered by these developing virtual cultures.

In an interview with Rudolf Arnheim (Peterson, 1972), he discusses a generation that had lost touch with its senses. Arnheim states:

> If you look at television for hours every day, you must grow up with the ghostly feeling that you live in a world of wraiths. You see, Jim, the mind finds it hard to grasp images that do not have significant form, and in grasping an object the mind finds meaning in that object… The visual sense in most men and women has been reduced to an economic minimum – the effort it takes to tell that the piece of paper is not a piece of bread. (p. 92) … We have lost the human ability to taste the feast of meaning that each event and object offers to our senses. (Ibid.: 55)

The mind cannot fully develop its imagination based on sensory input coming from an artificial medium, and this is more so for virtual worlds than it was in Arnheim's time.

Pearce (1985: 63) states that "[a]bstract imagery is not present to the senses; it must be created from within. We must then process that imagery, transfer it into images available to the senses out there. If we cannot, we have no imagination, and if we have no imagination we are automatically grounded in sensory-motor imagery". When the mind is bombarded with sensory input from an artificial medium, there is no place for acquiring and manipulating abstract imagery. There is no creation of images from within, and therefore no imagination.

In his warning to us about the dangerous aspects of children's exposure to artificial media, Latham (2003: iv) concludes that "young children's spontaneous imaginative capabilities may be neurologically foreclosed and become increasingly impoverished as exposure to screen-based electronic entertainment rises". The internal process of imagination is replaced by the outside exposure to the artificial media. Kline (1989) summarizes this shift as one in which "marketing, rather than entertainment, considerations dominate the design of children's characters, the fictions in which they appear, and hence the way children play" (ibid.: 311;

Levin & Rosenquest, 2001: 243). At the same time, "[p]lay, the most important modality of childhood learning is thus colonized by marketing objectives making the imagination the organ of corporate desire. *The consumption ethos has become the vortex of children's culture*" (ibid. – emphasis added).

Virtual worlds may therefore pose a fundamental harm to the development of children's imagination through the ways in which they distort children's sense perceptions. However, the harm posed to children's imagination by the use of virtual worlds is challenging in two ways: it is intangible, and there is a paucity of research into children's experiences with virtual worlds.

Empirical Research on Children and the Media: The Visualization Hypothesis

Most, if not all, of the empirical research regarding media and the imagination was conducted during the 1980s and therefore focused on television. For several reasons – undoubtedly the problem of quantifying imagination being one of them – this line of research has not been pursued further to other, more advanced artificial mediums. Therefore, we will review the existing research in this field, and the implications for the effects of more advanced artificial mediums will be drawn by analogy.

Two competing theories have been introduced regarding the effects of TV use on creative imagination: stimulation theory posits that TV stimulates creative imagination through its content; reduction theory, on the other hand, posits that TV hinders the development of creative imagination (Valkenburg and van der Voort, 1994: 324–325). While five types of reduction hypotheses have been proposed in the literature (Salomon, 1984: 650; Singer et al. 1984), only the visualization hypothesis is relevant and will be discussed here. The visualization hypothesis posits, in essence, that the visual nature of TV is responsible for the reductive effect that TV has on creative imagination. Unlike verbal media, such as radio and print, TV presents the viewer with ready-made visual images and thus leaves little room for forming one's own. When engaged in creative thinking, it is hard to dissociate oneself from the images supplied by TV, with the result that one has greater difficulty generating novel ideas and images from TV (Greenfield and Beagles-Ross, 1998: 74; Meline, 1976: 81; Webb, 1980: 10).

Valkenberg and van der Voort (1994: 336–337) have found some support for the visualization hypothesis. They reviewed a number of studies which indicated that children who watched a TV story more often used visual content as a basis for drawing story related inferences, whereas children who had heard the same story on a radio more often based their inferences on the verbal content, as well as information from outside of the story, such as personal experience (ibid.: 332; see also Beagles-Ross and Gat, 1983; Greenfield and Beagles-Ross, 1988; Meringoff, 1980; Vibbert and Meringoff, 1981). Goldberg (1994), too, found that "[TV] supplies the same image to millions of people at the same time. We process those images rather than create them" (p. 16). Goldberg (1994) and Latham (2003) support this line of thinking. Latham states:

> With images that are processed through the sensory system, rather than created in the mind's eye, we take in what Giegerich (1985) refers to as a 'distillation of image' (p. 17) … In the case of young children, neuronal pathways are being wired and shed according to their use patterns. When concentrated representational electronic images are observed through the visual sensory system, other body and sense modalities consequently receive less stimulation. (Goldberg, 1994: 11–12)

Further support for the visualization hypothesis was provided by Conway and Siegelman (1978), who found that "[h]eavy viewing destroys the natural ability of children to form mental images from what they hear or read. With too much TV, the young child's basic capacity of imagination, like an unused muscle, never reaches a level adequate for performing even the most elementary of creative acts" (ibid.: 191). Mander (1978), discussing the visualization hypothesis, wrote that "[m]ore than any other single effect, television places images in our brain. It is a melancholy fact that most of us give little importance to this implantation, perhaps because we have lost touch with our own image-creating abilities, how we use them and the critical functions they serve in our lives" (ibid.: 216).

This can have a negative effect on the development of creative imagination in children. Pearce (1992: 166) argues:

> Television feeds both stimulus and response into that infant-child brain, as a single paired-effect, and therein lays the danger. *Television floods the brain with a counterfeit of the response the brain is supposed to learn to make to the stimuli of words or music.* As a result, much structural coupling between mind and environment is eliminated; few metaphoric images develop; few higher cortical areas of the brain are called into play; few, if any, symbolic structures develop.

Pearce (ibid.: 167) concludes that "failing to develop imagery means having no imagination".

In their research on video game users and dreams, Gackenbach et al. (2009: 219 found that high-end users were associated with the lucid dream type, had more dead and imaginary characters in their dreams (Gackenbach, 2006: 108; Gackenbach et al., 2009: 219), and were coded as containing more bizarre elements in their dreams (ibid, 2009: 227). Gackenbach et al. (2009b) assume that dream bizarreness in high-end video game users is a result of a more developed creative imagination (ibid.: 228).

Similarly, a study conducted among users of the virtual world *Everquest* found that 80.6% of the female and 58.4% of the male players reported dreaming of the virtual world or having a dream taking place in the virtual world environment (Smahel et al., 2007). However, these findings may rather indicate the deep influence of video games (and consequently, virtual worlds) on the user. It might be said that the most 'sacred' space of the imagination – dreams – has been 'invaded' by the artificial medium, and that this is a warning sign as to its deep and embracing influence.

We argue that virtual worlds and virtual realities call upon us to extend the visualization hypothesis further – from the senses of vision and sound to higher psychological dimensions of perception, including of time, interaction and associated aspects as a narrative construction, and judgments concerning reality versus fantasy. We posit that these are weak and almost irrelevant in TV, stronger in video games and predominant in virtual worlds, as the user becomes more and more immersed in the medium, and more and more of the material is supplied for the user by the medium. This is the key theoretical advance that we propose in this chapter. Accordingly, we propose to rename this phenomenon the 'displacement hypothesis' in order to capture these new cognitive and sensory dimensions that are being displaced by the immersive virtual environment, and to emphasize that, when manufactured content is supplied ready-made to the individual, it displaces the creative imaginative processes that the individual would otherwise supply for him or herself. In children whose creative imagination is still developing, such continuous displacement could have permanent effects on the creative imagination. It is no longer the visual only that is displacing the images that could have been created by the imagination; time, space, interaction and narrative, even presence and being, are now being projected onto us and consumed from the artificial medium, where they are replacing the natural pace and creation of these mental processes within the person. This has much more significant effects on the individual than when only the visual sense is being displaced. The most internal object, the mind, is becoming externalized, nourishing itself falsely from the artificial medium dimensions, and leaving little space for the flourishing of the imagination.

Summary

This chapter has reviewed some of the extant literature on virtual worlds, particularly those aimed at children, as well as the imagination and its development. We have noted that there is a great potential for the use of virtual worlds to harm the development of the creative imagination in the child's developing mind. Furthermore, we posit that the likely pathway of this harm is that virtual worlds, like television, displace the imagination with ready-made images and narratives. Unlike television, however, virtual worlds further displace the child's imaginary universe, their sense of reality versus fantasy, and their creative and symbolic play. They do this while mimicking the imaginary world that children need to create on their own terms, displacing this experience as well. For this reason, children experience the virtual world not as a construct of their imagination, over which they have control, but as an external reality like any other. This can give rise to serious distortions of normal developing cognitive processes.

We are aware that there is little empirical research to date on the effects of virtual worlds on children's cognitive development, let alone the development of the creative imagination. With this review of the extant literature, and our proposed mechanisms for how virtual worlds disrupt children's normal development, it is our hope to suggest a testable hypothesis, and generate interest in further research. The displacement hypothesis that we herein propose has a long provenance in the literature and is an extension to new media theories for which there is already much empirical support. Healy (1998: 17) reminds us that "[t]echnology shapes the growing mind. The younger the mind, the more malleable it is. The younger the technology, the more unproven it is". The rapid development of new and untested technologies operating on younger and younger minds for longer and longer periods of time is in many ways itself a great experiment, and there seem to be good reasons to believe that it is an ill-conceived one, with potentially serious consequences. Until further research has been done, we conclude that children's storytelling through the use of virtual worlds should not replace more traditional methods of storytelling that more fully engage the child's creative, imaginative, and cognitive processes.

References

Adams, J., Sutherland, B., Kalb, C. and Raymond, J. (2003, August 25). The end of make believe. *Newsweek*. Retrieved from http://www.newsweek.com/end-make-believe-135693.

Arnheim, R. (1969). *Visual Thinking*. California: University of California Press.

Aronson, J. N., & Golomb, C. (1999). Preschoolers' understanding of pretense and presumption of congruity between action and representation. *Developmental Psychology 35(6):* 1414–1425.

Beagles-Ross, J. and Gat, I. (1983). Specific impact of radio and television on children's story comprehension. *Journal of Educational Psychology* 75: 128–137.

Berson, I. R. and Berson, M. J. (2009). Panwapa: Global Kids, Global Connections. *Social Studies and the Young Learner 21(4)*: 28–31.

Bitarello, M. B. (2008). Another time, another space: Virtual worlds, myths and imagination. *Journal for Virtual World Research 1(1)*: 1–18.

Britsch, S. (1992). *The Development of Story Within the Culture of Preschool*. Berkley: University of California Press.

Cash, H., Rae, C., Steel A. and Winkler, A., (2012). Internet Addiction: A Brief Summary of Research and Practice. Current Psychiatry Reviews 8(4): 292–298. Castronova, E. (2005). *Synthetic Worlds: The Business and Culture of Online Games*. Chicago: University of Chicago Press.

Chmielewski, D. C. and Pham, A. (2008, January 28). Disney Adds Fantasy Lands. *L.A. Times*, C1.

Club Penguin (2015). *Membership*. Retrieved on September 9th, 2016, from https://secured.clubpenguin.com/membership/US

Cobb, E. (1977). *The Ecology of Imagination*. New York: Columbia University Press.

Cohen, D. and MacKeith, S. A. (1991). *The Development of Imagination: The Private Worlds of Childhood*. London: Routledge.

Conway, F. and Siegelman, J. (1978). *Snapping*. Philadelphia: J. B. Lippincott.

Cooper, P. J., Collins. R. and Saxby, M. (1992). *The Power of Story*. Melbourne: MacMillan.

Dellinger-Pate, C. and Conforti, R. J. (2010). Webkinz as Consumerist Discourse: A Critical Ideological Analysis. In Berson, I. R. and Berson, M. J. (eds.). *High Tech Tots: Childhood in a Digital World* (pp. 249–270). Charlotte: Information Age Publishing.

Dubos, R. (1965). *Man Adapting*. New Haven: Yale University Press.

Egan, K. (1990). *Romantic Understanding*. London: Routledge.

Eldon, E. (2007, August 1). Disney buys Club Penguin in $700 million deal – virtual worlds have arrived? *Venture Beat*. Retrieved from http://venturebeat.com/2007/08/01/disney-buys-club-penguin-in-700-million-deal/.

Feldman, D., Csikszentmihalyi, M. and Gardner, H. (1994). *Changing the World: A Framework for the Study of Creativity*. Westport: Greenwood Publishing.

Gackenbach, J. I. (2006). Video game play and lucid dreams: Implications for the development of consciousness. *Dreaming 16*: 96–110.

Gackenbach, J. I. (2009). Electronic media and lucid-control dreams: Morning after reports, *Dreaming 19*: 1–6.

Gackenbach, J. I., Matty, I., Kuruvilla, B., Samaha, A. N., Zederayko, A., Olischefski, J. and von Stackelberg, H. (2009). Video Game Play: Waking and Dreaming

Consciousness. In Krippner, S. (ed.). *Perchance to Dream* (pp. 239–253). Hauppauge: Nova Science.

Gackenbach, J., Kuruvilla, B. and Dopko, R. (2009). Video game play and dream bizarreness. *Dreaming 4:* 218–231.

Gackenbach, J. I., Kuruvilla, B., Dopko, R. and Le, H. (2010). Dreams and Video Game Play. In Columbus, F. (ed.). *Computer Games: Learning Objectives, Cognitive Performance and Effects on Development* (pp. 127–136). Hauppauge: Nova Science.

Giegerich, W. (1985). *The Nuclear Bomb and the Fate of God: On the First Nuclear Fission.* Dallas: Spring.

Goldberg, D. A. (1994). Television From Jungian Perspective. *Psychological Perspectives 29(2):* 10–20.

Goldman, L. R. (1998). *Child's Play.* Oxford: Berg.

Golomb, C. and Kuersten, R. (1996). On the Transition From Pretense Play To Reality: What Are The Rules Of The Game? *British Journal of Developmental Psychology 14(2):* 203–217.

Greenfield, P. M. and Beagles-Ross, J. (1988). Radio vs. Television: Their cognitive impact on children of different socioeconomic and ethnic groups. *Journal of Communication 38(2):* 71–92.

Grimes, S. M. (2015). Playing by the market rules: Promotional priorities and commercialization in children's virtual worlds. *Journal of Consumer Culture 15(1):* 110–134.

Grimes, S. M. (2015). Configuring the Child Player. *Science, Technology, & Human Values 40(1):* 126–148.

Grossman, D. and Degaetano, G. (1999). *Stop Teaching Our Kids to Kill.* New York: Crown Publishers.

Hannaford, J. (2012). Imaginative Interaction with Internet Games. For Children and Teachers. *Literacy 46(1):* 25–32.

Harris, L. P. (2000). *The Work of the Imagination.* Oxford: Blackwell.

Healy, J. (1998). *Failure to Connect: How Computers Affect Our Children's Minds – For Better and Worse.* New York: Simon & Shuster.

Hew, K. F. and Cheung, W. S. (2010). Use of Three-Dimensional (3-D) Immersive Worlds in K-12 and Higher Education Settings: A Review of the Research. *British Journal of Educational Technology 41(1):* 33–55.

Hunter, D. (2003). Cyberspace as Place and the Tragedy of the Digital Anticommons. *California Law Review 91(2):* 439–519.

Jabs, C. (2009, February 1). Talking with Your Children About Online Avatars: Understanding the Difference Between Imagination and Reality. *Indy's Child,*

Online Column: Growing Up Online. Retrieved from http://www.indys child.com/Articles-i-2009-02-01-230763.112112_Talking_With_Your_Children_About_Online_Avatars.html.

Jenkins, C. (2009, June 26). Your Own Virtual World: Play God – Be God (Even If It's Only Electronically*). Articlesbase: Free Online Articles Directory*. Retrieved from http://www.articlesbase.com/computer-games-articles/your-own-virtual-world-996244.html

Jung, C. G. (1933). *Modern Man in Search of a Soul*. London: Harvest Books.

Kline, S. (1989). Limits to the Imagination: Marketing and Children's Culture. In Angus, I. and Jhally, S. (eds.). *Cultural Politics in Contemporary America* (pp. 299–316). New York: Routledge.

Kuss, J. D., Griffiths D. M., Karila, L. and Billieux, J. (2014). Internet Addiction: A Systematic Review of Epidemiological Research for the Last Decade. Current Pharmaceutical Design 20(25): 4026–4052. Kzero (2013). Virtual World and MMO Universe Chart: Tween/Teen segment for Q3 2013. Retrieved from http://www.kzero.co.uk/blog/category/kidstween-worlds/.

Lang, A., Dhillon, K. and Dong, Q. (1995). The effects of emotional arousal and valence on television viewers' cognitive capacity and memory. *Journal of Broadcasting and Electronic Media 39(3)*: 313–327.

Lastowka, G. F. and Hunter, D. (2004). The Laws of the Virtual Worlds. *California Law Review 92(1)*: 3–73.

Latham, C. L. (2003). *High Tech Image Influences On Development Of Young Children's Imaginative World Making*. Dissertation Abstracts International: Section B: The Sciences and Engineering Vol. 63(7-B), 3495 [ProQuest].

Levin, D. E. and Rosenquest, B. (2001). The increasing role of electronic toys in the lives of infants and toddlers: Should we be concerned? *Contemporary Issues in Early Childhood 2(2)*: 242–247.

Lillard, A. (2002). Just through the looking glass: children's understanding of pretense. In Mitchell, R. W. (ed.). *Pretending and Imagination in Animals and Children* (pp. 102–114). Cambridge: Cambridge University Press.

Mallan, K. (1991). *Children as Storytellers*. Newtown, Sydney: Primary English Teaching Association.

Mander, J. (1978). *Four Arguments for the Elimination of Television*. New York: Perennial.

Marsh, J. (2010). Young Children's Play in Online Virtual Worlds. *Journal of Early Childhood Research 8(1)*: 23–39.

Matte, C. (2016).Virtual Worlds for Kids: Pretend Play Online. *About.Com: Family Computing*. Retrieved on September 6th, 2016 from http://familyinternet.about.com/od/websites/tp/virtualworldskids.htm.

McLuhan, M. (1964). *Understanding Media: The Extensions of Man.* Toronto: Toronto University Press.

McGonigal, J. (2011). *Reality is Broken, Why Games Make Us Better and How They Can Change the World.* New York: Penguin Press.

Meline, C. W. (1976). Does The Medium Matter? *Journal of Communication 26(3):* 81–89.

Meringoff, L. K. (1980). Influence of the medium on children's story apprehension. *Journal of Educational Psychology 72:* 240–249.

Miller, C. H. (2008). *Digital Storytelling: A Creator's Guide to Interactive Entertainment.* Boston: Focal Press/Elsevier.

Misson, R. (2000, April 8–10). Imagination, the Individual and the Global Media. *Cross-Roads of the New Millennium, Proceedings of the Technological Education and National Development (TEND) Conference 2nd*, held in Abu Dhabi, United Arab Emirates.

Mitchell, W. R. (2002). Imaginative animals, pretending children. In Mitchell, R. W. (ed.). *Pretending and Imagination in Animals and Children* (pp. 3–22). Cambridge: Cambridge University Press.

Pearce, J. (1985). *Magical Child Matures.* New York: E. P. Dutton.

Pearce, J. (1992). *Evolution's End: Claiming the Potential of Our Intelligence.* San Francisco: Harper Collins.

Peterson, R. J. (1972). Eyes Have They, But They See Not, A Conversation With Rudolf Arnheim About a Generation That Has Lost Touch With Its Senses. *Psychology Today*, June 1972: 55–58.

Piaget, J. (1962). *Play, Dreams and Imitation in Childhood,* Gattegno, C., & Hodgson, F. M. trans. New York: W. W. Norton.

Plowman, L. (2004). Hey, Hey, Hey! It's Time to Play: Children's Interactions with Smart Toys. In Goldstein, J., Buckingham, D. and Brougere, G. (eds.). *Toys, Games, and Media* (pp. 207–223). Mahwah: L. Erlbaum Associates.

Raines, S. and Isbell, R. (1994). *Stories: Children's Literature in Early Education.* New York: Delmar Publishers.

Rideout, V. J., Vandewater, E. A. and Wartella, E. A. (2003). *Zero To Six: Electronic Media In The Lives Of Infants, Toddlers And Preschoolers.* Henry J. Kaiser Family Foundation. Retrieved September 6th 2016 from https://www.dcmp.org/caai/nadh169.pdf

Rogers, C. R. (1959). Toward a Theory of Creativity. In Anderson, H. H. (ed.). *Creativity and its Cultivation.* New York: Harper.

Rogers, J. (2008). A passive approach to regulation of virtual worlds. *George Washington Law Review 76(2):* 405–425.

Rosen, C., Schwebel, D. and Singer, J. L. (1997). Preschoolers' Attributions of Mental States in Pretense. *Child Development 66:* 1133–1142.

Salomon, G. (1984). Television is "Easy" and Print is "Tough": The Differential Investment of Mental Effort as a Function of Perceptions and Attributions. *Journal of Educational Psychology 76:* 647–658.

Sanchez-Vives, M. V. and Slater, M. (2005). From presence to consciousness through virtual reality. *Nature Reviews. Neuroscience 6(4):* 332–339.

Schwebel, D., Rosen, C. and Singer, J. L. (1999). Preschoolers' Pretend Play and Theory of Mind: The Role of Jointly-Conducted Pretense. *British Journal of Developmental Psychology 17*: 333–348.

Shiner, R. L., Masten, A. S. and Roberts, J. M. (2003). Childhood Personality Foreshadows Adult Personality and Life Outcomes Two Decades Later. *Journal of Personality 71(6):* 1145–1170.

Silvey, R., & MacKeith, S. (1988). The paracosm: A special form of fantasy. In Morrison, D. C. (ed.). *Organizing Early Experience: Imagination and Cognition in Childhood* (pp. 173–197). Amityville: Baywood.

Singer, D. G. and Singer, J. L. (1990). *The House of Make-Believe.* Cambridge: Harvard University Press.

Singer, D. G. and Singer, J. L. (2001). *Make-Believe: Games and Activities for Imaginative Play.* Washington, DC: American Psychological Association Books, Imagination Press.

Singer, D. G. and Singer, J. L. (2005). *Imagination and Play in the Electronic Age.* Cambridge: Harvard University Press.

Singer, J. L. (1975). *The Inner World of Daydreaming.* New York: Harper & Row.

Singer, J. L. (1975). Navigating the stream of consciousness: Research in daydreaming and related inner experience. *American Psychologist 30:* 727–738.

Singer, J. L., Singer D. G. and Rapaczynski, W. (1984). Children's imagination as predicted by family patterns and television viewing: A longitudinal study. *Genetic Psychology Monographs 110:* 43–69.

Smahel, David, Blinka, L. and Ledabyl O. (2007). *MMORPG Playing of Youths and Adolescents:Addiction and its Factors.* Vancouver: Association of Internet Researchers, *Internet Research 8.0: Let's Play.* Retrieved September 6th, 2016 from http://www.muni.cz/research/publications/726643.

Smilansky, S. (1986). *The Effects of Sociodramatic Play on Disadvanteged Preschool Children.* New York: Wiley.

Smolen, W. (2012, December 5). Making it to the Top: Tweens Rule the Virtual Worlds Space. *Kidscreen.* Retrieved from http://kidscreen.com/2012/12/05/making-it-to-the-top-tweens-rule-the-virtual-world-space/.

Spiegel, A. (2008, February 21). Old Fashioned Play Builds Serious Skills. *National Public Radio*. Retrieved from http:// www.npr.org/templates/story.php?storyId=19212514

Subrahmanyam, K. (2009). Developmental implications of children's virtual worlds. *Wash. & Lee L. Rev.* 66: 1065–1083.

Superdata. (2013, September 11). World of Warcraft is thinking of microtransactions, and that's a good thing. Retrieved from http://www.superdataresearch.com/blog/wow-microtransactions/.

Tüzün, H., et al. (2009). The effects of computer games on primary students' achievement and motivation in geography learning. *Computers and Education 52(1):* 68–77.

Ulanov, B. and Ulanov, A. (1991). *The Healing Imagination*. New Jersey: Paulist Press.

Valkenburg, P. M. and van der Voort, T. H. (1994). Influence of TV on Daydreaming and Creative Imagination: A Review of Research. *Psychological Bulletin 116(2):* 316–339.

Vibbert, M. M. and Meringoff, L. K. (1981). Children's production and application of story imagery: A cross-medium investigation (Tech. Rep. No. 23). *Project Zero*. Cambridge, MA: Harvard University. (ERIC Document Reproduction Service No. ED 210 682).

Vygotsky, L. S. (1978). Interaction between learning and development. In Vygotsky, L. S. (ed.). *Mind in society: The development of higher psychological processes* (pp. 79–91). Cambridge: Harvard University Press.

Vygotsky, L. S. (2004). Imagination and creativity in childhood. *Journal of Russian and East European Psychology 42(1):* 7–97 (English translation 2004, M.E. Sharpe, Inc., from the Russian text Voobrazhenie i tvorchestvo v detskom vozraste (Moscow: Prosveshchenie, 1967)).

Wadley, M. and Benda, P. (2007). Speaking in Character: Using Voice-Over-IP to Communicate Within MMORPGs. IE '07 Proceedings of the 4th Australasian conference on Interactive entertainment, Working Paper.

Walton, K. L. (1990). *Mimesis as Make-Believe*. Cambridge: Harvard University Press.

Wang, C. X., Berson, I. R., Jaruszewicz, C., Hartle, L. and Rosen, D. (2010). Young children's technology experiences in multiple contexts. In Berson, I. R. and Berson, M. J. (eds.). *High Tech Tots: Childhood in a Digital World* (pp. 23–48). Charlotte: Information Age Publishing.

Watkins, M. (1990). *Invisible Guests: The Development of Imaginal Dialogues*. Boston: Sigo Press.

Watters, A. (2010, October 1). Number Of Virtual World Users Breaks 1 Billion, Roughly Half Under Age 15. *Redwriterweb.com*. Retrieved from http://www.redwriteweb.com/archives/number_of_virtual_world_users_breaks_the_1_billion.php.

Webb, E. (1980). Images Of Television: Some Reflections. *Use of English 32(1)*: 10–17.

White, P. (2012, October 29). Kids Virtual Worlds. *TBIvision*. Retrieved from http://tbivision.com/highlight/2012/10/kids-virtual-worlds/19038/.

Winnicott, D. W. (1971). *Playing and Reality*. Tavistock Publication.

Wittgenstein, L. (1992). Last Writings on the Philosophy of Psychology. *The Inner and the Outer*, Vol. 2. Oxford: Blackwell, 1949/199.

Wulff, S. B. (1985). The symbolic and object play of children with autism: A review. *Journal of Autism and Development Disorder 15*: 139–48.

Vincenzo De Masi & Han Yan

The Digital Turn in Storytelling and Creative Industries in China: A report

Abstract In recent years, creative industries in China have had an important role both economically and socially, and the sectors of animation and video games have had the chance to develop significantly. Animation, as a form of storytelling, can have a strong educational power (Van Riper, 2011): this is the basis of the new industrial strategy adopted by China in the creative sector, as far as the animation field is concerned (Tan, 2006). Over a few years, the animation industry was able to achieve a great development with the creation of products mainly for broadcast on TV. Animation now represents around 220,000 minutes per year. For this reason, China became the number one producer of animation in the world in 2010. But to achieve this, the Chinese government had to encourage and try to structure the entire animation industry (Lu Bin, 2013). In the early 2000s, the animation industry in China increased the production of animation contents, thanks to the introduction of computers in industrial production, bringing about an increase in minutes and quality (Tan, 2006). This new technological condition was somehow facilitated by the government that pushed the major animation production studios to adapt to new technological standards and keep pace with other countries competing in this area (Qing, 2006). The digital turn in storytelling seems to have increased the capacity of the government to promote traditional values, rather than improving the chances of the independent authors and private studios to create new stories. The development of technology and the entry of computers in many Chinese homes also generated a change in the spread of animation products, as many users, especially students, began to watch online products made abroad. Moreover, it has created a new generation of authors, who, although few, have begun to create new stories and have a clear idea of how to use new technologies – even criticising, in some animations, the social situation of modern China. At that moment, there was still a predominance of foreign productions, mainly Japanese and American: almost the totality of the merchandise was in the hands of foreign companies (Lu Bin, 2014).The digital turn in storytelling has made propaganda productive: not a cost for the government but actually a profitable business to reach in few years. This article will relate the historical and technological development, government policies in favour of this industry and it will analyse the reasons of the theatrical feature animation films success, highlighting the most representative works produced over the past 15 years.

The Civilising Mission in History

Education and a civilising purpose inspired Chinese animation from its beginning, when China was suffering from the cultural and territorial invasion of foreign imperialism. Against this background, Chinese animation took on the responsibility for the education of common audiences of all ages. Marie-Claire Quiquemelle wrote that the Brothers Wan produced six "educative" and "patriotic" films for Lianhua before moving to Mingxing Film Company in 1933, where until war was declared in 1937, they made nine short films and lived "for the first time in comparative comfort and security" (Quiquemelle, 1991: 177). At that time, the ideological and moral education animations with strong patriotic themes included: *Citizens, Wake Up* (国人速醒, Guó rén sù xǐng, 1931), *Blood Money* (血钱, Xuě qían, 1932), *United Together* (精诚团结, Jīng chéng tuán jíe, 1931), *The Leak* (漏洞, Luò dòng, 1933) and *The Year of Chinese Goods* (国货年, Guó huò nián, 1933). The overtly anti-Japanese propaganda films were: *Dog Detective* (狗侦探, Gǒu zhēn tàn, 1931), *National Sorrow* (民族痛史, Mín zú tòng shǐ, 1934), *New Tide* (新潮, Xīn cháo, 1936) and *The Motherland Is Saved by Aviation* (航空救国, Háng kōng jiù guó, 1933). There were also animations based on animal fables to educate people, including *Tortoise and Rabbit Have a Race* (龟兔赛跑, Guī tù sài pǎo, 1932), *Sudden Catastrophe* (飞来祸, Feī lái huò, 1932) and *Locusts and Ants* (蝗虫与蚂蚁, Huáng chóng yǔ mǎ yǐ, 1932).

After 1949, animation films became an effective method to spread "enlightenment": a large number of people need not only moral education but also scientific popularisation. Shanghai Animation Film Studio produced many animations at that time: *Zhu Bajie Eats the Watermelon* (猪八戒吃西瓜, Zhūbājiè chī xīguā, 1958), *A Clever Duckling* (聪明的鸭子, Cōng míng de yāzi, 1960), *Where Is Mama?* (小蝌蚪找妈妈, Xiǎo kē dǒu zhǎo Māmā, 1961), *Snow Kid* (雪孩子, Xuě háizi, 1980), TV series such as *Sheriff Black Cat* (黑猫警长, Hēi māo jǐng zhǎng, 1983–1987) and so on. Shanghai Studio fully exploited enjoyable and educational animation features, and from then on, the educational mission became a very important part of the Chinese animation industry.

The animation suitable for television made in China at the end of the 70s and 80s has features of storytelling very similar to the previous ones, but the new technologies and the easy access of Chinese families to television were changing the way of telling stories. In fact, Chinese products were becoming more and more similar to the international standards giving less importance to the educational aim (Qing, 2006). An outstanding example of the change is *Sheriff Black Cat* (1983–1987). This change in storytelling and the globalisation of the canon were to be even stronger in the productions of the digital age.

The First Stage of Chinese Animation Development

According to the Bluebook (2015 edition), government policies implemented over the past 15 years boosted the investment and production of animation with new private Chinese investors and encouraged those businesses that were still in their early growth phase. The established studios started focusing on industrial production in some way, in many cases abandoning artistic content and creating animations with global and commercial content (Tan, 2006; Bluebook Animation, 2015).

In order to counter the entry of foreign animation films into the market and to develop the domestic animation industry, the Chinese government has enacted and created several laws to support the companies in the production with new technologies and the storytelling that has the educational and traditional content of the Chinese culture.

In line with these new ideas, in 2000 the State Administration of Radio, Film and Television (SARFT)[1], on behalf of the government, issued regulations focusing on broadcasting cartoons on TV in order to help Chinese animation producers. One of these rules stated that every television channel had to submit all foreign animation products for approval to SARFT before their broadcasting. In addition, the approved products could be aired only if broadcast in the same proportion (expressed in minutes) as Chinese cartoons.

In the *Tenth Five-Year Development Plan* issued in 2002, the government demanded that companies operating in the animation sector create a television channel devoted to the broadcasting of original animations made by the same companies.

In August 2003, SARFT invited the provincial and local governments to support and encourage development policies focused mainly on the animation industry (Qing, 2006).

In 2004, thanks to these policies, there was a 15% growth in the production of animation with an increment of 7 percentage points over the same period in the previous year. Despite this successful growth, about 70% of productions were still of foreign origin, in particular Japanese productions, which had about 50,000 broadcasting minutes against the 23,800 minutes of original Chinese animations. According to official data published in the same year, it was estimated that the total demand for animation products for TV was about 260,000 minutes, highlighting that this area had potential for development in China.

The main aims of the government policies were not only economic but also ideological and moral: this is one of the important aspects for the Chinese government, which aimed to improve the education of the younger generation. To

1 The State Administration of Press, Publication, Radio, Film and Television of the People's Republic of China (SAPPRFT or SARFT, 国家广播电影电视总局, Guójiā Guǎngbō Diànyǐng Diànshì Zǒngjú), is the government institution that checks and manages all media in China.

receive government funding, producers had to ensure that their animations had educational and moral content in their storytelling (Tan, 2006).

From this period (2000–2004), one of the most significant productions following the aim of the government is *Magic Umbrella* (可可的魔伞, Kěkě de mó sǎn, 2000), which used 2D and 3D in a mix of animation and real sequences (Bluebook Animation, 2013), produced by the Chinese government-controlled Shanghai Animation Film Studio (SAFS), which is also the oldest still operating animation studio in China. Equally interesting is the animated TV series *Wars of Millennium Bug* (大战千年虫, Dà zhàn qiān nián chóng, 2001), in part publicly funded and considered as the answer to famous American TV series such as *Rugrats* (1991–2004), *Histeria (1998*–2000) and *The Simpsons (1989*-present*)*. This animated series was made with the cooperation of Beijing Green Olives Animation, Animation Chang'an Beijing and Shanghai Red Dragonfly Animation, and aired on CCTV[2] in 2001.

From a technical and narrative point of view, this series is interesting not only for its stylistic level, far from the Chinese school of animation, but also because it deals with topics close to a global culture rather than purely Chinese ones (Deng, 2011). The animated series *Music Up* or *Crazy for the Song* (我为歌狂, Wǒ wèi gē kuáng, 2001) deals for the first time with the topic of pop stars, referring to typical Japanese animation style such as that of *Ai Shite Knight* (1983–1984) or the American series *Jem* (1985–1988). *Music Up* is made up of 52 episodes and it is a co-production between SAFS and Shanghai TV, broadcast on CCTV in 2001. The series is remembered mainly because of its high production cost of 18 million yuan (about two million euro), and also because it was only moderately successful in China. Later, the series performed well, financially speaking, thanks to its successful merchandising policy (Lu Bin, 2015).

In the early 2000s, CCTV broadcast 3D productions of foreign origin. This period was also marked by productions that had relatively high production costs and little success, both at the box office and on TV. According to scholars, this failure was due to the low quality of many of these productions such as *Platoon Urbano* (城市野战排, chéng shì yě zhàn pai 2001), an animated series of 26 episodes produced and broadcast by CCTV. Among the successful animations is *Zetrix* (2004), in high-quality 3D, made by Hong Kong-based Imagi Studio. It is a 3D

2 China Central Television (中国中央电视台, CCTV) is the Chinese public TV company, which owns 45 channels, such as CCTV 14 devoted to animations and children's programmes and CCTV-Shinco Animation (CCTV-新科动漫), which is a pay channel.

animation with no Chinese cultural characteristics distributed in many countries, including Japan, Germany and the United States (Lu Bin, 2012).

On 26 February 2004, the Communist Party's Central Committee and the State Council drew up a document entitled "Recommendations on further strengthening and improving of the ideological and ethical construction of Minors", which clearly stated a willingness to help companies in the production of original animation, "following it step by step, for the formation of national cultural characteristics which must be suitable for minors".

In particular, the document states:

> First, strengthening and improving the ideological and moral construction of minors is an important and urgent strategic task.
>
> Children are the future builders of the socialist cause with national characteristics. At present, minors under the age of 18 are about 367 million. Their moral condition is directly related to the overall quality of the Chinese nation, tied to the country's future and destiny. The Government gives great importance to education and training of the next generations and strives to improve their ideological and moral quality. It is right to pass on the fine tradition of our party to children because they will be an important guarantee for our country.[3]

Furthermore, the document stresses the importance of the creation and production of products for children to achieve these goals:

> Strengthening the creation and production of films and television for children, actively supporting the creation of domestic animation, filming, production and broadcasting, and gradually forming a national character, with features suitable to minors, showing the fine tradition of the cartoon series of the Chinese nation. It is necessary to actively develop the socialist market economy to improve the distribution of films for children.

The achievement of these objectives was primarily related to a series of actions carried out by the government in order to improve the situation of the sector and to protect the market and culture from the "invasion" of foreign products.

On 20 September 2004, SARFT issued the "Regulations of the Drama Review", stating that the creation of audiovisual products such as fiction (including TV cartoons) had to meet certain mandatory requirements established by the regulations and, in addition, that all the pre-production material (synopsis, test boards, titles and dialogues, subtitles, songs etc.) had to be delivered to the local institution (office of SARFT) for approval. With this initiative, SARFT wanted to establish

3 中共中央 国务院 关于进一步加强和改进未成年人 思想道德建设的若干意见 (2004年2月26日), http://www.gov.cn/gongbao/content/2004/content_62719.htm, last visited Aug. 31, 2015.

control over the national cartoons in order to ensure their educational aspects and content (Lu Bin, 2011). In October of the same year, the central government approved a document stating it would have to "support the industrial development of animation and video games" because that was considered a "special and strategic job". In this document, the Ministry of Culture was commissioned by the central government to put in place a strategy for the improvement of the "National Animation and technical quality of the Games" (Document 2004 SARFT).

In the same year, to address the foreign cultural and economic influence, SARFT issued a law regulating the broadcasting of foreign-origin products, the share of which should not exceed 40% of total prime time programming because 60% had to be covered by Chinese original animation[4] (Cooper-Chen, 2010).

In 2004 and 2006, in order to speed up the educational aim and create places devoted to the development of the sector, the Chinese government appointed the cities of Guangzhou, Chengdu, Beijing and Shanghai as the "basis for the development of the national network of the industry of game and animation".[5]

On 20 January 2005, SARFT introduced a new regulation concerning the licensing for broadcasting cartoons of Chinese origin on television: it stated that from 1 July 2005 all domestic cartoons (new productions and even those already broadcast) had to apply for a licence before being broadcast on TV. These new regulations encouraged the production of new cartoons that aimed to educate children and strengthen ideologies. In addition, they were given more TV broadcasting time; the national television channels were almost forced to pass domestic animations as they could not show more than a certain number of foreign animations in their daily programming (Tan, 2006).

One of the animation products directly or indirectly related to the new government policies described above is *DragonBlade: The Legend of Lang* (龙刀奇缘, Lóng Dāo qí yuán 2005), produced in 3D by China Film and DCDC Studio in 2005. The film was made in Hong Kong because the Chinese studios did not have the right technology for 3D animation products. For this reason, the first Chinese 3D animations were co-productions with Hong Kong.

4 This law also regulated prime time advertising and, if an animation product had a duration of more than 60 minutes, prescribed only two commercial breaks, one at the beginning and one at the end of the broadcast.

5 "Basis for the development of the national network of the industry of game and animation" 我国部分城市国家级动漫产业基地的发展模式, "国家动漫产业振兴基地", Beijing Cultural and Creative Network, http://www.iccie.cn/web/static/articles/catalog_ff8080813165bac4013165cf01d10020/article_2c909489318dca5b01318dca77ac0037/2c909489318dca5b01318dca77ac0037.html, last visited on 29 August 2015.

In line with the previous animation is the film *Thru the Moebius Strip* (魔比斯环, mó bǐsī huán, 2005), made in Shenzhen by the Institute of Digital Media Technology in co-production with the United States. The animation technique and language are very similar to those of American series but the narrative structure is very complex. This may be one of the reasons why the film was not very successful (Bluebook Animation, 2013).

To cope with the strong foreign influence, CCTV and Beijing Golden Pinasters Animation Company produced an animated series (26 episodes of 20 minutes each) called *The Dreaming Girl* (梦里人, Mèng lǐ rén) in 2005. It can be considered as the first television adaptation in the form of animation of the comic *Dream Men* (梦里人, Mèng lǐ rén, 2005) by Yao Feila (姚非拉), which is very famous in China. The series was produced with the specific aim to address a teenage audience using the language of Japanese cartoons, much loved by the young generation in China (Sun, 2011).

The Chinese animation industry was growing because, thanks to state contributions and support from the central government, production of animation became more interesting in terms of income. For the production houses, selling their products to CCTV was not only a opportunity to gain visibility for their products throughout China but also a way to achieve better financial results.

In this period, there was the change from the production of individual products to a more industrialised production characterised by the realisation of animation developed in a large number of episodes. An early example of this change is *Century Sonny: The Adventure of the Extra-Galactic Prince* (精灵世纪, Jīng líng shì jì, 2006), made up of 105 episodes of 18 minutes each. It is a high-definition 3D animation that cost about 1.1 billion yuan (150 million euros) and was able to make big profits because it was broadcast first on CCTV, Beijing TV and Shanghai TV and then on 500 other TV stations throughout China (Xinmin Weekly, 2006).[6]

Also worth mentioning is another animation titled *SkyEye* (天眼, Tiān yǎn, 2005), a series of 500 seven-minute episodes with a total production cost of 15.6 million yuan (2.5 million euro). Its production involved the participation of three prominent media leaders: CCTV, the Central Academy of Dramatic Arts and the Beijing Film Academy.

The year 2005 saw the birth of a series dedicated to young audiences: *Pleasant Goat and Big Big Wolf* (喜羊羊与灰太狼, Xǐ Yang Yáng yǔ Huī Tài Láng). Considered the most important production of all time in China, *Pleasant Goat* was

6 Xinmin Weekly (2006), 新民周刊, Editions 1–25, Xinmin Weekly Club, 新民周刊社.

produced by Creative Power Entertaining.[7] The series, made up of 1,500 episodes lasting 25 minutes each, is still in production. There were also cinema films based on the television series, which were successful for eight consecutive years. Made with Flash animation, with simple graphics and simple stories, *Pleasant Goat* is a cartoon that does not have particularly interesting aspects: from the aesthetic point of view, it does not present any Chinese cultural features, and it has been designed as pure children's entertainment with a moral ending. Children are attracted by the ease of language and by the aesthetic features of the characters, all accompanied by traditional music suitable for children. *Pleasant Goat* was able to obtain government funds despite the lack of traditional Chinese features. It also represents a real turning point for Chinese animation because, for the first time, a domestic production was able to generate the kind of revenue achieved until then by foreign productions only[8] (Lu Bin, 2011).

On the contrary, the film *Little Soldier Zhang Ga* (小兵张嘎, Xiǎo bīng Zhānggǎ, *Zhang Ga or The Soldier Boy*, 2005) by director Sun Lijun (Deputy Director of the Beijing Film Academy) is a film with Chinese cultural features made entirely with private funds. Based on a true story, the film tells the life story of little soldier Zhang who fights against the Japanese army. The original story was modified to attract younger audiences and was later released to theatres in 2005 to celebrate the 60th anniversary of the end of the war against Japan. To lower the production cost, which were about 9.2 million yuan (1.2 million euros), the director used the contributions of Beijing Film Academy's students. Although it is not a propaganda film, *Little Soldier Zhang Ga* revived the idea of nostalgic films like *Red Star*, that is those films with communist propaganda as their main topic (Jiu, 2008).

One of the latest 3D animations created in this period is *Tortoise Hanba's Stories* (憨八龟的故事, Hān bā guī de gùshì, *Tortoise Hanba's Stories, The Story of Hanbagui* or *Hanbagui*, 2006), consisting of 500 episodes of 13 minutes each (still in production), broadcast by CCTV and other national and local networks. Produced by Shenzhen Toonring Animation, the animation became famous for its main character, a turtle, which is still very popular in China. Even in this case there are no Chinese cultural references in the animation. The educational aspects of this animation are very simple, such as respect for others, friendship and love, and general themes that in some way can be found in many other animations.

7 In 2012, the rights for the series were purchased by Toon Express Group.

8 In fact, Chinese animation films had never achieved as significant revenues as foreign animations.

Government Commitment & New Policies in Support to the Sector

In China the new digital era has led the government to indirectly intervene on storytelling through the SARFT control over projects and scripts. Only those companies that followed the guidelines, the stylistic and narrative canons dictated by the government could receive funding. This strategy has led many companies to create propaganda products with no relevant educational content in order to access to funding and financial incentives dedicated to the sector.

Since 2006 the government has been committed in supporting Chinese animation with a series of interventions such as tax breaks given to companies dealing with animation. Furthermore the Ministry of Culture was appointed to take care of the animation industry considered important for the "ideological education and moral construction of minors".[9] The Ministry of Finance was appointed to create special funds for the sector. As mentioned before, the Chinese government tries to support the animation industry since it is considered important in the formation and orientation of education of the youngest generation.

For this reason the government has entrusted the television broadcasts to control the series and animations in order to cut out any cultural content in opposition to the national cultural identity.

To strengthen the Chinese culture and its animated products the government issued a new regulation in August 2006 that prevented all broadcasters to air Chinese animations from other countries in the time slot from 17:00 to 20:00 (Tan, 2006), starting from the 1st of September of that year (Tan, 2006; Qing, 2006; Lu Bin, 2013).[10]

According to statistics released by the State Administration for Industry and Commerce and by SARFT in 2006, sector interventions by the public institutions, started in 2000, have promoted the birth of 447 universities offering animation courses in China and more than 5000 animation production companies.

---

9 Official data at http://www.gapp.gov.cn/caiwusi/oldcaiwusi/contents/2981/137488.shtml, last accessed on 22 November 2014.

10 In addition to the funds allocated to the production, the government set an animation transmission prize for original productions. The award consisted of 1,775 yuan (about 230 euro) for each minute broadcast on CCTV and 926 yuan (about 120 euro) for each minute broadcast on channels that were operating in cities and provinces that had joined this initiative.

Thanks to these laws, in 2006 there was a boom of cartoon production for national TV, with a total of about 81,000 minutes, while in the previous year there were only 42,000 minutes[11].

Worthy of mention is the animation *Rainbow Cat and Blue Rabbit* (虹猫蓝兔七侠传, Hóngmāo Lántù qī xiá zhuàn, *The story of Hongmao and Lantu*, 2006), a series of 108 episodes of 15 minutes each aired on CCTV for a few years with the aim to educate and entertain the young but recently suspended because considered too "cruel, violent" and eliminated from CCTV Children's Channel. Based on the series, broadcast by 800 TV stations, there were also several video games, 20 comic books, novels and eight different CDs. With the sale of the books based on the comic (Changchun Film Studio 2007) alone, Hunan Greatdreams Communications Studio (湖南宏梦卡通传播有限公司, Hunan hóng Meng kǎtōng Chuanbo yǒuxiàn gōngsī) gained 16 million yuan (2 million euros).[12]

Another film from this period is *Monkey King vs Er Lang Shen* (孙悟空大战二郎神, Sūnwùkōng dà zhàn Èrlángshén, 2007), made for the cinema with a cost of 6 million yuan (800,000 euro) by the producer and director Yuan Cheng Liang Hansen (China Film Press 2009).[13] The film is very innovative and therefore interesting from a stylistic point of view because it uses 3D animation with the traditional art of puppet animation: here, the producers' aim to refer to Chinese culture is clear.

Another important series (still being aired in its fifth season with over 100 episodes of 21 minutes made), is *Qin's Moon* (秦时明月, Qín shí míng yuè, The Legend of Qin Dynasty), in high quality 3D. It is an adaptation of a novel by Wen Shiren dating back to ancient China. The animation was translated into seven languages (Italian, Spanish, English, German, French, Arabic and Russian) and was distributed in 37 countries, including Italy, the US, France, Spain, Canada, Russia etc. (Sun, 2011).

Another film in line with Communist ideology and propaganda is *Sparkling Red Star* (闪闪的红星之孩子的天空, Shǎnshǎn de hóng xīng: háizi de tiān kōng, 2007) directed by the famous director Dante Lam from Hong Kong and produced by Puzzle Animation Studio, one of the most famous production companies based

11 The productions in 2006 were still subject to the laws and regulations of the 2000–2005 period because an animation series or a 3D movie requires a processing time ranging from 3 to 5 years.

12 Changchun Film Studio (2007), 电影文学 (Literature of Film), Editions 7–12, 长春电影制片厂 (Changchun Film Studio), page 164.

13 China Film Press (2009), 中国电影年鉴 (Cinema Yearbook 2009), 中国电影出版社 (China Film Press), pages 191, 491–2.

in Shenzhen. Made during the Cultural Revolution, the animation tells the story of a boy and his friends who want to help the Red Army. *Zhang Ga* and *Sparkling Red Star* represent a return to communist culture by the animation.

According to data reported by the 2008 *BlueBook*, China had more than 2,000 television channels, 25 channels dedicated to children, 289 TV programmes offering a section dedicated to children, 123 million users who had access to the internet and 430 million people using mobile phones (Bluebook Animation, 2008) in 2007.

Here is a short list of the significant measures implemented by the central government:

- From 1 May 2008, all television stations, including the local ones, could not broadcast any kind of foreign animation between 5pm and 9pm.
- In 2009, the Ministry of Culture stated that companies producing animation could enjoy five tax breaks, including VAT exemption.
- On 12 October 2009, SARFT announced that it would strengthen control on animation broadcasting and that, from the 1st of January 2010 onwards, the amount of time dedicated to Chinese animation had to increase; from 5pm to 10pm, only Chinese animations could be broadcast.
- In November 2009, SARFT allowed Jiangsu TV to create a channel for children on the satellite TV called Cady (优漫卡通卫视, You Man kǎtōng Weishi).

Thanks to all these incentives and government measures, in early 2009 the number of children's channels increased to more than 34. In 2009, the production reached 322 titles, or a total of 170,000 minutes, an increase of 31% when compared to the previous year.

Among the most significant animations of this period is *Storm Rider Clash of the Evils* (风云决, Fēng yún jué, 2008), directed by Dante Lam who preferred, again, issues related to Chinese culture. Produced by Puzzle Animation Studio and Shanghai Media Group, the film is based on a popular series of Wuxia Manhua (China martial arts comics) entitled *Fung Wan* (风云, Fēng yún, since 1989) by the Hong Kong author Ma Wing-shing (马荣成, mǎ Róngchéng) and uses a Japanese animation technique that manages to seamlessly integrate 3D into 2D in the same scenes.

An animation with original content is *Ming Kee* (茗记, Míng jì, 2008), produced by L-Key Studio. Its topic is the student life and romances of high school students in the 1990s in a small Chinese town. The series consists of three episodes with three separate stories: *Ming Kee – second life* (茗记 – 2nd Life, Míng jì: 2nd Life, 2006), *Ming Kee – Weaving Love* (茗记 – 初织恋, Míng jì: chū zhī liàn, 2008) and *Ming Kee – Trade-off* (茗记 – 取舍, Míng jì: qǔ shě, 2010). The author has shown that even Chinese artists are able to tell stories of teenage love in a deep and delicate way, taking as inspiration the Japanese animations from both stylistic and narrative points of view.

Internet and New Productions

The use of new technologies and new software has allowed many artists to express themselves and to tell stories without being censored, at least for a limited period. As Internet platforms such as Google, Twitter, YouTube, Facebook cannot be accessed in China, other platforms were created that are very similar to the original ones and sometimes even better. For example, Youku is a video hosting service platform that replaces YouTube; Weibo is similar to Twitter, Renren to Facebook.

Youku is one of the favourite platforms of young artists, and it is the first video platform that also allows for a certain independence from the government. It is sometimes possible to find very interesting documents that might, in some way, irritate the government.

A very important artist of this new trend is Pi San, who since 2005 has been analysing the Chinese modern society through his animations and the problems related to social policies adopted by China in recent years. For example, in the animated series *Kuang Kuang Kuang*[14] (哐哐哐, Kuāng kuāng kuāng, 2009) there is a sort of criticism with biting irony against the school system of the 1980s in China. Some episodes uploaded to Youku still survive but others such as *Kuang-kuang, The Little Rabbit* (小兔子哐哐, Xiǎo tùzi kuāng kuāng, 2011)[15] were immediately censored after their release on all sites across China. In fact, the episode *The Little Rabbit* recounts the scandal of contaminated milk powder. The Hutoon studio by Pi San now produces many series; some, such as *Miss Puff*, are funded directly by Youku, and in some cases are broadcast on the public television CCTV.

The period from 2009 to 2014 is the most productive for China in the field of animation. Since 2010, China has been holding the world record for producing animation, ahead of Japan. In this new production context, there are two interesting films: *Lee's Adventures*[16] (李献计历险记, Lǐ Xiànjì lì xiǎn jì, 2009)

14 Please see the website https://www.youtube.com/watch?v=p04oJUTVYZo, last accessed on 11 February 2016.

15 Please see the website https://www.youtube.com/watch?v=rNzjClqE1pY, last accessed on 11 February 2016.

16 Please see the video in Chinese at https://www.youtube.com/watch?v=2elRiYNwgkk, last accessed on 11 February 2016.

and the film called *A Jewish Girl in Shanghai* (犹太女孩在上海, Yóu tài nǚ hái zài Shànghǎi, 2010).

The first film is very important because it was created as an independent animation and shows a new way to tell a story, far from the classical patterns of Chinese animation. The director Li Yang[17] wanted to experience new languages by adapting the film to the new Chinese social context. The video, posted on the internet, was very successful with the young audience and was awarded as the Best Animated Short at the Tudou Video Festival. Later, it was made into a 90-minute live action film based on the original story and directed by Li Yang and Frant Gwo.

The second film *A Jewish Girl in Shanghai* is also worth mentioning; it is based on Wu Lin's comic and directed by Wang Genfa and Zhang Zhenhui. The film tells the story of the Jewish ghetto in Shanghai where, during the Second World War, Chinese people helped Jews to escape from Nazi persecution. The main characters are three children, who fled from Europe because of racial persecution, living in Shanghai occupied by the Japanese allied with Hitler. The characters establish a great friendship with the locals and try to reject the Japanese army in the city.

In 2011, there was another interesting film released entitled *Little Big Panda* (熊猫总动员, Xíong māo zǒng dòng yuán), considered the first Chinese 3D animation film.[18] *Little Big Panda*[19] is a co-production between China, Germany, France and Belgium, and it is a film with a moral dedicated to children (50 million euros) (Bluebook Animation, 2013).

The technique used to achieve 3D vision is very original; the characters' animation was drawn by hand using traditional Chinese painting technique and the 3D illusion was created by powerful animation software. The backgrounds were created using traditional ink painting. The production of this film took about five years.

The animation called *The Dreams of Jinsha* (梦回金沙城, Mèng huí Jīn Shā Chéng, 2010) is also remarkable for its great artistic quality and narrative. It deals with educational themes that speak about respect for nature. A distinctive feature

17 Li Yang graduated in ICT sciences in Germany and studied at the school of animation at the Academy Film in Bejing.

18 CNTV "China and Europe making 3D panda film", September 15, at http://china.org.cn/video/2010-09/15/content_20933354.htm, last accessed on 22 May 2013.

19 Considered as the answer to the great success of *Kung Fu Panda* created by Dreamworks in 2008, it was the first animation movie to earn a revenue of 100 million yuan in China, a record reached by no other film.

of this film is the choice of 2D and B2K as a standard resolution, and it is considered one of the best quality digital films showing in cinemas during that period.[20]

Sweetheart Princess (甜心格格, Tián xīn gégé, 2011) is an animated series that uses irony to tell the story of a princess who helps everyone. The series presents certain cultural aspects of Chinese tradition.

Thanks to its cultural, aesthetic and innovative features, the series *Rainbow Sea* (星游记, Xīng yóu jì, 2011) is an important product – it uses both 3D and 2D techniques. The series was produced by KAKU TV, a private television funded by advertising (99%), and You Yang Beijing Culture Media Co. (北京优扬文化传媒有限公司) (Shenzen Yearbook, 2009).

Another film with Chinese traditional content is *The Legend of Rabbit* (兔侠传奇, Tù Xiá chuán qí), released in July 2011 and produced by Tianjin Film Studio and Beijing Film Academy. It is an animated 3D film made in response to the great success of Disney's 2008 hit *Kung Fu Panda*. Sun Lijun, the film director and director of the school of animation at the Beijing Film Academy, said that "this film has achieved a moderate commercial success, but there is still some way to go" for the industry of Chinese animation.

Unlike previous films, *Kuiba* (魁拔, Kuí bá, 2011) uses 2D and 3D animation typical of Japanese animation but tells a story that refers to traditional Chinese culture.

An independent production with new narrative content and distributed on the internet is *One Hundred Thousand Bad Jokes Big Film* (十万个冷笑话, Shí wàn gè lěng xiào huà, 2015), released in China at the beginning of 2015. It is a funny story full of cyberlanguage which soon became popular among young people. The series even spread to Taiwan where Taiwan's ETtoday evaluated it as the Chinese version of *Gintama* (ぎんたま, gintama). It is remarkable because it is an adaptation of an internet animation series. On 26 March 2013, *One Hundred Thousand Bad Jokes* started its crowdfunding project on the web, asking for a hundred thousand ordinary people to fund the movie. Thanks to the internet, this project attracted more than 5,000 investors and 1.3 million yuan.

In the same year, Geng Xue (耿雪), a student at the school of animation at the Academy of Film, created *Mr. Sea*[21] (海公子, Hǎi Gōngzi, 2014), a very original independent horror animation that is very successful on the internet. The animation short film *Mr. Sea* is based on the traditional Chinese horror story *Mr. Sea*,

20 The film can be shown on a 30-metre screen preserving its full colours and its soft lines.

21 Please see the website https://www.youtube.com/watch?v=64WfOYr09AY, last accessed on 11 February 2016.

which is about a young man's quirky experience being lured by a beautiful hooker (a snake spirit, actually) and attacked by a huge snake (Mr. Sea, actually) on a desert island. The attraction of this animation film lies not only in the interesting story but also in its special style, a stop-motion animation using Chinese ceramics.

A short note is also needed for the independent animation *A Prequel of the Assassin*[22] (刺客聂隐娘前传, Cì kè Niè Yǐnniáng qián zhuàn, 2015) created by Weng Jie (翁劼), who was successful especially for his narrative style and Chinese element. It is based on a Tang Dynasty legend story about a little girl who was stolen and trained to be an assassin.

Finally, the role of the government policies introduced in 2000 to support the production of films and animation series with an educational and cultural purpose was decisive for the production of animation in China because prior to this, animation was considered one of the minor industries of the audiovisual sector in China.

As far as the creative factor and the creation of stories: SARFT cannot change the storytelling productions but it can decide which of these products can benefit from the contributions and support of the institutions. As mentioned above, animations wanting to obtain financing should respect the narrative and stylistic canons (even the possible opportunities of economic success) defined by the government guidelines. In fact, SARFT has to select scripts, storyboards and the estimated costs that companies are obliged to deposit before the production phase.

Following a long period of funding for majority companies, SARFT began a new campaign in 2011, funding only those companies or projects that managed to achieve important quality standards and exhibited a high level of educational and entertainment (edutainment) content.

According to the government, the use of animation as a tool for education is very important because the simple language used by animation films can catch the attention of new generations and hence form them in the Chinese tradition and the culture of modern China. In addition, the government aims at animation because this sector can create new jobs for people with a great intellectual and creative ability. Finally, there is another important goal that is purely economic: since the market is occupied mostly by productions from North America, Japan and Europe, the Chinese government aims at winning over a part of this market with new strategies.

---

22 Please see the website https://www.youtube.com/watch?v=3p79oGwxZZo, last accessed on 11 February 2016.

The introduction of new technologies has mostly favoured a change in the production of animations useful for educational purposes, but the government uses them as a means of propaganda and industrial development rather than as a creative means. In this new context, new generations aim to tell new stories with different points of view and, thanks to new technologies, today they are able to create their stories and find internet platforms for dissemination, managing to reach the international public and displaying the new point of view of modern China.

References

Bluebook Animation (2015). *Chinese Animation Industry Development Report* (2015). Beijing: 社会科学文献出版社 (Social Sciences Academic Press).

Bluebook Animation (2013). *Chinese Animation Industry Development Report* (2013). Beijing: 社会科学文献出版社 (Social Sciences Academic Press).

Bluebook Animation (2011). *Chinese Animation Industry Development Report* (2011). Beijing: 社会科学文献出版社 (Social Sciences Academic Press).

Cooper-Chen A. (2010). *Cartoon Cultures: The Globalization of Japanese Popular Media*. Peter Lang.

Deng, L. (邓丽丽, 2011). 十一五"期间中国动漫产业基地发展思考 (The Analysis of Development of China's Animation Industrial Base During the Phase of 11th Five-Year Plan). In *BlueBook*. Beijing: 社会科学文献出版社 (Social Sciences Academic Press).

Lu Bin, Niu Xìng, Zhen Zheng Yuming (卢斌, 牛兴侦, 郑玉明, 2015). 动漫蓝皮书 中国动漫产业发展报告(2015). In *BlueBook of Animation: Annual Report on Development of China's Animation Industry*. Beijing: 社会科学文献出版社 (Social Sciences Academic Press).

Lu Bin, Zheng Yuming & Niu Xingzhen (卢赋, 郑玉明, 牛兴侦, 2011). 动漫蓝皮书: 统筹兼顾, 多管齐下, 实现从动固大国到动渥强国的跨越 (Make Overall Arrangements, Leave Multicelly Together, Promote the Transformation from a Big Animation Country to a Powerful Animation & Comics Country). 社会科学文献出版社 (Social Sciences Academic Press).

Lu Bin, Niu Xìng, Zhen Zheng Yuming (卢斌, 牛兴侦, 郑玉明, 2012). 动漫蓝皮书 中国动漫产业发展报告. In *BlueBook of Animation: Annual Report on Development of China's Animation Industry*. Beijing: 社会科学文献出版社 (Social Sciences Academic Press).

Qing Xijie (2006). *An Economic Research of China's Animation Industry* [*Zhongguo donghuapian de chanye jingjixue yanjiu*]. Beijing: China Market Press.

Sun Lijun, Liu Yuejun (徐铮, 李楠, 2011), 数字互动时代的第三代电影研究与开发 (The Research and Development of 3rd Generation Film in Digital

Interactive Era). In *BlueBook*. Beijing: 社会科学文献出版社 (Social Sciences Academic Press).

Tan Ling, Yin Jun (2006, 谭玲, 殷俊), 动漫产业/21世纪文化产业前沿丛书 (Dòngmàn chǎnyè/21 shìjì wénhuà chǎnyè qiányán cóngshū, Animation industry / culture industry forefront of the 21st century books). Sichuan University Press.

Van Riper A. B. (2011). *Learning from Mickey, Donald and Walt: Essays on Disney's Edutainment Films*. Jefferson, NC: McFarland.

Xinmin Weekly (2006). 新民周刊. Editions 1–25, Xinmin Weekly Club, 新民周刊社.

Nathalie Hyde-Clarke

Story-Telling and Narrative Inquiry as a Gateway to Methodology

Abstract Across campuses, the very word 'methodology' elicits negative reactions and utterances of dismay from students even before they have embarked on a course. Deemed to be boring or a 'necessary evil', learners often arrive for their first class demotivated or disinterested. Yet, as all educators know, without a solid foundation in research methods, students will flounder in their research reports at the end of their undergraduate degrees and will continue to battle into postgraduate studies. How then can the usually compulsory methodology course be structured in such a way as to create a constructive and engaged learning experience? This paper examines the effectiveness of introducing story-telling techniques, through the use of narrative enquiry and reflective practices. The objective is to introduce different methodologies and allow students to apply those research methods to everyday events based on their own encounters, experiences and understanding, thereby demonstrating the need and relevance of a firm understanding of these approaches and concepts.

Keywords Story-telling, narrative inquiry, methodology

Introduction

By the second class, the numbers had doubled. Yes, doubled – a bizarre occurrence as it was a methodology class that experience shows students will do their best to avoid at all costs. But there they were, sitting eagerly at the desks waiting to hear the next installment and have their chance to participate. And so, a pilot study in the first class guided us through an entire course with almost 100% attendance and all assignments submitted on time. What had changed? It was so simple: the 'me me me[1]' generation had found the pleasing combination of being allowed to talk about themselves, analyse their own behaviour in minutiae, and thus place themselves in the very centre of their own learning experience. It was about them making research relevant to their immediate realities. Through the use of narrative enquiry, the world of methodology had been demystified.

This methodology course caters to communication, culture and media students. In their minds, they are going to be the next international news desk anchor, Pulitzer

1 A reference to the *Time Magazine* article by Joel Stein (May 20, 2013) about the millennials, people born between 1980–2000, who are labelled as exhibiting traits of excessive narcissism, entitlement and a general lack of motivation to succeed through hard work.

winner, acclaimed director, or working behind the scenes in sound, editing and production. For them, methodology is just another course to get through so they can graduate and move on. More often than not, students who do arrive instantly immerse themselves in activities on their digital devices paying little attention to the rest of the class. This creates a dual challenge for those of us teaching: firstly, they clearly do not see the relevance of this knowledge now or for later; and secondly, as the course is generally theoretically based, more practically minded students see it as a strange and terrifying hurdle best avoided. At the start of every methodology course, I always allay the latter fears by pointing out that

> there is nothing new about methodology – you have been doing it all the time. You just haven't realised. So now, we will start to identify the steps and name them so you can use them in a systematic way later. You will be amazed at how often you will use these tools in industry and how much difference this will make to your job performance. You will just get better and more credible information when you use them correctly.

The point that is emphasised through this process is that we all engage in a cycle of inquiry and analysis on a daily, even hourly, basis and that very few of the methods that we as communication and media students use are all that different from what we as individuals have been using all along. The methods in research are simply more systematic, more meticulously selected and designed, sometimes conducted on a large scale, and include people other than ourselves.

But how to address the former challenge of a general lack of interest demonstrated by the continuous use of personal communication devices in the class? The key to getting 'buy-in' or engaged academic participation really only occurred when I introduced narratives and narrative inquiry as a means to opening the gateway to methods in research. As keen producers, consumers and reviewers of digital content, they felt a need to tell others about their experiences which outweighed their inclination to disengage. Basically, we tell each other our own stories, and then we retell them – identifying and defining key steps in a research process. We reflect on the experience described in the story and discuss how we could have changed the result or got a better result had we approached it differently. By the end of the course, learners clearly understand and are able to implement the steps in a research proposal. They are accurately identifying which research methods will work better for various types of data collection needs. They understand reliability, validity and ethics. But most importantly, they understand the relevance of what they have learned.

This chapter examines how narrative inquiry is being increasingly used as an educational tool. It suggests that the inclusion of story-telling techniques allows the 'digital native' learner to better understand academic approaches and make those more relevant to their educational process in a methodology course. For the purposes of this paper, methodology will refer to "a set of skills, assumptions and practices that the researcher employs as he or she moves from paradigm to the empirical world" (Denzin & Lincoln 2005: 25, as cited in Lal et al. 2012: 2). At the same time, it is important to note the multiple influences the use of narrative inquiry has had on the course. Not only does it act as a means of interpretation and introduction at the individual level, it also serves to mould curriculum planning and development. In other words, both the 'digital turn' and the 'narrative turn' are influencing the educational space quite significantly. The chapter starts with an introduction to narrative inquiry and then considers its application as an educational tool.

Narrative Inquiry

The 'narrative turn' – a phrase coined to capture the sudden and increased interest in the use of narrative inquiry in social sciences – highlights the importance of meaning and social interaction through storytelling within situated contexts (Monteagudo 2012: 297). While the initial purpose may have been to analyse the structure and content of stories, there has now been a shift to exploring how those narratives may have political, social and educational functions (Rutten and Soetaert 2013). It is increasingly viewed as an "ethnographically-oriented social science approach" (Stanley and Temple 2008: 275) to be included as a research tool of analysis for visual, oral and written texts. It has been effectively applied across disciplines, including literary studies, cultural studies, psychology, sociology and education.

Narrative inquiry first appeared in research from the Chicago School of Sociology in the early 1900s, although it really only garnered noticeable interest in the 1960s (Lal, Suto and Ungar, 2012: 4). Viewed as a seminal author in the field, Jerome Bruner published a number of texts on narrative, the construction of reality, and the possibilities for education from the late 1980s to mid-1990s. In his article titled *The Narrative Construction of Reality* (1991: 6), he refers to narrative as

> an account of events occurring over time…The time involved, moreover, as Paul Ricoeur has noted, is 'human time', rather than abstract or 'clock time'. It is time whose significance is given by meaning assigned to events within its compass.

It is through the narration of those events that theories are developed to guide people in terms of understanding, as they manifest through "temporality; generic particularity; interpretability; implied canonicity; negotiability; ambiguous reference and historical extension" (Bruner 1996: 133–147 as cited in Monteagudo

2012: 298). Bruner goes on to argue that there must be some form of agency in narrative, as agency is based on selection and action. A person chooses to present chosen events in a specific way in order to either explain or interpret their or other's behaviour. Connelly and Clandinin (2006: 375, as cited in Clandinin and Huber 2010: 436) refer to narrative inquiry in the following way:

> Story…is a portal through which a person enters the world and by which their experience of the world is interpreted and personally meaningful. Narrative inquiry, the study of the experience of the story, then, is first and foremost a way of thinking about experience. Narrative inquiry as a methodology entails a view of the phenomenon. To use narrative inquiry methodology is to adopt a particular view of experience as phenomenon under study.

There is clearly intent in the sharing of a story. The narrative of the self is thus largely used as a tool to make sense of personal experience or expectations. Of course, this means it is important for any researcher to note that the meaning is based on and located within an existing set of values, beliefs and desires. As such, narratives are complex and are characterised by "problems, dilemmas, contradictions and imbalances" (Monteagudo 2012: 298).

One of the narrative features explored by Bruner (1991: 8) is hermeneutic composability:

> The telling of a story and its comprehension *as* a story depend on the human capacity to process knowledge in this interpretative way.

By this, he postulates that the act of constructing a narrative is more than simply choosing events. The particulars selected need to be constituted as relevant to the story, becoming its parts and functions. In this way, the construction of reality and experience has two clear phases: how it is created as a purpose of explanation; and then how it is interpreted. It is often difficult to separate the two, as, depending on the audience, the selection and interpretation of events are also based on the intention to elicit an expected response or outcome. Context is then a mitigating factor for interpretation. Of course, it would be remiss not to acknowledge that the 'millennials' are perhaps less concerned with reception than dissemination – demonstrated by the 'overshare' culture – but certainly the proliferation of 'likes' has had some influence in this regard in more recent times.

Narratives are understood in terms of 'who speaks' and the situations in which they speak. For example, in generic terms, one may be more tolerant of children's embellishments, more supportive of friends and families' versions, and more sceptical of stories told by those we deem untrustworthy or manipulative. We also highlight points of emphasis in other people's narratives based on our own levels of importance or understanding. It is normal for narratives to change with each telling, as people focus more on what holds true or significant to them, and not necessarily on what was of interest or significance to the original narration. Even if an individual retells a story of their own experience, it has been altered based on their first telling and subsequent response to that story, and how they have changed their understanding of that story. Less positive aspects of their own character or role they played may be toned down, or parts of the story deemed less interesting to the listener removed and those more interesting extended. In the digital sphere, the narrative may also be shortened due to space and characters available, this limiting the individual in their account of events. It would be difficult to imagine any situation where a story remains completely true to its original form in each retelling. This trend is significant when incorporating narrative inquiry into a course on methodology as a means to steer the introduction of key concepts; and the notion of subjectivity needs to be discussed very early in the process so that learners are aware of the critical aspects of the approach adopted.

Increasingly, studies indicate that the education setting can be enhanced through the use of a shared construction of meaning, presenting the opportunity to introduce and apply set frameworks, and approaches that allow learners to both elicit and interpret that meaning. Lal, Suto and Ungar (2012: 7) argue that

> narrative inquirers believe that humans communicate their experiences using co-constructed narratives that offer an epistemological portal through which experiences can be viewed and interpreted and then re-presented using storied forms.

Narrative-centred environments can therefore create a foundation for active participation and discovery learning to occur (Lee, Mott and Lester, 2011). Given the oral and written narrative traditions in most cultures, students are already intrinsically aware of basic 'research assumptions and objectives' connected to narratives, and it is through the combination of three factors that effective learning and engagement may be created. These have already been entrenched through the analysis of stories outside the self, using previously established norms and conventions. For example, in narrative theory, the first factor suggests that a character must be believable and embedded in the plot. As the plot presents circumstances to which the character should react, there is a need for agency as a selection of choice must be demonstrated to further the narrative. There is a symbiotic relationship between the character and the plot. Thus, both constructs, narrative and agency, are required to create an experience that is self-determined and purposeful (Lindgren and McDaniel 2012). Simultaneously, in order for the character to contribute to the outcomes of the plot, some form of problem-solving must occur (Lee, Mott and Lester, 2011). This is the second factor, and means that characters, or in this case, the self, cannot simply be depicted as unidimensional, but rather as complex individuals who are influenced by events or circumstance, and who share a willingness to better understand these 'realities' through constructive means. In order to best engage with the subject and the circumstances, the audience/ reader needs to exert agency and interact meaningfully and systematically with that narrative. In this third factor, elements such as purpose, aim, objectives, and the method of data collection and analysis should form a clear framework for consideration. A study by Lindgren and McDaniel (2012: 352) found that content with an explicit narrative and clear requirements for student agency increased levels of critical comprehension, improved academic skills, and increased ratings of personal development. But how best to introduce those tools to maximise the learner's information experience?

The Application of Narrative Inquiry as an Educational Tool

When using narrative inquiry as a means to introduce the research process in a methodology course, it is difficult to miss the cyclical nature of our actions. Essentially, we are analysing and – in some ways – re-structuring a narrative in order to demonstrate the creation of a different narrative based on the findings of the first. It is indeed a combination of telling, engagement, restructuring and retelling[2]. It is also important to note that the storytelling of one event or experience may occur through a variety of media and representations. Participants may use one or more techniques separately or simultaneously to express their experience to the listener: discourse, dialogue, drawings, notes, online content etc. In any face-to-face conversation, the researcher is also taking cues from non-verbal communication expressed through facial and body movements. And so one narrative may present itself as a 'sum of all parts'. This is a key aspect to emphasis in terms of data synthesis.

As narratives are complex both in terms of their content and delivery, the student needs to understand that it becomes the researcher's task to collect and possibly sort the necessary data associated with the narrative in order to make it comprehensible, to extract meaning, and to draw out the steps of the process for analysis and contemplation. Narrative inquiry is therefore a good entry to discuss alternative methods such as interviews, discourse and content analysis as well as auto-ethnography.

Clandinin and Huber (2010) identify several steps to designing a narrative inquiry: justification, naming the phenomenon, living the narrative inquiry,

2 In reference to Huber et al. (2013: 212) the extraordinary potential of living, telling, retelling, and reliving stories of experience.

positioning, ethical considerations, and issues in representation. First, the purpose of the research should be motivated by personal, practical and/or social concerns. Next, the phenomenon under investigation for analysis should be considered within three common places of narrative inquiry – temporality, place and sociality. This is important as it demonstrates the shifting nature of the phenomenon, as opposed to other methodologies that suggest a phenomenon is fixed or unchanging throughout the duration of a study. In the third step, Clandinin and Huber (2010: 10–11) raise a point that is significant to both design and pedagogy. A narrative inquiry is a lived experience. Not only is it changing, but it also has a life cycle that predates the time under study and will continue thereafter. Narratives are related to experience and in the telling and retelling inform and influence that experience. Thus, research is a recursive process. Learners and researchers should be prepared to revisit ideas more than once. In the final stages of presentation, there may be a need to create a chronological time frame; as Bruner (1991: 6) pointed out, narratives are shared in terms of personal importance and time may be attached accordingly. This again points to the relational role played by the researcher. Simultaneously, the researcher will probably select and sort information in order to identify what is most suitable for the purposes of the study. The combination of the above factors means that narrative inquiry is more likely to present interim instead of definitive results based on a manageable amount of information. The fourth step in design is the need for positioning the study in relation to other research and existing literature. In a methodology course, this allows for natural introduction of alternative ways of presenting and analysing information. In this manner, narrative inquiry can be an inclusionary and complementary mechanism in the curriculum. Ethics are included as a fifth step – a topic to be discussed in more depth shortly. Consideration should be given to informed consent, anonymity, confidentiality and sensitivity. Researchers should also reflect on the strategy of selection and the shaping of narratives. Finally, issues of representation refer to how participants and 'voice' are presented in the research text, essentially a shared narrative with a diverse audience.

If we were to stay true to these design stages in a course, we would always begin with a story. However, in a classroom context, that is not always the case. I have found that I need to discuss 'ethical' storytelling very early in the process, and now even include references to it in the first instructions. As Cole (1989: 31 as cited in Huber et al. 2013: 218) states:

> Their story, yours, mine – it's what we all carry with us on this trip we take, and we owe it to each other to respect our stories and learn from them.

Basically, learners should be encouraged to identify and discuss if, when and to what extent there is a need for clear parameters and regulations regarding the choice of stories according to social, ethical and institutional policies and contexts. There are literally hundreds of news reports about 'over-share gone wrong' and the lack of personal privacy in the digital age. So, in theory, the current generation should be aware of the concerns surrounding storytelling in a public space. That said, as these cases continue to receive international media attention, the message for careful and ethical storytelling can always be reinforced. As Stocchetti (2016) points out, there is both power and ambivalence in storytelling, and it is our role as educators to alert learners to that potential. This exercise is also a good practical example of 'shared constructed meaning'. Ethics may be implemented in two ways. Firstly, ground rules could be set by participants ahead of the selection of narratives. For example, no vulgarity should be allowed or tolerated. Alternatively, students may be instructed to 'think of a story' and then consider how they chose it and whether it is appropriate to be shared with the class. In other words, critical self-reflection in relation to the community becomes a key consideration – even more so in a class of future content producers.

This first step may be a contested one in terms of the role of the researcher and the informed consent of participants. Do regulated environments hamper creativity or self-expression? Is it possible to encourage the 'digital native' to understand the ethics of sharing a story, when it is so integral to their reality? Perhaps in the field the first concern may impact original contribution, but as this occurs in an educational setting and is driven not by research on student perceptions but rather the creation of a portal to better understand the research process, originality is less important than participation and understanding. It has always troubled me, when reading academic texts on methodology, that the ethics chapter is often towards the end, and that in research proposal templates (and even the design mentioned above) the penultimate question the researcher is asked is: 'any ethical considerations?' For researchers (experienced and emerging) to conduct more socially responsible studies, this should really be prefaced – especially in subjective qualitative studies, such as narrative inquiry, where the self is at the forefront and heart of the process. From the beginning of this course, emphasis is thus already placed on context (setting and purpose) and the recognition that audience and location impact on the framing of narrative.

Then we return to the first stage of the narrative inquiry design: we start with a story. I have tried two approaches: choose your own; and respond to the following scenario. The latter has proved the most effective as it removes the concerns of personal privacy from the first interaction. It also allows learners to construct a common understanding around a process in order to commence with the initial steps of creating research around a selected topic. This is more in keeping with what will be expected later in their degrees.

Here is an example of one scenario I have used in a second-year class (20-year-olds):

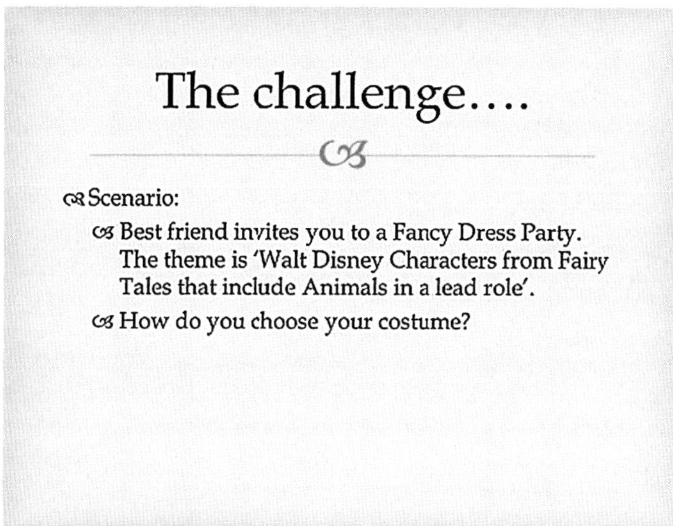

Of course, the first step should be to recognise that this is a culturally specific scenario. It requires that learners have some familiarity with the stories and characters. It should obviously be tailored based on the interests and knowledge of the students in the class. Students are given some time to think about the challenge, conduct an online search if they wish (usually by phone) and jot down a few ideas. Depending on the size of the class, they are then encouraged to share their ideas with one or more students in their vicinity. They are then encouraged to discuss their ideas with the class. This is a very organic process in that students are given (ethically responsibly) free rein to share their ideas or tell their story. Aside from verbal communication, learners include images from personal digital devices and anecdotes about previous experiences or something they have seen or heard about elsewhere.

Then comes the second phase: if this were a research project, what would we ask or test? What would be our hypothesis or research question? And so the research process starts. By the end of this class or workshop, a very basic proposal structure is presented to reinforce the notion that research is something we have been doing all along but a good understanding of methodology will allow us to do it better:

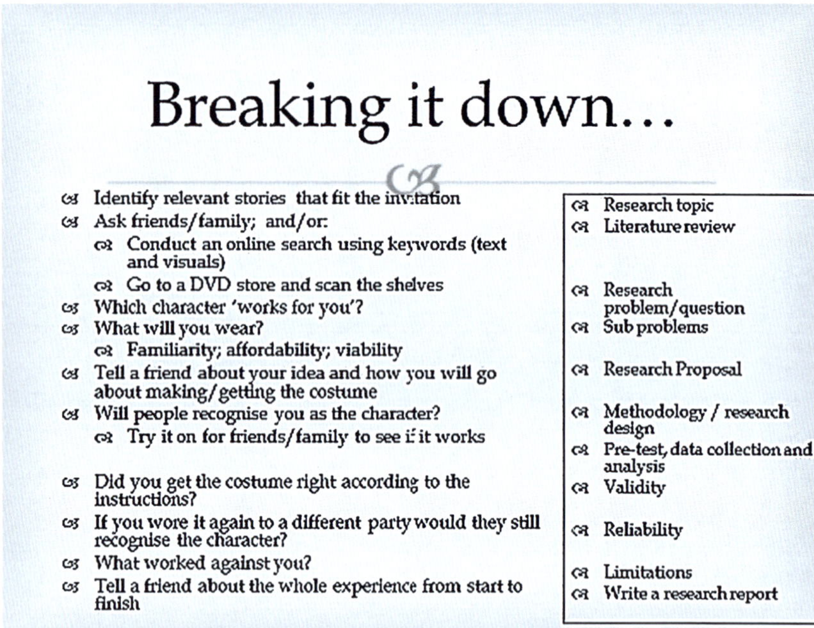

Thus, when leaving their very first session, students will have been exposed to foundational research design and practice. While the definitions and application will follow, they have at the very least heard several key terms and concepts, and through the use of narrative enquiry, they are starting to realise the accessibility and usefulness of a variety of methodologies. It can also be an empowering experience as they become aware that they already have some of the competencies required and now need to hone them to make themselves better at getting and compiling reliable and compelling data. They have also discovered, by default, that some online sources are more credible or compelling than others.

The difficulty with implementing narrative inquiry when teaching methodology is that it may place undue emphasis on that approach, causing students to favour it over other qualitative methodologies or alternative quantitative studies. Similarly, narrative inquiry is a subjective process. Narrative inquiries are deemed to be 'overly personal or interpersonal' (Clandinin and Connelly 2000: 181 as cited in Lal, Suto and Ungar 2012: 13). The close relationship between the researcher and the participant in constructing the narrative means that it may be difficult to create boundaries. This is further complicated if the researcher is the participant, or in this case, if the learner seeks to analyse the narrative of the self. It is sometimes difficult later when introducing methodologies that require more distance between the researcher and the subject.

This brings us to the next aspect of narrative inquiry as an educational tool. It can and does influence curriculum planning, as there must be a collaborative relationship between the class and the lecturer in terms of engagement and participation. The curriculum becomes part of the recursive process. If a particular approach is not effective, the students should be able to communicate that concern in order to effect change or at least receive feedback as to why the approach was chosen or will continue. This feedback mechanism is of course present in most courses regardless of the method of teaching. However, in narrative inquiry, much of the content takes its lead from the emphasis in the shared research narratives. So, for example, in a recent course with senior students, it was apparent from their storytelling exercises around possible thesis topics that we had a group emphasis on interviews. The course content therefore altered slightly to include more discussion around the interview process as it was perceived to be more relevant to their educational process. Of course, such emphasis does not exclude alternative methods that should also be introduced in a general methods course.

Concluding Remarks

Student comments at the end of the course referred to the lectures as "fun", "interesting" while "informative". In a conversation at the end of a class, a student told me: "we keep coming because we want to know what happens next". Perhaps without realising it, the learner completes the narrative cycle: just like with any good story, the audience only returns if they want to know more or when they feel part of or invested in the story. Arguably, there is little novel about what is presented in this chapter, except the explicit notification that narratives steer the way we experience our educational development. However, the positive influence of narrative inquiry in the presentation of a methodology course is profound and worth sharing. While storytelling gets more and more attention in terms of its digital contributions, it is its very malleable nature that garners increased interest in academic circles. The difference between a methodology course based on a narrative inquiry design and one that is not, is that due to years of understanding life experiences through narrative, it becomes easier for the current generation of learners to engage with research designs previously perceived as inaccessible so that they may go on to create cohesive studies.

References

Bruner, J. (1991). The Narrative Construction of Reality. *Critical Inquiry 18(1):* 1–21.

Clandinin, D. and Huber, J. (2010). Narrative Inquiry. In B. McGaw, E. Baker, & P. Peterson (eds.). *International Encyclopedia of Education 3rd ed* (pp. 436–441). New York: Elsevier.

Huber, J., Caine, V., Huber, M. and Steeves, P. (2013). Narrative Inquiry as Pedagogy in Education: The Extraordinary Potential of Living, Telling, Retelling, and Reliving Stories of Experience. *Review of Research in Education 37*: 212–242.

Lal, S., Suto, M. and Ungar, M. (2012). Examining the Potential of Combining the Methods of Grounded Theory and Narrative Inquiry: A Comparative Analysis. *The Qualitative Report* 17(21): 1–22.

Lee, S., Mott, B. and Lester, J. (2011, September 28). Modelling Narrative-Centred Tutorial Decision Making in Guided Discovery Learning. Retrieved from http://link.springer.com/chapter/10.1007%2F978-3-642-21869-9_23.

Lindgren, R. and McDaniel, R. (2012). Transforming Online Learning through Narrative and Student Agency, *Educational Technology and Society 15(4):* 344–355.

Monteagudo, J. (2011). Jerome Bruner and the challenges of the narrative turn. *Narrative Inquiry 21(2):* 295–302.

Rutten, K. and Soeteart, R. (2013). Narrative and Rhetorical Approaches to Problems of Education. Jerome Bruner and Kenneth Burke Revisited. *Studies in Philosophy and Education* 32: 327–343.

Stanley, L. and Temple, B. (2008). Narrative methodologies: subjects, silences, re-readings and analyses. *Qualitative Research* 8(3): 275–281.

Stocchetti, M. (2016) ed. The Politics of Education and the Digital Turn in Storytelling: A Critical Introduction. In Storytelling and Education in the Digital age, Frankfurt: Peter Lang, pp. (13–30).

Cristina Aliagas-Marín[1] & Ana M. Margallo

Digital Storytelling, Book Trailers and Literary Competence in Initial Teacher Education[2]

Abstract Storytelling and digital skills are core abilities that trainee teachers should be confident in as future educators in primary and secondary classrooms, and therefore both sets of skills should be integrated into formal instruction in initial teacher education courses in higher education. How can technologies and storytelling be combined in the ITE classroom in order to enhance the literary competence and pedagogic insights of our future teachers? What are the pros and possible cons of making a vernacular literacy practice such as digital storytelling central in formal learning? Can the new forms of expression, exploration, cooperation and communication associated with digital storytelling involve relevant areas of learning? This chapter analyses, in the light of these questions, an educational intervention on digital storytelling through the writing of a book 'trailer', designed as an assignment in a module on literary education for the BA in Primary Education at the Autonomous University of Barcelona (Catalonia/Spain, academic year 2012–13). The study shows the contribution and possibilities that digital storytelling brings to initial teacher education, and the impact that it has on the development of literary and technological skills of trainee teachers.

1 With the support of the Secretary for Universities and Research of the Ministry of Economy and Knowledge of the Government of Catalonia and the COFUND programme of the Marie Curie Actions of the 7th R&D Framework Programme of the European Union (Beatriu de Pinós 2011-A).

2 This paper is part of two R&D projects financed by the Ministry of Science and Innovation in Spain for the period 1/1/2012 to 31/12/2014, with an extension until 2015: "School 2.0: Digital literacy practices. Materials, classroom activity and online linguistic resources" (EDU2011-28381; directed by Dr. D. Cassany at the Pompeu Fabra University. Site: https://sites.google.com/site/ies201x1/home) and "Digital children's literature: production, reader's uses, reception and teaching practices" (EDU2011-26141; directed by Prof. T. Colomer at The Autonomous University of Barcelona. Site: http://gretel.cat/en/projectes-de-recerca/literatura-infantil-i-juvenil-digital-produccio-usos-lectors-recepcio-i-practiques-docents/#more-3268). We are grateful to the undergraduate students studying for the BA in Primary Education who participated in the activity, and in particular to Aiana and Mònica, who recorded themselves working at home while designing the book 'trailer'. We are also grateful to Peter Skuce, who has contributed helpful and challenging linguistic revisions of this paper.

1. Introduction

The digital age has given rise to new challenges for the educational community. One of the most salient of these is surely the incorporation of new technologies within formal learning, which is associated with a new learning culture that makes the best of the communicative, informational, collaborative, interactive and creative advantages such technologies afford (Adell and Castañeda, 2012). This methodological renewal is mediated by digital tools and artefacts that give new significances to what is learned. In this chapter we focus on digital storytelling, which enables the production of unprecedented multimodal artefacts to build and share ideas and stories. How does digital storytelling contribute to this methodological renewal? What are the risks, the challenges and the opportunities of including digital storytelling in formal learning? How can it be integrated meaningfully into the curriculum?

In many developed countries, the digital focus of the Common Core State Standards – which guide teaching policies in the integration of digital media, emphasising information gathering, critical appraisal, communicative skills and meaning-making through the digital medium – emphasises that teachers should be confident in digital competences. This is because they are seen as agents of the curriculum change (Priestley, Biesta and Robinson, 2013) that seeks to move from the 1.0 mind-set to the 2.0 mind-set (Lankshear and Knobel, 2006). When our undergraduate students in initial teacher education (ITE) come to perform as teachers, they will have studied in print-centric classrooms but lived in a digitally driven world and thus accumulated their own "funds of (*technology*) knowledge" (González, Moll and Amanti, 2005); and they will work in schools with disparate ideologies regarding the educational uses of technology (Aliagas & Castellà, 2014). For all these reasons, we see university classrooms in ITE as spaces wherein new digitally enabled teacher identities can develop.

A route to unchaining a real change in education is to give technology-based learning experiences to trainee teachers (Davies and Merchant, 2014), so they can appreciate the learning advantages. Digital storytelling affords a comprehensive approach to technology as it requires a variety of tools for recording information (e.g. photography, audio/video recording) and editing (e.g. *iMovie, Movie Maker* and suchlike software) besides giving a narrative mould to learning. How can technologies and storytelling cooperate in ITE in order to offer new avenues to learning that might enhance (or extend) the literary competence, the storytelling and pedagogical skills of future teachers in relevant ways?

These are tough questions that we will tackle in this chapter by sharing our research-based analysis of an educational intervention on digital storytelling through a book 'trailer' designed as a pair-based assignment on literary education. In this chapter we give an account of our experience integrating the book trailer artefact into the ITE curriculum as a tool for 'breaking' the classical print-focused approach to thinking about how to teach literature in primary classrooms, and we analyse the impact this task had on the learning of the trainee teachers.

2. Digital Storytelling

Digital storytelling comes from oral storytelling, which is the art of telling an ephemeral story through a three-fold partnership of mutual influences between a storyteller, a listener and a spoken story. Storytelling is interwoven with social life and related to the basic human need to find order, explanations and intellectual clarification. Storytellers were particularly important in illiterate societies and their stories had a ludic/imaginative and moral/pedagogical function similar to the one performed by cathartic theatre in Ancient Greece. Storytellers are still alive in urban society in strong association with children, in literary events in libraries or bookshops or at children's parties (Poveda, Morgade and Alonso, 2009). Even teachers (and parents) become storytellers when they retell traditional tales or set up puppet theatres.

Digital storytelling (Ohler, 2008; Robin, 2008; Lambert, 2010) extends ephemeral storytelling into a narrative that blends voice, text and multimedia content through a "creative process" (Ohler, 2008) of meaning-making in which technological tools (e.g. a computer, video camera, sound recorder) and semiotic codes (e.g. visual, linguistic, graphical, auditory) are combined in order to create, tell or retell a short story that can be a traditional tale, a personal narrative or an instructive tale. It can adopt a variety of forms, ranging from a recorded oral story to complex narrative artefacts such as *book trailers* or *draw your life* videos. According to Lambert (2006), in digital storytelling, seven main elements are articulated:

- the *point* (*of view*) of the author(s)
- *a dramatic question*
- *emotional content* about issues that are tackled personally
- *the storyteller's voice*, which personalises the story
- *the power of the soundtrack*
- *economy* of language and information
- the *pacing* of the story

The landscape of the internet is expanding with digital storytelling artefacts that allow people to express their ideas to a wider audience. More recently, this landscape is being enhanced with education-driven artefacts that students create as part of their formal learning. The successful integration of digital storytelling in education seems to be related to the expressive opportunities that it brings to the classroom in terms of literacies and multimodal communication, through which students can better connect their insights on academic content with their identities and vernacular ways of communicating in online life. However, some dissenting or sceptical voices have warned of the dangers of techno-centrism and the marketisation of education (Cuban, 2001; Ferneding, 2003), ideologies that carry a model of "student as a consumer" and that are supposedly infiltrating education through the digital storytelling movement. From this point of view, digital storytelling is seen as a promotional or persuasive form driven by market forces.

2.1 Why Digital Storytelling in the Classroom?

The pedagogical uses of digital storytelling are gaining popularity across the educational spectrum; in the elementary classroom (Nixon, 2013), in secondary education (Yang and Wu, 2012) and in higher education (Villalustre and del Moral, 2014). What are the pedagogical foundations that support digital storytelling as a teaching/learning approach?

The integration of digital storytelling in the curriculum is aligned with the sociocultural conceptualisation of literacy and learning represented by New Literacy Studies (NLS; Pahl and Rowsell, 2005). In its aspiration to reframe literacy in policy and practice, NLS has argued that connecting formal learning to vernacular, digital literacies helps to overcome the disconnect between the print-centric classroom and the more digital-centric world. From this point of view, the recognition in the curriculum of multiliteracies, multimodality, the use of Web 2.0 and the participatory nature of life online (Pahl and Rowsell, 2005; Cassany, 2012) have all been defended. The NLS position is sustained by the *funds of knowledge* approach (González, Moll, and Amanti, 2005), which works towards a culturally sensitive pedagogy capable of turning the cultural resources that learners bring to the classroom, in terms of literacy and ways of knowing, into valid resources for learning.

Moreover, the integration of digital storytelling in the classroom aligns with the constructivist approach to teaching/learning (Sadik, 2008) that has oriented the latest educational reforms, which have attempted to replace the knowledge-based pedagogy with a learner-centred one in which the student becomes the subject who critically reconstructs knowledge (Freire, 2004). In that sense, digital storytelling goes along with particular ideas developed in this tradition such as Vygotski's conceptualisation of learning as a cultural process, Piaget's idea of the learner as a meaning-maker and Ausubel's call for meaningful learning. It also connects with particular constructivist forms of teaching/learning such as the project-based approach originated in Freinet's works, where learning is organised in a way that gives resources and agency to the student to solve a problem or to produce an output at the end of the didactic sequence. Moreover, digital storytelling fits in with the competency-based approach, since its process mobilises several competences such as reading, writing, talking and listening. As Pitler (2006) argues, the integration of technology in learning is more powerful when it is combined with situations where the students discuss before, during and after the project (e.g. cooperative and collaborative learning).

Within the socio-constructivist approach, the pedagogical applications of digital storytelling have been described as multiple: as a tool to acquire and share knowledge (Ohler, 2008; Lambert, 2010), as a powerful way to make abstract content more understandable (Robin, 2008) and as an effective teaching strategy to motivate struggling learners (Sadik, 2008). Others have shown that learning is reinforced through identity reflexion (Nixon, 2013) and through "vernacular creativity" (Burgess, 2006) – digital storytelling uses the discursive codes that consumers develop in everyday life (e.g. cinema, television) to tell its stories.

2.2 Why Use Book Trailers?

A book trailer is a brief multimodal artefact that encompasses images and sound in order to promote a book by showing its appealing features, as a movie trailer does for a movie; it merges a promotional discourse with narrative pleasure. As a result of this, its rhetoric is moulded by certain features (e.g. brevity, concision), time conventions (1–2 minutes in length) and attributes associated with the trailer format (Kernan, 2004) such as an opening that addresses the target reader and situates the book in a genre tradition, an introduction to the main character(s), and a montage of scenes from the source text.

In addition to being used commercially by the publishing houses, the book trailer has become a strategy for promoting reading among teens through competitions announced by libraries and schools. Instead of seeing book trailers as a snare, the emphasis is on promoting books in order to 'hook' new readers and readers who are closer to the cinema. Certainly, using book trailers in educational settings brings a range of discourses into the classroom, such as ones on social, media and consumer life (Ferneding, 2003), but in favour of nourishing, in line with the wider argument of NLS, more critical consumers of the publishing houses' sales strategies.

The extended educational uses of the book trailer typically consist of employing the trailer format to encourage the reading of a book (e.g. Villalustre and de

Morral, 2013). Creating a book trailer is a challenge, since it requires reading the book, defining its allure and showing an awareness of the target audience, besides some technological skills for the digital montage. The reasons why we chose the book trailer format include its affinity with our subject and what it can offer to primary classrooms. As we explain in the following section, we adapted the book trailer format to the pedagogical rationale of our subject with the goal of giving the students an alternative path to develop their competence regarding literary education in primary classrooms.

3. Making Sense of Storytelling in our Classroom Through Book Trailers

3.1 The Context

We implemented a book trailer-based activity in a course on literary education given during the academic year 2012–13 in four groups from the third year of the BA in Primary Education at the Autonomous University of Barcelona (Catalonia, Spain), with a total of 216 participants, all Spaniards. The sessions aimed to develop the required 'pedagogical imagination' to teach literature-based comprehension meaningfully, something which demands literary, storytelling and pedagogical skills.

3.2 The Adaptation

We adapted the book trailer format with the aim of reinforcing specific competences and, in particular, addressing the requirement of planning activities to help the schoolchildren develop a wider comprehension of the book. This presents a challenging 'thinking space' with which many trainee schoolteachers struggle due to difficulties related to a) the exercise of adopting a coherent, literary-driven reading of the book, b) the design of a set of activities with a clear literary-centred purpose (e.g. avoiding a moralistic perspective) or c) a combination of the two. This challenge deepens when the students are asked to offer literary and pedagogical reflections to support their proposal. If the management of that reflexive thought oscillating between literary appraisal and pedagogical imagination is complex per se, encapsulating it in academic writing further hinders the process and in many cases causes the students to produce descriptive or nebulous essays with rambling teaching proposals.

In our specific context, we appropriated the book trailer as an artefact to facilitate that complex thinking between literary appraisal and teaching methodology, in tune with Robin's (2008) idea that digital storytelling can improve how teachers are trained, since it facilitates the articulation between knowledge about content, pedagogy and technology, and thus makes conceptual aspects easier to grasp. This is the case because digital storytelling, besides being a motivational tool for both teachers and students, is a powerful tool for converting data into information and transforming information into knowledge. The emphasis on (historical or personal) stories and the integration of visual images and written text are also two elements that reinforce both expressivity and comprehension.

3.3 Modelling the Task

We asked the students to create a two-minute trailer for a children's book using the programmes *iMovie* or *Movie Maker*. The book trailer had to articulate freely two insights into the book:

- a *trailer* for the book emphasising its main literary aspects (e.g. genre, theme, plot, characters, settings) to arouse appealing anticipation of the story, and
- a classroom-oriented proposal as to how they would use the book in a primary classroom to mobilise particular literary skills

The trailer was expected to focus on the process of retelling the book's storyline and the classroom-oriented proposal of giving the students a narrative space for reflecting on their choices. In order to give a meaningful context to the activity, we set up a scene linked to the role of schoolteacher: our students were schoolteachers participating in a staff meeting and had to propose a book to read for the next academic year. The headteacher encouraged them to create a book trailer in order to upload it to the school's website after a vote. This imagined context framed the narrative and analytical dimensions of the activity, and positioned the students as storytellers, digital meaning-makers and teachers who make proposals and take decisions.

Given that the integration of technology in formal learning is more powerful when it is developed through peer talk (Pitler, 2006), the participants in the activity were organised in pairs (108 in total). They had to select a book from a list of twelve children's novels (see Annex 1), which included universal classics, recognised works of Spanish children's literature, and other genre novels such as detective stories. The students shared the book trailer through a YouTube link in the classroom's online environment. Afterwards, they individually chose one book trailer for each of the following categories:

a) the overall best executed book trailer
b) the book trailer that offered the most powerful literary arguments
c) the book trailer presenting the strongest didactic arguments

These choices had to be explained in an online form[3] created with Google Docs. The students individually chose one book trailer per category and then had to justify their choices with pedagogical and literary arguments using a maximum of 70 words. A list of the results, complete with anonymous explanations, was also made public. The winning book trailers were linked to on our research group's webpage.[4]

The students were given three weeks from receiving the instructions to the delivery of the book trailer, and had one more week to watch the other trailers and vote. In terms of assessment, the criteria employed by the teachers focused on the following points: a) the general quality of the presentation of the book trailer, b) the identification and analysis of the literary strengths of the story, c) whether the digital artefact was globally convincing and d) the appropriateness of the written and oral language employed. Which book trailers won, according to the students' votes, did not influence the academic assessment.

As shown in Diagram 1, literary appraisal and pedagogical strategies were the two pillars of the content that the students were asked to integrate into the book trailer. These learning goals were driven through the discursive features of digital storytelling (Lambert, 2006) and those of the book trailer in particular, the most salient being: the narrative structure, the informational conciseness, multimodality as a meaning-making resource and the awareness of their audience (conceptualised as an 'expert' one, since they had to convince the schoolteaching community). These were our criteria for the analysis of the corpus.

---

3 Online form for participating in the vote: https://docs.google.com/forms/d/1D_qKi14hPN759CqkMBNC2-b2_143oawEcFH6b6QNvX0/viewform?c=0&w=1

4 GRETEL's webpage: http://gretel.cat/materials-docents/book-trailers-de-llibres-lij/

Diagram 1. The underlying principles of the activity

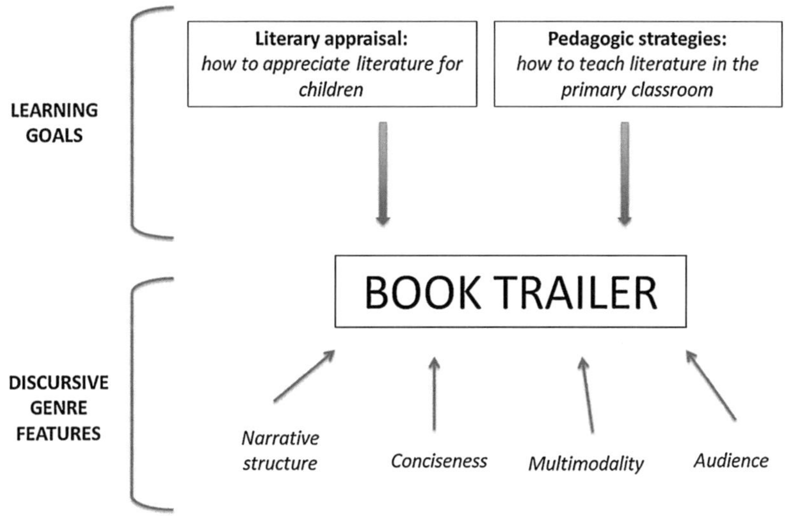

4. The Research Lenses

4.1 Corpus and the Goals of the Analysis

The analysis of this educational experience is supported by 65 book trailers made in pairs, which correspond to three of the four courses in which the book trailer activity was implemented (those given by the co-authors), with a total of 136 trainee teachers, and the students' individual online forms (from two groups) in which they voted. The corpus also includes one audio recording of a pair of students working at home on the book trailer, made in response to our request to the class for voluntary participants.

Data analysis was driven by the following research question: what did the book trailer task bring to the students' understanding of the subject, in terms of literary analysis and pedagogy? The book trailers were analysed by looking at the underlying principles of the activity in terms of the discursive genre features of the output (Diagram 1).

4.2 Analysis

In this section, we present the results of our analysis by focusing on how the discursive features of digital storytelling and the book trailer in particular mediated learning and meaning-making. The analysis is enhanced with illustrative excerpts from the interaction between the two students (one of whom was repeating the subject) who voluntarily recorded themselves while working on the book trailer of a recognised novel of Spanish children's literature, *Xolak badu lehoien berri* (*Xola and the lions*) by Bernardo Atxaga, a Basque author. It is a story about a tiny dog called Xola who, after listening to a conversation between her owner and a friend who had been to Africa, believes that she is a lion and behaves accordingly.

The Narrative Mould Afforded Different Operative Accesses to the Conceptualisation

The narrative structure or mould of the book trailer encouraged the students to find alternative ways of tackling the demanding task of defining the literary strengths of the books that best supported their classroom-oriented proposal. Many students imposed a sense of drama on the trailer's contents by enumerating the book's literary appeal or the reader's challenges in original ways, such as syncing the emergence of information with music. Those book trailers in which the content was successfully integrated into the narrative mould tended to display a more refined literary analysis than those that presented the information through schematic slices or random enumerations of general points. Refined literary analysis was usually articulated in the usage of metaliterary language, the identification of the literary elements (e.g. genre, narrative voice) and the expressive function (e.g. humour). The example analysed in the next section shows that literary analysis might be facilitated through visual presentation.

The reflective content overlapped with visual elements or stories that lent the literary analysis a congeniality that was appropriate to the book trailer format. This was the case with a book trailer about *Jim Button and Luke the Engine Driver*, in which the density of an opening abstract reflection on the functions of a literary reading was set off against an introductory self-made film in which a little girl is walking along a railway track and decides to read Ende's book just as we hear a steam locomotive approaching. The scene was clearly connected to the novel's plot, which involves a train trip that symbolically represents an imaginative journey into friendship.

These observations suggest that the narrative mould helped the trainee teachers to appropriate abstract content (Robin, 2006) by experimenting narratively with the hybrid academic content between literary analysis and pedagogy, whilst the situation of 'feeling' like a storyteller encouraged them to impose a dramatic tension on their analyses or to illustrate them with allusive stories.

Conciseness Fostered Focalisation on the Essential Points

The economy of language was a requirement imposed by the time constraints inherent in book trailers, since the spectator expects a brief trailer that will not overload the story with too much information. This feature represented an effective incentive to drive the literary analysis to focus on the essential points, which also needed to be worded clearly. The following extract from a book trailer on *A Christmas Carol* shows how the authors managed to present the story by weaving a discourse that combined an anticipatory approximation of the plot (2–4) with literary analysis (5–9), and how they used this discourse successfully to frame the story in just a few written headlines:

1 *It will immerse the students in a revealing trip to the Christmas of the main character*

The past

3 *present*

and future Christmases of Ebenezer Scrooge

5 *It is a tale peculiar for its…*

humoristic profile

7 *mysterious plot*

caricaturisation of the main characters

9 *and for its brilliant and varied style.*

The need for conciseness led to a 'hidden' exercise involving synthesis of the content and finding effective ways to represent it multimodally. This underlying process surfaces in the following snippet from the dialogue between the students working on the book trailer of *Xola and the lions.* Aiana[5] proposes a schematic approach to the book's main theme (the duality of real and imaginary worlds) by adding brief headlines to two photos (1). Afterwards, she proposes to link that topic to their didactic proposal in a longer phrase (2–3) that caught Mònica by surprise (4).

1 Aiana *we can put these images, "real world" and "imaginary world" and afterwards "and the fact that Xola is undergoing this psychological process through the book gives us a basis to work on the duality"*

4 Mònica *but how would we set it? talking?*

5 Names are pseudonyms.

5 Aiana *yes, talking, with a voice-over, because it would be no good* [to write it] *best not to get into the whole writing thing*

The awareness of how inappropriate it would be to "get into the whole writing thing" led them to choose the voice-over technique (6) as a complementary way to introduce the lengthy content. This awareness was also explicit in the final competition vote, in which many students associated brevity with accuracy and subtlety, whilst any written excess was seen as "annoying" and "bewildering".

In short, the need for brevity led the students to search for non-textual strategies when the information was copious or complex, or other solutions to shorten it through headlines or visual elements. Conciseness also encouraged them to define and convey the essential points of their literary interpretation and teaching proposal, and thus the apparent simplicity of book trailers concealed a demanding exercise in analysis, thought and peer exchange.

Drawing on the Benefits of Multimodality – a Digital Tool to Create Meaning

The multimodal repertoire came from the pieces of editing software proposed for the task (*Movie Maker* and *iMovie*), which facilitate the assembling of diverse types of raw material (image, video, text, sound) by manipulating them (e.g. through cutting, embedding, crossfading) and enhancing the content with a range of effects (e.g. motion, soundtrack, filters). These features helped the students to find their own ways of 'textualising' their ideas as shown in the interaction between the students working on the *Xola and the lions* book trailer. Once they had conceptualised the theme, a complex process was unchained for selecting the most appropriate multimodal resources to narrate the idea. The search for meaningful resources led them to creative solutions, like mixing real photos of a dog and a lion (2–3) with an illustration from the book (3–4) where Xola looks at herself in the mirror, which reflects the image of a lion, and how this process was combined with the voice-over:

1 Mònica *it would be, like… the lion story begins, whatever, I don't know, voice-over, and the lions, whatever, then "the real world", photos of the dog, "the imaginary world", photos of the lions eh… "duality", that mirror photo, and then the voice-over "how she sees herself and how others see her, the psychological process that she's going through"*

5 Aiana *exactly!*

6 Mònica *and what if when Xola talks we use a different voice-over, like a little girl, you know? Aaaa she talks like that* [imitating the suggested voice] *and then when we talk it's more like the narrator*

Regarding the voice-over, the students decided to separate the voice of the narrator (10), which had the function of guiding the contents, from the voice of the dog (8–9). Overlaying a voice in the artefact was an extensively commented aspect in the final peer assessment. The students valued the effectiveness of the voice-over, usually performing as a teacher, and the contribution of dramatised voices performing main characters; for instance the grandmother in *George's Marvellous Medicine* was usually performed in a slow, slightly malevolent voice to emphasise her scheming and cunning qualities. This exercise certainly contributed to the students' oral storytelling abilities.

The artistic possibilities expanded the students' expressive resources. The musical effects were used deliberately to liven up the interpretation of the book, and so Aiana and Mònica set the images of a lion in the jungle to an African melody that gave a humoristic, happy-go-lucky feel to the scene; others working on a detective story chose intriguing soundtracks, such as *The Pink Panther*. The use of background music, image, sound and voice gave new weight to words and ideas, as was evident in a book trailer about *Tom Sawyer*. The plot's setting was portrayed with a photo of the Mississippi river, which helped the audience to situate itself in a distant reality. Meanings were also enhanced with other creative elements such as devices of emphasis (e.g. encirclings, highlighting options) and animation (as when an effect was applied to an illustration, creating the illusion of movement, or when a zoom-in was used to create narrative tension). The meaningful use of these resources was evidence of a layered process of meaning-making that concealed complex, creative choices for 'materialising' ideas multimodally.

The Audience: Developing Teacher Identities and Fostering an Online Community

The book trailer became a 'conceptual space' within which talking as a teacher was possible, and thus the activity encouraged the students to situate their idea between literary interpretation and pedagogy. The process of creating the digital storytelling artefact encouraged them to incorporate terminology and ideas to which they had been exposed during the course. In the following snippet, the students, while working at home, talk from the position of a teacher who has to structure a reading activity considering the strengths of the book. The way these stances were articulated during the interaction (indicated in bold) suggests that adopting the identity of a teacher was a driving force in the elaboration of the activity.

1 **Aiana** *this reference about* ***why it's important*** *would be nice 'cos* ***we have to know how to appreciate this book,*** *because* ***we're promoting it***

Mònica *I know …*

4 **Aiana** *and* ***we can work on the duality through*** *this character* ***because*** *she's undergoing a psychological process*

6 **Mònica** *ok, or… how she sees herself and how others see her, you know?*

7 **Aiana** *of course, and* ***we can use*** *the voice-over to say that* ***this triggers humour*** *and…* ***why and how we tackle it****, you know?*

The incorporation of a teacher's voice, which implies using specialised discourse and particular ways of thinking about pedagogy, was propelled by two features of the activity's design. Firstly, the simulated reality that framed the activity put the students in the position of defending their ideas in front of a forum of teachers. Secondly, the book trailer format challenged their positions as students and their identities attached to written essays. If the task of writing an academic essay typically positions trainee schoolteachers as learners, the book trailer 'space' positioned them in a more agentive way, as teachers.

Some of the nuances in their voices were triggered by the consciousness of having a larger audience beyond the teacher, since the book trailers would be available in the class online environment and on YouTube. This involved a new horizon that changed the students' audience from being a teacher *acting as a critical reader* to being *critical peer teachers* as a wider audience. In our case, the virality that publishing houses usually seek when launching book trailers to reach potential buyers had a positive effect on the activity, since the students had to watch all their classmates' digital artefacts in order to participate in the final debate and online vote. This last voting task positioned the students as critical teachers and compelled them to appropriate the activity guidelines as the basis of their criteria for the peer assessment, as this assessment of a book trailer for *The Adventures of the Black Hand Gang* demonstrates:

> *This book trailer shows in a synthetic and explanatory way what the most powerful literary elements are, and this is displayed clearly because, without reading the book and with just a few images and texts, we can see that one of its strengths is to make the schoolchildren participate in the story, to become detectives.*

The students' justifications also revealed their positionings as emergent teachers, with enthusiastic assessments (e.g. "these examples are a source of inspiration"), projections towards the future (e.g. "the aftertaste is that I want to work on this book with children") or the construction of their own assessment criteria, such as deeming the link between the didactic proposal and the children's everyday life to be of value.

Moreover, the fact of uploading a learning-based task to YouTube (usually in public mode, although some decided to make their content private) positioned the students as contributors of an original artefact that put unique ideas at the disposal of other learners, teachers and internet users. As evidence, winning book trailers uploaded to Gretel's webpage (see footnote 28) accumulated between 100 and 600 views over the following two years. In this sense, these book trailers became part of the students' legacies on the net, their online identities, evidence that they might use to enhance their *curriculum vitae*, or just an available artefact with attached experiences, knowledge attainments and senses of a teaching community that they will re-visit in the future.

6. Conclusions

Despite the limitations imposed by case studies, the analysis of our educational experience focused on how book trailers contribute to some key issues in the larger debate about the functions of digital storytelling in education. These include: a) digital storytelling as a strategy for methodological renewal in pedagogy, b) the use of digital storytelling in breaking with the written text as the exclusive code for sharing/constructing academic knowledge, and c) the use of technology for the marketisation of education.

Digital storytelling provides a feasible 'working space' from which to propel the methodological renewal in pedagogy that, as prescribed by many Common State Standards in developed countries, seeks to integrate the digital learning culture into classroom *praxis* (Pahl and Rowsell, 2005; Adell and Castañeda, 2012). Our study has shown the possibilities offered by digital storytelling for driving pedagogy in this direction, if and when it is integrated into activities under a socio-constructivist approach. In particular, in our educational experience, the framing provided by the project-based learning methodology is key in positioning the student as a *meaning-maker* and as a 'valid' contributor of original ideas. This also reinforces *learning by doing*, learning through *collaboration* and *peer talk*, and the idea of *participation* in a community of practice (in our case in the schoolteacher community). These socio-constructivist principles, integrated into the task of creating a book trailer of a children's book, also emphasised certain features of the digital-driven learning culture, such as *multimodality*, *participation*, *shared knowledge* and *peer interaction* (Cassany, 2012), and thereby shaped learning as a professionally *meaningful* activity.

However, to make digital storytelling meaningful within the curriculum, its classroom integration requires an exercise of adjustment by *appropriating* it in particular learning contexts rather than just *applying* it. Our account, making sense of digital storytelling as a resource to support formal learning, highlights the importance of making a diagnosis of specific learning needs and a selection of the discursive features that might focus learning on the development of key competences. In our case, the reflective process led us first to choose the book trailer as a specific form of digital storytelling and then to adapt it for shaping an activity that, by stressing particular discursive features and learning goals, sought to mobilise our students' thinking between literary appraisal and pedagogy.

One of the pedagogical strengths of digital storytelling is that students learn about content and technology for academic purposes simultaneously. In that regard, ours and previous educational experiences (Ohler, 2008; Nixon, 2013) indicate a general function of digital storytelling in education focused on the possibility of enhancing learning with other "ways of knowing" (Pahl and Rowsell, 2005) beyond the written essay; it affords an alternative route to 'materialising' ideas multimodally, in addition to offering new ways of tackling abstract content, since, as Robin's (2008) argues, it is a powerful tool for converting data into information and transforming information into knowledge. The implications of this are profound, since any student will have accumulated identities as a more or less 'good' student and writer in particular subjects across his/her academic trajectory and these carried identities certainly influence the textual choices made and the risks taken by the student when writing, in terms of form, voice and ideas. In that regard, the resources that multimodality offers for meaning-making (e.g. image, voice, sound) position students in a more agentive way by allowing vernacular culture to support their learning (Erstad and Silseth, 2008).

At our specific level in ITE in literary education, digital storytelling constitutes a powerful approach for tackling digital and specific competences such as oral retelling of children's tales (Villalustre and del Moral, 2014) and, as our study suggests, literary appraisal and literary-focused pedagogy. Regardless of the dangers that have been identified concerning the marketisation of education and others associated with the 'infiltration' of consumerism into formal learning (Ferneding, 2003), we perceive the everyday-academic crossover as having strong learning benefits. The inclusion in the book trailer activity of the student's own "funds of (*technology*) knowledge" allows her/him to explore them as meaningful resources for formal learning. The positive effect of this coalescence reinforces our vision of trainee schoolteachers as "agents of the curriculum change" (Priestley, Biesta and Robinson, 2013).

We cannot finish this summary of the educational contributions of digital storytelling without broaching some unanswered questions about further implications. Firstly, a question that is still to be explored is whether digital storytelling has the same positive effects in all student profiles or whether, as our data imply, those students more at ease with academic writing encounter greater difficulties in using the book trailer's discursive features to mobilise conceptual content. A second underexplored question is to what extent technical competence affects the final results of the exercise. In other words: is there a correlation between previous experience using the software proposed and the production of effective digital artefacts? Does the learning of new software intimidate new users? Can a lack of technical experience be detrimental within academic parameters? Can it hinder creativity or the assimilation of educational content? Thirdly, considering the need to appropriate digital storytelling in each particular educational context through a reflexive exercise of programming, we wonder to what extent this might hinder its establishment in education, or lead to simplistic or ill-considered applications that might under-exploit its power. With these concerns in mind, we close this chapter by stressing the necessity of designing learning-focused, classroom-oriented applications. We would also suggest, in line with Barret's (2005) arguments, focussing educational research into digital storytelling on the collection of data from the process, in order to widen our understanding of the impact that it has on learning.

References

Adell, J. and Castañeda, L. (2012). "Tecnologías emergentes, ¿pedagogías emergentes?" In J. Hernández, M. Pennessi, D. Sobrino and A. Vázquez (eds.). *Tendencias emergentes en Educación con TIC* (pp. 13–32). Barcelona: Espiral.

Aliagas, C. and Castellà, J. M. (2014). Enthusiast, reluctant and resistant teachers towards the one-to-one programme: a multi-sited ethnographic case study in Catalonia. In M. Stochetti (ed.). *Media and education in the digital age. Concepts, assessments, subversions* (pp. 237–258). New York: Peter Lang.

Barrett, H. (2005, November 18). Digital storytelling research design. Retrieved from http://electronicportfolios.com/digistory/ResearchDesign.pdf

Burgess, J. (2006). Hearing Ordinary Voices: Cultural Studies, Vernacular Creativity and Digital Storytelling. *Continuum: Journal of Media & Cultural Studies 20(2):* 201–214.

Cassany, D. (2012). *En_línea: Leer y escribir en la red.* Barcelona: Anagrama.

Cuban, L. (2001). *Oversold and Underused.* London: Harvard University Press.

Davies, J. and Merchant, Gu. (2014). Digital Literacy and Teacher Education. In P. Benson and A. Chik (eds.). *Popular Culture, Pedagogy and Teacher Education* (pp. 180–192). London: Routledge.

Erstad, O. and Silseth, K. (2008). Agency in digital storytelling. Challenging the educational context. In K. Lundby (ed.). *Digital Storytelling, Mediatized Stories: Self-representations in New Media* (pp. 213–232). New York: Peter Lang.

Ferneding, K. (2003). *Questioning technology*. New York: Peter Lang.

Freire, P. (2004). *Pedagogia da autonomia*. São Paulo: Paz e Terra.

González, N., Moll, L. and Amanti, C. (eds.) (2005). *Funds of Knowledge*. Mahwah: Lawrence Erlbaum.

Lambert, J. (2002). *Digital storytelling*. Berkeley: Digital Diner Press.

Lankshear, C. and Knobel, M. (2006). *New Literacies*. Maidenhead: Open University Press.

Nixon, A. (2013). Engaging Urban Youth in Meaningful Dialogue on Identity through Digital Storytelling. In J. Avila and J. Pandya (eds.). *Critical Digital Literacies as Social Praxis* (pp. 41–61). New York: Peter Lang.

Ohler, J. (2008). *Digital storytelling in the classroom*. Thousand Oaks: Corwin Press.

Pahl, K. and Rowsell, J. (2005). *Literacy and Education*. London: Sage.

Pitler, H. (2006). Viewing technology through three lenses. Retrieved on Sept 2nd, 2016, from http://www.naesp.org/resources/2/Principal/2006/M-Jp38.pdf.

Poveda, D., Morgade, M. and Alonso, B. (2009). Storytellers of Children's Literature and their Ideological Construction of the Audience. *Oral Tradition 24(1):* 227–248.

Priestley, M., Biesta, G. and Robinson, S. (2013). Teacher agency and Emerging Models of Curriculum. In M. Priestley & G. Biesta (eds.). *Reinventing the Curriculum* (pp. 187–206). London: Bloomsbury.

Kernan, L. (2004). *Coming attractions*. Austin: University of Texas Press.

Robin, B. (2008). Digital storytelling: a powerful technology tool for the 21st century classroom. *Theory into practice 47:* 202–228.

Sadik, A. (2008). Digital storytelling: a meaningful technology-integrated approach for engaged student learning. *Education Tech Research Dev 56:* 487–506.

Villalustre, L. and del Moral, E. (2014). Digital storytelling: a new strategy for storytelling and acquired competencies by future teachers. *Revista Complutense de Educacion 25(1):* 155–132.

Yang, Y. and Wu, W. (2012). Digital storytelling for enhancing student academic achievement, critical thinking and learning motivation: A year experimental study. *Computers and Education 59:* 399–352.

Annex 1: Complete list of children's novels (titles have been listed in the original version and then translated into English although read in Catalan language).

Atxaga, Bernardo: *Xolak badu lehoien berri* [*Xola and the lions*].

Dahl, Roald: *George's Marvellous Medicine.*

Ende, Michael: *Jim Knopf und Lukas der Lokomotivführer* [*Jim Button and Luke the Engine Driver*].

Gaiman, Neil: *The Graveyard Book.*

Nöstlinger, Christine: *Konrad oder Das Kind aus der Konservenbüchse* [*Conrad: The Factory-Made Boy*].

Press, Hans Jürgen: *Die Abenteuer* der *»schwarzen hand«* [*The Adventures of the Black Hand Gang*].

Burnett, Frances Hodgson: *The Secret Garden.*

Collodi, Carlo: *Le avventure di Pinocchio* [*The Adventures of Pinocchio*].

Dickens, Charles: *A Christmas Carol.*

Jané, Albert (adaptation): *Odýsseia* [*Odyssey*].

Lancelyn Green, Roger (adaptation): *King Arthur and His Knights of the Round Table.*

Twain, Mark: *The Adventures of Tom Sawyer.*

Simge Esin Orhun

An Interdisciplinary Approach for the Digital Media Landscape of the 21st Century: Storytelling as an Instrument in Design Education

Abstract Recent technological advancements have started to lead the development of products and services in all areas of design. However, these innovations have been suspected of having diverse effects on human beings due to the new needs and original activities that they have introduced into our lives. In order to weaken the dominating position of today's digital media, the scholars in design education need to base their approaches on the consciousness of human beings by introducing the aspects of real time and physical space as primary components of the design process. Owing to the advantage of bringing people, places and actions real time, storytelling is recognised for its potential to act as an active mechanism that communicates events and provides the needed contextual information. This research looked for interdisciplinary ways to improve interactive media design education through storytelling, involving the exchange of information between spatial, material and media entities. In the frame of this study, the concept of interactive exhibiting was chosen to work for the creation of the experiences that require bodily performances with respect to the architectural qualities of space and time, and storytelling was used as an instrument to provide a setting to create the participatory experience. An approach supporting this aim was applied for the development of conceptual spatial communication projects with the students of Communication Design Program between 2009 and 2012. The analysis of the students' works reflected the benefits of integrating the place-based and time-based aspects into design education on the basis of storytelling, especially for members of the young generation, who are already natives of such media landscape.

Introduction

Our interaction with information technologies moved on to a new level of understanding with the introduction of the term "ubiquitous computing" coined by Mark Weiser in 1991. While this term denoted the concept of "being present at every time and everywhere", it also pointed to the invasion of these technologies in our daily life through their characteristic "invisibility". Although these hybrid products and services support our daily tasks by providing faster, more comfortable and safer alternative networking modes, they also display a tendency to create their own customs by shaping the users' daily life and basic habits. In fact, all new technologies carry the risk of creating their own needs that force new requirements on the users, as they not only add or exclude but also change all relations and root structures fundamentally (Norman, 2010). Especially in the twenty-first century, the arguments are based on the belief that these technologies are not created to provide for the needs of the people and that the needs related to these technologies are being created afterwards; however, they are created "only because it's possible to do so" (Postman, 2004). From the perspective of the discipline of design, however, it should always be remembered that the quality and essence of any designed product, varying from a building to a web site, lies in the expressiveness in terms of its content and how well it can fulfil its function (Norman, 2010). This conflicting condition of the digital media landscape has been primarily affecting the behavioural and perceptual systems of the young generation. As educators, the most important point we confront in the area of design education is to bring our students up as contextually strong and highly sophisticated designers of tomorrow (Tasa and Orhun, 2013). Therefore, the educational approaches used in this discipline need a reconsideration of the strategies for teaching design on the basis of the transformational effects of these technologies.

By extension of the studies carried out, stories are identified as an important source in building blocks of knowledge, the foundation of memory and learning, as they reflect the human experience as a set of connected events with roots in space and time. While stories address many functions, storytelling provides an area for designers to develop methodologies that arouse the users' creativity and intuition. The storyteller has to prepare the necessary language, tools and media in order to present the message of a story effectively and efficiently (Tally, 2012). As stories are composed of time, spatiality, drama, causality and personification, the art of storytelling is recognised to be a fresh yet solid educational tool for design education to guide describing a context or a situation, illustrating problems, launching design discussions and exploring a design concept (Bruner, 1990; Quensenbery and Brooks, 2010). The aim of this study is to make use of storytelling as an instrument for design students to generate better user experiences and to bring consciousness to their design tactics.

In this study, we tried to combine the constructive nature of storytelling for developing a context for the digital media landscape with the support of the concept of interactive exhibiting, as the meaning emerges from the contextual experience (Salen and Zimmerman, 2004). This research examines the conceptual interactive exhibition design student projects, which are based on narratives for special contexts, developed for the Spatial Interaction Design Course in the Communication Design Department of Yildiz Technical University between 2009 and 2012 with the aim of assessing the benefits of storytelling as an instrument in design education. It is our claim that such an approach will enable interactions, develop more engaging interventions in the frame of suitable contexts and support the innovation of future products and services.

The Effects of Digital Technologies and Tools on Users

In the last 20–30 years, digital technologies have spread out and thus are referred to with the term "pervasive computing". Wi-Fi, Bluetooth, GPS and similar satellite and networking technologies are integrated with tools, which enables the involvement of virtual reality in physical architecture and enhanced spatiality in the fourth dimension (Bullivant, 2005). The effects of technology on an individual's daily life can be observed in his interaction with other people, devices and settings. Intellectual and cognitive processes are not just products of neurological activities but also the outcomes of complex and mutual interactions between the brain, the body and the designed context that we live in (Clark, 2010). As the digital arena starts to override the analogue ways of doing things, we encounter the designed contexts to be based on reductive and deconstructing systems. For example, the internet technology that forms the substructure of the web has a pattern designed to protect the whole, even if some parts are missing. In parallel with the information architecture, this fragmented information appears in data packages connected to each other without a central structure. Each piece of data follows a different path in the packaging structure, which can be considered to be meaningless on its own as the content of every package is a tiny segment. At the end, it is impossible to track which part of the information comes from where and to consider a transparent information flow (Lanier, 2010). So, we actually are working in systems that are represented by bits, categorised and listed separately in the multiple-choice databases.

These technological advancements also cause a variety of transformative effects on the perceptual capabilities of their users through their active visibility and affordance that enable the users to manipulate these tools just by knowing how to operate them, without having an idea on how they actually operate. The first generation computer users had to learn the hardware and logic in detail in order to be able to use the computers; users today, however, perceive everything by its interface value. They are content with this superficiality and thus become inactive (Turkle, 2004). For example, the Google search engine, being one of the most favourable ways to access information on the internet, is said to be spoiling the reading habits of human beings and promoting undetailed and depthless interpretations (Carr, 2008). Location-based applications not only affect the way individuals obtain, practice, spread and interact with spatial information, but also shape their capabilities and perceptions concerning locale and are suspected of enlarging the hippocampus glands in the brain (Hirtle, 2011; Bateson, 2000). Studies have shown that the excessive use of mobile devices causes certain mental and behavioural disorders like "imaginary wobbly syndrome", "obsessive compulsive disorder" and "attention deficit hyperactivity disorder" (Burrough, 2012). Similarly, messaging through mobile devices and the social media as a new means of meeting people and a widely spread communication method are suspected of being the causes and effects of the weakening physical interaction and friendship practices especially among the new generation. It has been found that when people stay connected more through the virtual network, the danger of feeling lonely increases, which triggers real pathological communication and identity problems and may result in addictions due to the unbearable isolation people experience (Turkle, 2011).

As a matter of fact, the technologies that we embrace today were most likely selected to be realised from among hundreds of alternatives due to the factors of chance and budget. This circumstance results in the development and establishment of inaccurate designs that become the infrastructure or the standard by itself, which generates consecutive systems dependent on that design without any reformation (Lanier, 2010). Therefore, it becomes important to identify the gaps in the design of products in order to compensate for them in the design process of future products.

We reviewed the areas of engineering, technology and science that constitute the background of the concept of interactivity featured in digital media tools. The areas of human-computer interaction and cognitive sciences, which are recognised for their dominance, showed similar evolutions in time in their approaches to the reduction and deconstruction of information. Both areas had not featured the human experience and favoured the process-based traditional approach at the start. However, the indications found in the last 20–30-year span argue for the fact that the cognitive act regarding cognitive science is not independent from the sensorial and movement course of the body and that these sensorial and motor courses depend on the biological, psychological and cultural context on an extended platform (Lakoff and Johnson, 1999). Likewise, in the 1990s, the mainstream approach in the area of human-computer interaction based on interaction-based data processing method was opposed by the concept of "embodied cognition", which emphasised the importance of "context" and "bodily involvement" (Dourish, 2004).

Meanwhile, advanced technologies are able to provide solutions to the problem of "being at the same place at the same time" by maintaining new modes of communication for humans that connect data from different geographies and time dilemmas (Mitchell, 1999), whereas the contexts for their use remain unclear. For example, a tablet, which is a mobile gadget, is mostly used by the young generation for playing games, reading, listening to music, watching films and connecting to social media. This tool can be suspected of affecting the mental model and social development of a young person negatively when used in this immobile manner. However, from our point of view, a tablet can fulfil its potential through its form and technological competence when it functions to provide non-periodic and asynchronous data for a mobile individual. As in the example of the agricultural project named Tarbil concerning precision farming (Fig. 1), farmers are given tablets to view and control the condition of their crops as they walk through the land. The sensors placed underground both send spatial information via temporal terrestrial monitoring stations and satellite images for the realisation of remote sensing-based agricultural analysis, and disseminate the outcomes to the farmers through these mobile devices (Bagis and Ustundag, 2013).

Figure 1. Varying mobile and immobile technologies in the frame of TARBIL agricultural project for precision farming

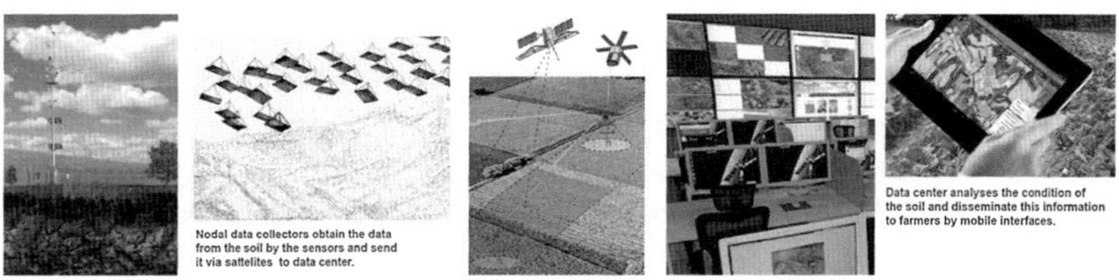

In line with these developments and the scope of this study, it becomes important to know the context in which these devices are used. In cybernetic systems, "the user" sees his/her relationship with any larger system composed of other people and stuff differently from the others and this is identified as a context. For instance, a letter means something only in a word, that word in a sentence and that sentence in a text (Bateson, 2000). When we look back in history, the demolishing of contextual barriers can be first identified with the invention of telegram, which reduced and deconstructed the concepts of "time" and "space" (Postman, 1985). Clocks, calendars and maps are the basic devices we use in abstracting and conceptualising, which lack the process, experience and other related dynamics (Mollison, 2011). Nevertheless, the transformation of these two concepts into a quantitative perception separated and isolated them more from each other and human experience. This study focuses on the ways to address this problem caused by the digitisation of information within the design education to support the creation and realisation of new products that are suited to the mental processes of human beings.

Making Use of Cognitive Sciences for the Discipline of Digital Design Education

As indicated in the introduction, these technological developments and their extensive uses have been affecting young generations most intensely through the use of digital tools. Meanwhile, the design of all future applications, services and tools will be created by the youngsters of today, who are already digital natives. This fact urges us to look for alternative design education tactics for interactive digital media. Recent approaches used in digital design education have shown that the students, who already have chosen this field due to their interest in virtual worlds and interaction design, are generally instructed to solve problems pertaining to fictional and virtual cases that have little reference to real physical conditions. So the educational environment can be described as the student working for imaginary cases that are be based on digital interaction and realised by code. Student design projects guided by this and similar approaches signalled deficiency in structural efficiency and were observed to result in perceptually and physically weak usability. We believe that an educational approach that supports the relationship of human beings with time-based and location-based aspects will be beneficial in decreasing the effects of digital media. So, in order to figure out how we can combine design education with the concepts of time and space in the frame of cognitive sciences, the following areas are examined:

1. **Awareness of temporal factors:** Every action or interaction occupies time. Time is an abstract concept and, thus, not inherently visual. Much of the terminology we use for time is based on our concrete experience of space and of the physical environment. Human beings tend to structure time spatially in parallel with their philosophical and intellectual tendencies, which can be classified into two groups: The first group structures time as horizontal navigation in the space that reflects the order and timing of occurrences in relationship to locale (Tversky, 1993). This linear condition defines history as an irreversible sequence of unrepeatable events, a definition which refers to time either as stationary and us moving through it in the direction of the future, or as a moving object that moves toward us (Meirelles, 2013). Contrary to modern western

mentality, the second group maintains their relationship with the context of time through observing nature, which can be defined as cyclic and intrinsic. Day and night, the seasonal changes that affect the vital living conditions like migrations, the stages of all living things are the visible processes of this cyclic condition, which determine and guide the measuring of time (Alexander, Ishikawa and Silverstein, 1977; Meirelles, 2013). This cyclic condition points out the existence of the fundamental states in time, which are always present and never changing, and thus builds the important bonds and supports the perceptions of human beings to cope with life. **Either perceived as linear or cyclic, moments are positioned to tell a story of connected events in one direction and are arranged to come one after the other**. So it is possible to say that the designs have to include and structure experiences and interactions in specific sequential orders or hierarchic connections.

2. **Responsiveness to spatial factors:** Human beings represent their spatial thoughts by mental representations. They use spatial metaphors that refer to movement and orientation in order to conceptualise abstract concepts as well as space-based conceptions concerning the arrangements of objects and their spatial relevance (Tversky, 1993). The content of the product is affected due to the architectural quality of the space in which it has been located and how it is located. Thus, spatial context can be perceived as the physical and characteristic qualities of locale to be transformed into a parameter for the usability of a designed product (Rapoport, 1982). **The spatial bond defines the relationship between objects and other objects, objects and humans and between human beings in a specific sequence of events or in a structure**. It does not only maintain the layout of objects, but also undertakes the organisation of the meaning upon which the users communicate with social and cultural values (Nasar, 1988). The spatiality of the products developed for media space can be realised within their virtual boundaries. In any case, these products refer to the existential space, which can be explained as the schemata developed by the brain in the frame of cognitive psychology (Norberg-Schulz, 1979). Non-spatiality is out of question due to the loss of context and meaning caused by the disseverance of the cognitive connections, including perceiving, memorising and scheming (Lang, 1987).

As seen from the brief explanation above, time is structured spatially and space gains momentum with the integration of time. Due to the fact that the concepts of "time" and "space" regulate each other meaningfully, this study gives emphasis to spatio-temporal context, rather than approaching space and time separately. This cognitive skill, which can be identified simply in the perception of travelling between two points, can be used in everyday life, in the workplace and in science to structure problems, find answers and express solutions, and can also be learned and taught formally to students using appropriately designed tools, technologies and curricula (National Research Council, 2006).

In parallel with the identifications mentioned above, we looked for suitable concepts and practices that can both serve to ground any design problem and be able to refer to both space and time. On a general level, **both contexts refer to the idea of perceiving objects, interactions and human beings in relation to other things, rather than a solid geometry or an isolated experience**. These aspects guided us to review the art of storytelling that hosts and customises a structured account of connected events which can be supported by both physical and media space.

The Interplay Between Storytelling, Spatio-Temporal Cognition and Design Education

According to the discussions and identifications above, storytelling is recognised to be a beneficial instrument that can support the idea of creating awareness for spatio-temporal context. While it is a well-known area to be used in design education for triggering students' creativity, we examined this subject in order to detect ways or methods of relating to spatio-temporal context that would reduce the transformational effects of technological tools and services by providing an alternative workspace. Driven by its own nature, a story assumes a certain time and space, whereas storytelling undertakes the function of conveying the intended message of a story by giving additional meaning (Quensenbery and Brooks, 2010). All of the components of events occur at various places at different times. A preceding event sets the context for the next event. Thus, events in an episode are linked together to form a chain. Due to the direct connections between these events, time ordering becomes an important parameter of the story (Satish, Jain and Gupta, 2009). So, on the basis of the story, the designer is directly connected to the concepts of space and time and has the capability to improve the concepts to be contexts by making use of storytelling.

In order to fulfil its function, the art of storytelling has always used every possible media and technology. A story can be told in writing, through pictures or moving images, or spoken live or through recorded audio or video. Digital technologies are valuable for offering some level of entertainment by performing the above-mentioned ways in digital space; yet they will be most beneficial when they are recognised and used for instituting interactivity (Miller, 2008). In today's experience-based culture, the element of interactivity is recognised to be an important element enriching the skills and strengthening the knowledge related to interactive applications ranging from video games to online training and education. Having expertise in this area of design, interaction designers can benefit from storytelling by creating personas, describing the context of use and identifying personal goals.

As a matter of fact, stories do not only belong to the storyteller but to the audience, too. Each person imagines and experiences the story in a different way (Quensenbery and Brooks, 2010). With the integration of technological tools and applications, storytelling becomes an immersive and participatory area in which members of the audience become active players and can influence the narration and its progress. At the end, each individual will be expected to have a unique and personal imagery of a completed story (Porteous, Cavazza and Charles, 2010). With the support of both digital and physical data, digital designers can make use of storytelling to generate methodologies and obtain results for the solution of design problems that may give birth to new technologies, tools or complex information architectures.

There is not a single way to construct a story, especially where digital technologies are concerned. However, in the frame of spatio-temporal cognition, two different streams are recognised:

1. **Spatio-temporal structures** that refer to the representation of time (Meirelles, 2013; Vasiliev, 1997; Peuquet, 1994): i. Time geography aiming at the visitors experiencing how much time it took for events to happen in space, when the time is that one specific object visited one specific place, ii. Historic geography reflecting what has happened in past times, what objects were present at a specific time in a specific place, iii. Cultural geography concerning where events have happened through time, what the location of one specific object at a specific time was.
2. **The type of changes that occur to spatio-temporal context** over time (phenomenological perspective) (Bok, 2000): i. existential changes that include the appearing, disappearing and reviving of objects and relationships; ii. changes in the spatial properties of objects such as location, size and shape; iii. changes in thematic properties.

Making use of the art of storytelling for the spatio-temporal context in the frame of these definitions and classifications for the design of interactive digital interactions and products looks promising. The following section involves the approach for adapting this idea to design education through the stages of briefing, conceptualising, planning and executing processes for this interdisciplinary approach.

An Interdisciplinary Approach for Making Use of Storytelling in Design Education

As indicated by its natural qualities, storytelling is recognised for its potential to provide the needed contextual information in the frame of design education. The power of the social practices shaped in such an approach is believed to be beneficial for the students to devise meaningful tools that bring the user, the system and the context of use into a productive relationship (International Organization for Standardization, 2009). The discipline of design covers a wide range of expertise areas like architecture, industrial design, communication design, graphic design, fashion and textile design, interior design etc., and storytelling can be applied in each of these areas, if this practice is perceived rather as a process or a medium for sharing, interpreting and offering the content and meaning of a story to an audience. Besides, it is impossible to neglect the possibility of integrating digital technology with the products of each area or to avoid the contributions for the advancements in design and innovation.

In parallel with the discussion above and the scope of this study, a design brief that could be worked on with digital design students was planned on the basis of two objectives: 1. Focusing on the performative aspects of body with respect to time with the aim of generating embodied interactions, 2. Increasing the awareness of spatio-temporal context with the support of storytelling.

These ideas were structured into a design brief on the basis of interactive exhibiting. Guided by this concept, the brief was based on the idea of communicating a story in a three-dimensional space using participatory digital technology that linked varying interactive narrative experiences (Lorenc, Skolnick and Berger, 2006). Space was expected to become a meeting point for the potential audience and the actors for interacting with a range of responsive digital applications and tools (Betts, 2008; Bullivant, 2007). These experiences would be created to support the content of the story, while the tools, objects and actors were to constitute the language of the storytelling (Hughes, 2010). The design of the setting became an important aspect to enhance and reveal the text and the story, which can be described as the translation and adaptation of the architectural qualities of space with dramatic time (Parker, Wolf and Block, 2008). At the end, the conceptual exhibition projects were expected to involve a storytelling in which the user's primary form of interaction becomes the moving within the story that is composed of the organisation of the spaces or the information. The works were required to support multi-layered communication that involved the design of navigation for both the physical and digital space.

Figure 2. The project named "Cultural Entertainment Forms through Bodily Performance" by Özge Genç focused on the different approaches of cultures to entertainment rituals. In it, she selected bodily performances and organised them in the physical working area according to the spatial needs of the performances. The aim of the project was to allow the visitors to experience how much time it took for events to happen in space.

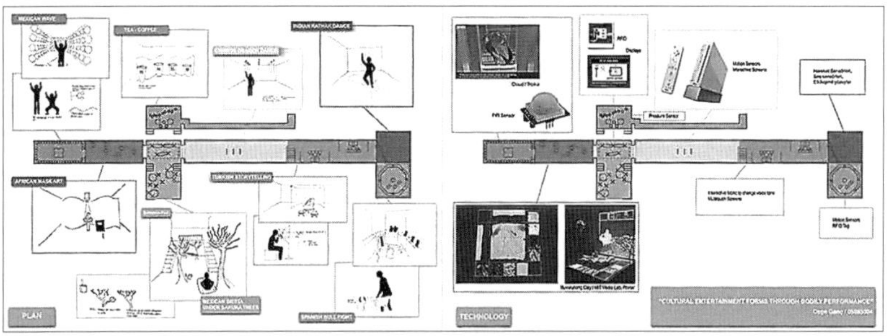

The preliminary design decisions

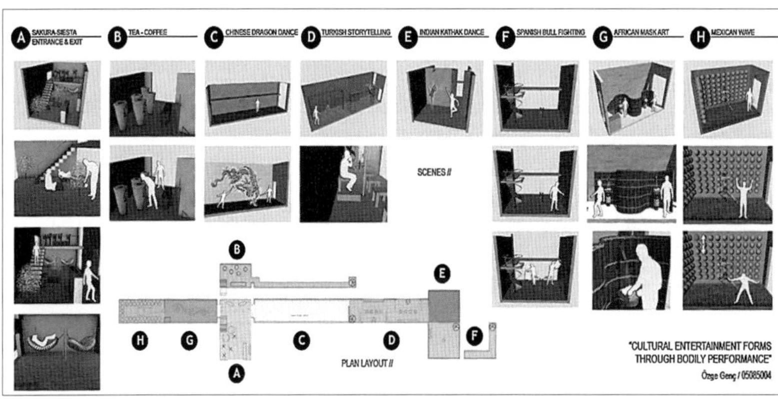

The detailed project

This approach was studied with the undergraduate students of the Department of Communication Design in the studio design course. As advised by the art of storytelling, the students were guided to develop their projects through two stages. At the first stage, they would conduct research and shape their theme and story together with the possible interactions, technologies and tools, and at the second stage they would focus on the customisation of the project that is suitable for the potential audience through the design of the spatial organisation and navigational aspects (Satish, Jain and Gupta, 2009). The conceptual designs will be developed for a specific physical space and are expected to take account of the spatial data. The stages of developing the design projects are shown in Figure 2. The upper scheme includes the research concerning preliminary design decisions for the selected theme and the suitable technological solutions that support the experiencing of the story. The folio below involves the finalised and submitted version of the design project that involves the staging of experiences, spatial layout and the scene design, which make up the language of the storytelling.

At the beginning of the studio design course, the design brief was clearly explained to the students, in terms of the objectives, the process and the physical working site. Afterwards, five weeks were dedicated to accomplishing the tasks of the first stage. At the end of this period, the students submitted their design decisions as preliminary sketches and layouts to the jury and got feedback. Subsequently, at the second stage, the students were guided to structure the theme through storytelling, which involved the design of the sequence of interactions that were organised spatially. On the completion of the students' work at the end of the twelve-week period, the same jury evaluated their success in achieving the objectives of the studio.

The Analysis of Designs for Maintaining the Spatio-Temporal Context Through Storytelling

This design brief was applied between 2009 and 2012 in the Spatial Communication Design Studio of the Department of Communication Design at Yildiz Technical University. The students assigned to the course had no prior experience with spatial organisation methods in architecture, scene design and industrial design but were accustomed to graphic and interaction design and trained to create novel user interfaces for interactive tools to manipulate digital information.

At the start of the studio, the students experienced difficulties with adapting to working with physical data, as they were used to working in a digital environment in their prior studios. Nevertheless, as they were forced to abandon their habits, they started to understand the dynamics of physical space and time and to generate ideas. At the end of the process, 90 percent of the 72 students were able to achieve the goals set out in the brief with varying levels of success.

In the scope of this study, our curiosity lay in the tendencies to structure the storytelling. The student projects were sorted into two groups based on the way they refer to spatio-temporal context:

1. Representation of time through geographical compositions: The stories in these projects were composed of a sequence of events and they involved a linear style

of storytelling, in which one event is experienced after the other. The examples shown were given to express how storytelling contributed to the realisation of time geography (Figure 2), historic geography (Figure 3) and cultural geography (Figure 4). The common approach to design was the perception of time as a static form. With the support of storytelling, the students were able to reflect the spatio-temporal aspects of design by providing the visitor with interactions based on bodily performance.

Figure 3. The aim of Evrim Aytemur's project named "Prehistoric Times" was to allow the user to experience the activities of early times and organised the space in a sequence corresponding with the development stages of mankind in prehistoric times. With the idea of making use of the linear condition of the architectural space in parallel with the historic sequence, this student developed a series of events and experiences that were supported by times gone by. Visitors' experience of the exhibition began with cave life, agriculture and art, and ended with the visit to the early settlement. In each section, visitors experienced the specific activity of that time dilemma with the support of digital technologies. In other words, time was represented as a still object and the visitors moved in time, in parallel with the geometry of the physical space.

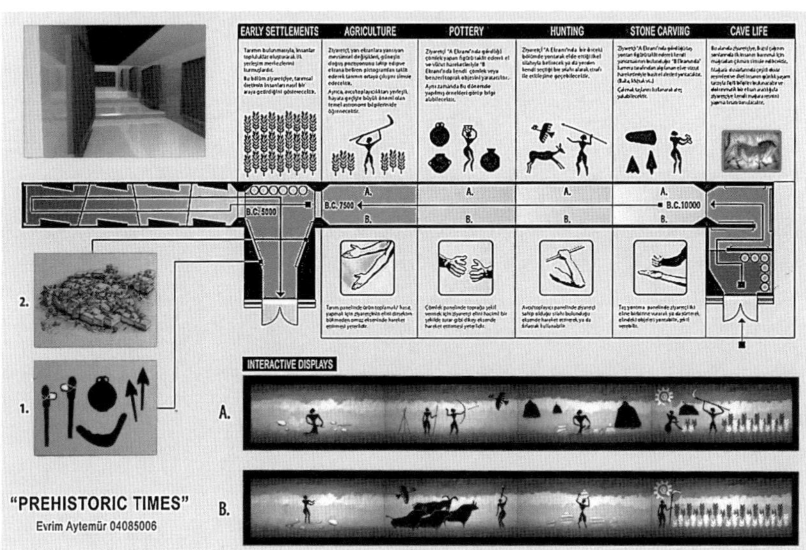

Figure 4. The project by Osman Can named "Childhood memories" focused on how a child perceives his home environment, starting from the living quarters and ending up in the private area. This project was based on a child's schemata and perceptions of the different parts of his house, in parallel with what had happened there. The project was based on cultural geography concerning and focused on developing themes, where the events had happened through time. Interactive tools placed in the thematic areas guided the activities in those areas so as to enhance the communicative aspect of the project. Each section in the house was depicted by suitable metaphoric objects and interactions to reflect how a child perceives that specific area. The scene design and the scaling of the tools were intended to remind the visitors of their childhoods through the provided cultural-geographical structure.

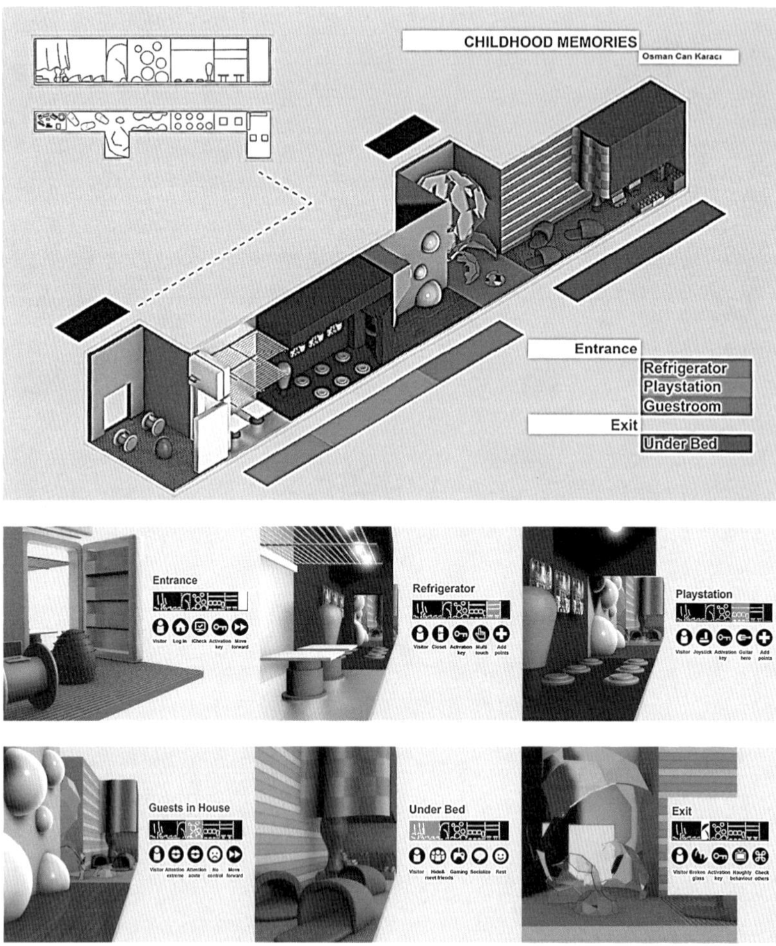

2. Representation of space and time through creating awareness in experience: The works that can be included in this group developed their storytelling either in parallel with thematic changes (Figure 5) or existential changes (Figure 6).

Figure 5. The project by Öykü Çataltepe named "Stories of Childhood" was based on the thematic changes caused by each story that refers to the changes in the values or attributes of space. The storytelling focused on the visitors' varying experiences and imaginative perceptions triggered by the stories. Different iconic elements from well-known children's stories were featured in order to make the visitor more familiar with the experience. The integration of interactive technologies enhanced the storytelling and contributed to the unique character of the exhibition.

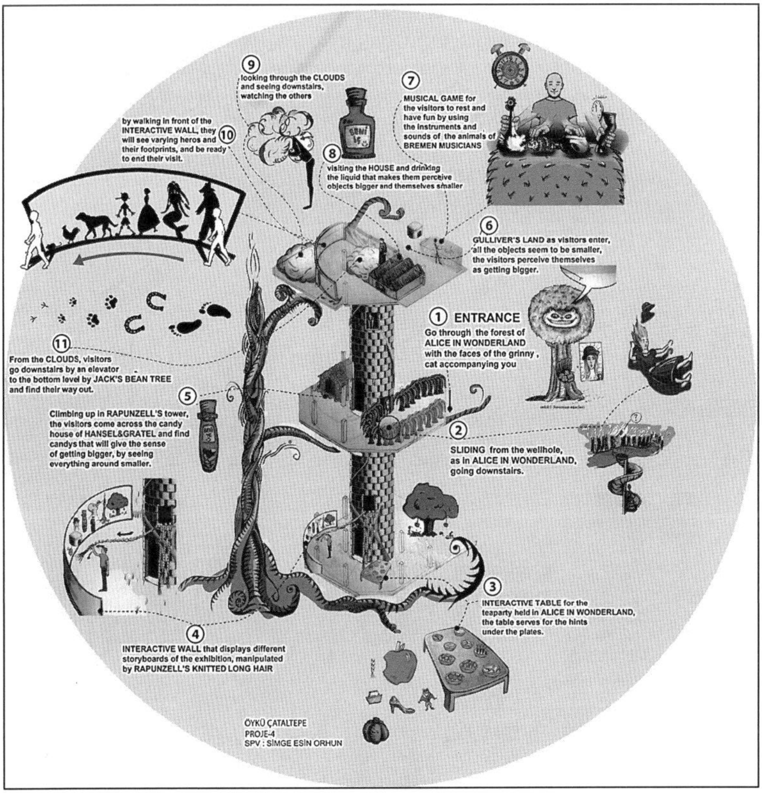

Most important factor that guided and inspired the development of storytelling in terms of representation of time was the architectural quality of the space. In a linear space it was possible to generate a direct connection between events, whereas in multi-storey spaces it was very difficult. Some works involved storytelling that studied the spatio-temporal context from the phenomenological point of view and composed novel scenarios that focused on user experience. Especially the category of existential themes yielded fruitful results in raising the awareness of space and time to the upmost level, together with the innovative approach of connecting three floors with an additional mobile or wearable object in order to maintain the unity of the exhibition and the experience. These tools were generated in line with the storytelling and were intended to be used by the visitor during his visit. All of these tools were meant to collect location-based data, which would affect later interaction or the route or the end result.

Figure 6. The project by Yasemin Yildirim named "House of Media", showing each visitor the extent of unnecessary information collected and consumed through social media, in terms of their personal approaches. The main actors include household items divided into three floors: the garden at the entrance, common areas on the first floor and private sectors at the top. Plant seeds were sown in the garden, and every visitor was given a flashlight for collecting and disseminating information for varying uses within the house. In parallel with a reasonable collection and use of information, the plant of each visitor reflected the existential changes in growth until the visitor left the exhibition. If the information was collected unnecessarily and consumed for unrelated functions, the plant would die.

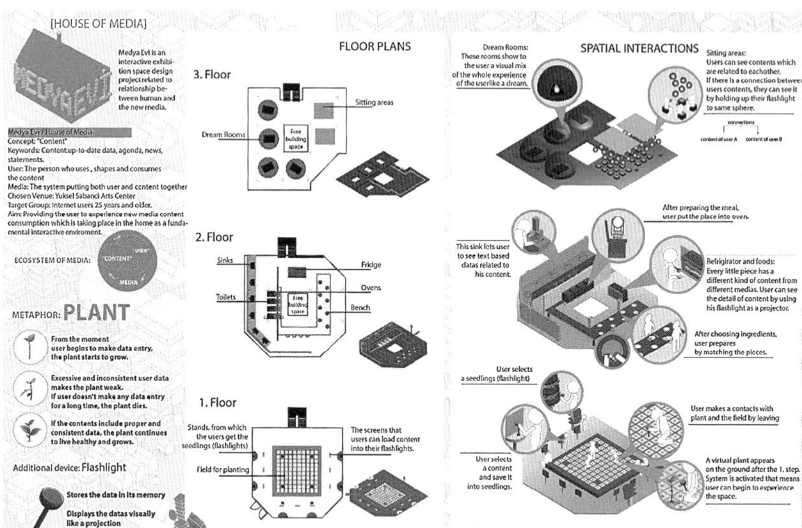

When the earlier works of this group of students were compared with their works created in this design studio, the scale of sophistication, creativity and contextual consistency of design of the latter stood out positively. In the surveys, the students highlighted the constructive learning outcomes due to the integration of the physical environment in the design brief and indicated the satisfaction they got for being able to understand the potential of interactivity in their projects with a solid content.

Concluding Remarks

In today's world, science is constructed into technological advancements, which has intense effects on daily life other than social theories, philosophy and psychiatry. It is believed that the overbearing role of technology can be weakened by increasing the visibility of the techniques of doing, rather than accepting the technology as it is. In order to achieve this objective, bodily involvement gains in importance together with the integration of spatio-temporal factors in design, both of which were separated from daily activities due to the alternative modes of communication provided by networking technologies and digital tools.

One reason to suspect digital technology of transforming the perceptual and behavioural aspects of human beings lies in the inappropriate or non-designed contexts in which most gadgets have been used. This aspect becomes increasingly important in the area of digital design education as the young generation are already digital natives and alien to the analogue way doing things. It is the argument of this study that the concept of interactivity, which is the most beneficial aspect these technologies can offer, can enhance the design of digital tools, if this concept is lifted to a higher level by the art of storytelling, and bring about a better definition and terms of use for the gadgets by the provided context.

In the frame of this study, the concept of interactive exhibiting was chosen for the creation of the experiences that require bodily performances and refer to the architectural qualities of space and time. This concept was also found suitable for the work with the students of communication design, as the discipline deals with design problems that involve interaction and the displaying of information. Within the frame of the course, the students were asked to work on developing conceptual exhibition design projects for a specific physical space. The designs were expected to involve the use of spatial aspects and organisation methods merged with the idea of creating motion and interaction in physical space.

On a general level, it is possible to say that the works created in the design studio were successful in providing diverse examples of storytelling supported by interactive tools to create the participative experience. The conceptual designs either focused on the representation of time or chose to deal with spatio-temporal phenomena. The first group of projects focused more on the bodily performances in space and less on technological innovations. A linear style of storytelling was favoured in most of the designs, with time perceived as a series of events. The second group of projects, on the other hand, showed a greater keenness to discover the extent of interactivity and experiencing a theme. Besides structuring the physical and virtual information, they also bound these two with a mobile tool in order to create a much more individualistic experience. The tools included tablets, eyeglasses, gloves, headphones, flashlights, helmets, memory sticks and cards, and were chosen according to need and guided by the narratives. With the aim of making the visitors experience the story in multiple ways, complex information architectures connecting three different layers of information were studied by the storytelling. The mobile tool, either carried or worn, is able to create an endless number of combinations that are based on the navigation and interaction of the individual. It can also be integrated with the whole story to define the ongoing steps or routes and to guide the visitor. This group of solutions were recognised not only to improve the capabilities and design skills of the students, but also to enhance creativity with regard to future tools and technologies through well-defined needs. Obtaining such outcomes from this approach proved the need for the integration of spatio-temporal aspects into design education and showed an alternative method for the development of digital technologies and tools in line with the real needs and design ethics.

The findings have shown us that every spatial and temporal condition brings its own circumstances, which may lead to different results. Another important outcome gleaned from this study, one which concerns designers working in the area of human-computer interaction, is the need to identify each design problem as constituting a challenge that cannot simply be solved by the integration of a tool. So it becomes important for designers to work with the art of storytelling in selected contexts within the planning stage in order to maintain suitable tools for user experience.

Designers working in the area of digital media today are facing opportunities that can lead them to be the innovators of the products and technologies of the future. The interactive experiences, tools and technologies will continue to progress and become more advanced, which in turn will call for new scenarios with changing settings. As innovativeness and creativity become valuable assets in today's world, the undesirable effects can be reversed and the technology can be utilised to bring positive outcomes for the society.

References

Alexander, S., Ishikawa, S. and Silverstein, M. (1977). *A Pattern Language: Towns, Buildings, Construction.* NY: Oxford University Press.

Bagis, S. and Ustundag, B. B. (2013). A spatiotemporal synthetic NDVI generation model for agricultural fields. Proc. Of *Agro-Geoinformatics (Agro-Geoinformatics), 2013 Second International Conference.* IEEE Xplore Digital Library, p. 82–86. DOI: 10.1109/Argo-Geoinformatics. 2013. 6621884.

Bateson, G. (2000). *Steps to an Ecology of Mind.* Chicago: The University of Chicago Press.

Betts, M. (August 22, 2008). Video Game Storytelling: Is It Really a New Medium? Retrieved from http://mikebbetts.wordpress.com/2008/08/22/video-game-storytelling-is-it-really-a-new-medium/.

Bok, C. (2000). Monitoring Change: Characteristics of Dynamic Geo-Spatial Phenomena for Visual Exploration. In Freksa, Ch. Brauer, W., Habel, C., Wender K.F. (eds.). *Spatial Cognition 2* (pp. 16–30), LNAI 1849. Berlin, Heidelberg: Springer-Verlag.

Bruner, J. (1990). *Acts of Meaning.* Cambridge: Harvard University Press.

Bullivant, L. (2007). *Interactive Architecture 4D Social: Interactive Design Environments.* London: Wiley and Sons *77(4).* (pp. 6–14)

Burrough, X. (2012). *Networks, Case Studies in Web Art and Design.* New York: Routledge.

Carr, N. (2008). *The Big Switch: Rewiring the World, From Edison to Google.* New York: W. W. Norton & Company.

Clark, A. (2010). Out of our brains. *New York Times,* 2010/12/12.

Dourish, P. (2004). *Where The Action Is: The Foundations of Embodied Interaction.* Cambridge: MIT Press.

Hirtle, S. C. (2011). Geographical Design: Spatial Cognition and Geographical Information Science. *Synthesis Lectures on Human-Centered Informatics,* 4(1) Morgan & Claypool.

Hughes, P. (2010). *Exhibition Design.* London: Laurence King Publishers.

International Organization for Standardization (2009). *Ergonomics of human system interaction – Part 210: Human-centered design for interactive systems (formerly known as 13407).* ISO FDIS 9241-210.

Kaptelinin, V. and Nardi, B. A. (2009). *Acting with Technology.* Cambridge: MIT Press.

Lang, J. (1987). *Creating Architectural Theory: The Role of Behavioural Sciences in Environmental Research.* New York: Van Nostrand Reinhold.

Lakoff, G. and Johnson, M. (1999). *Philosophy in the Flesh: The Embodied Mind and Its Challenge to Western Thought.* New York: Basic Books.

Lanier, J. (2010). *You are not a gadget: A manifesto.* New York: Penguin.

Lorenc, J., Skolnick, L. and Berger, C. (2006). *What is Exhibition Design?* Mies: Roto Vision SA.

Meirelles, I. (2013). *Design for Information: An Introduction to the Histories, Theories, and Best Practices Behind Effective Information Visualizations.* Beverly: Rockport Publishers.

Miller, C. H. (2008). *Digital Storytelling: A creator's guide to interactive entertainment.* Amsterdam: Focal Press/Elsevier. Mitchell, W. (1999). *E-topia: Urban Life, Jim – But Not As We Know It.* Cambridge: MIT Press.

Mollison, B. C. (2011). *Introduction to Permaculture.* California: Tagari Publications.

National Research Council (2006). *Learning to Think Spatially: GIS as a Support System in the K-12 Curriculum.* Washington, DC: National Academies Press.

Norberg-Schultz C. (1979). *Genius Loci: Towards a Phenomenology of Architecture.* London: Rizzoli.

Norman, D. (2010). Technology first, needs last. *ACM Interactions 17(2).* (p. 38)

O'Sullivan, D. and Unwin, D. (2002). *Geographic Information Analysis.* Hoboken: John Wiley & Sons.

Parker, W. O., Wolf, R. C. and Block, D. (2008). *Scene Design and Stage Lighting* (9th edition). Boston: Wadsworth Cengage Learning Publishing.

Peuquet, D. J. (1994). It's About Time: A Conceptual Framework for the Representation of Temporal Dynamics in Geographic Information Systems. *Annals of The Association of American Geographers 84(3):* 441–461.

Porteous, J., Cavazza, M. and Charles, F. (2010). Applying planning to interactive storytelling: Narrative control using state constraints. *ACM Transactions on Intelligent Systems and Technology*: ACM 1(2).

Postman, N. (1985). *Amusing ourselves to death.* New York: Penguin.

Quensenbery, W. and Brooks, K. (2010). *Storytelling for User Experience, Creating Stories for Better Design.* New York: Rosenfeld Media.

Rapoport, A. (1982). *The Meaning of the Built Environment: A Nonverbal Communication Approach.* Beverly Hills: Sage Publications.

Salen, K. and Zimmerman, E. (2004). Rules of Play: Game Design Fundamentals, London: MIT Press. In Triantafyllakos, G., Palaigeorgiou, G. and Tsoukalas, I. (eds.) (2008), *Collaborative Design as Narrative.* Department of Informatics, Aristotle University of Thessaloniki, Greece.

Satish, A., Jain, R. and Gupta, A. (2009). *Tolkien: an event based storytelling system. Proc. VLDB Endow. 2:* 1630–1633.

Tasa, U. and Orhun, S. E. (2013) Changing Landscapes in Interactive Media Design Education. In Chakrabati, A. and Prakash, R. V. (eds.). *ICoRD'13: Lecture Notes in Mechanical Engineering* (pp. 1189–1200). New Dehli: India: Springer.

Tully, R. (2012). Narrative Imagination: a Design Imperative. *Irish Journal of Academic Practice* 1(1, Article 8). Retrieved on September 2nd, 2016, from http://arrow.dit.ie/ijap/vol1/iss1/8.

Turkle, S. (2011). *Alone Together.* New York: Basic Books.

Tversky, B. (1993). Cognitive maps, cognitive collages, and spatial mental models. In Frank, A. U. and Campari, I. (eds.). *Spatial information theory: A theoretical basis for GIS* (pp. 14–24). Berlin: Springer-Verlag.

Weiser, M. (1991). The Computer for the Twenty-First Century. *Scientific American* Sept.: 94–104.

Vasiliev, I. R. (1997). Mapping Time. *Cartographica 34(2)*: 1–51.

Julie Faulkner & Greg Curran

Personal Stories and the Visual Turn: Exploring Digital Stories as Identity Representation

Abstract While the rhetoric surrounding digital technologies in education has occasionally been breathless, the reality is that formal learning and ICT have a messier relationship (Selwyn, 2011; Ferneding, 2003). However, considered exploration of digital technologies for personal storytelling offers promising suggestions for learning under certain conditions. In this chapter, two educators discuss digital stories as an effective mode to articulate and extend meaning-making in different ways. In the first case, digital introductions offered authors opportunities to play with multimodal potentials and reflect on aspects of technology and stories of personal identity. In the second case, digital stories were employed to give voice and form to author experience, often traumatic, that cannot easily be expressed in oral or written language. Moreover, these stories are ones which have been and continue to be actively suppressed by government institutions. In each instance, the designers of the curriculum tasks were influenced by notions of authentic purpose, meaning-making and audience.

Introduction

In 1951, Isaac Asimov published a short story, "The Fun They Had", about schooling and computerisation. Set 200 years into the future, it tells of two children who discover a book in their attic. While speculating on the book's purpose, Margie and Tommy compare its educational appeal to their own programmed, depersonalised schooling. Their curriculum is mediated by an inspector, and delivered via individual computer punch cards. The novel idea of a human teacher and learning in a single room with peers grows on the children. Increasingly, they consider the "fun" that schoolchildren of yesteryear must have had.

Asimov reputedly wrote the story for a friend, and was surprised by its popularity. The power of story to engage on a number of levels leads us to speculate, wonder and predict. Asimov's writing of digital learning is prescient and, in the tradition of many short stories, ironic.

The story stays with us for what Asimov, as a science fiction writer, got wrong as well as right. The children's home technology adjusts to generalised age levels, and computer malfunction means students cease formal learning. Margie has to submit work via a punch code which she learned when she was six. Coding has now been part of UK primary school curriculum since 2014, working from the assumption that children are enabled through knowledge of the "architecture" of the digital. We continue to wrestle with questions around engagement and influence of digital technologies on our learning and social practices.

A prevailing discourse around computers in the mid-20th century is that of mechanistic, controlling forms of technology which render users passive. The "big brother" capacity of the computer held more fear than excitement for those anticipating the future. While traces of this encroachment thinking continue in contemporary representations of digital technology, we generally view our devices and their potentials in far more social and active ways. Since the advent of social media, it is the "communications" dimension which dominates the information and communications technologies (ICT) concept. The implications of such a rapid and shifting digital embrace have deep implications for learning and teaching. In this chapter, we will explore the "communications" potential of new media, specifically for digital storytelling, and critically consider some of the ways in which such forms of expression might impact on education in the 21st century.

Background

Narratives have long been recognised as central to our human experience. Stories are "primary" ways (Hardy cited in Meek, 1978) to create a sense of events and exchange, as we organise our experiences into socially meaningful episodes. To do this, we call upon combinations of prior knowledge, assumption, expectation, inference, pattern matching and metaphor. Storytelling ranges across cultures and sees different representations of human experience. Through rich stories, students are offered access to understanding themselves and their world, as both creators and readers/listeners of stories. Here, stories are used as powerful forms of personal, social and cultural representation. Moreover, their power is contingent on ways that they might legitimate or contest more dominant narratives, or metanarratives. The extra dimension in the discussion that follows is the role of the digital in the storytelling, and the ways it might serve to shape and distribute the producer's content, particularly in terms of audience and purpose, two concerns fundamental to literate practices. The examples discussed in this chapter attempt to move the lens between the microprocesses involved in creating personal stories to larger political and cultural issues within which the stories sit.

In the first instance discussed in this chapter, digital introductions offer authors opportunities to play with multimodal potentials and reflect on aspects of technology and personal identity. In the second case, digital stories are employed to give form to author experience, sometimes traumatic, that cannot easily be expressed in oral or written language.

In each instance, the designers of the curriculum tasks were heavily influenced by notions of authentic purpose, meaning-making and audience. To fully engage, writers need to hear the sound of their own voices as well as those of others, a capacity central to human interaction. Feeding the imagination through oral storytelling, however, has dropped off the school curriculum radar, partly as a consequence of high stakes testing and, pertinently for this chapter, the rise of digital technologies in schools. Phillips (2000: 5) notes that "for many years storytelling has been forgotten in many educational environments, as our world of visual imagery has rapidly flourished".

This chapter argues for a classroom re-emergence of storytelling as a convergence with digital technologies. A key affordance of ICT is that of writer (of the technologies) as knowledge producer rather than reproducer, a shift from many of the more traditional learning approaches of the past. Further, the rapidly expanding number of ways that digital tools can mediate ideas is a feature of 21st century design. As a teacher educator (Julie) and an English as an Additional Language teacher (Author) in two universities in Melbourne, Australia, we sought openings for learners to find their voice through authoring their own narratives. Although by the time of writing, we were working at different universities in Melbourne, we had worked closely together previously and shared curriculum ideas around narrative and digital technologies.

As educators, we sought openings for learners to find their voices as knowledge producers through authoring their own narratives. Contained within this authoring notion are practices of assembling, selecting, pacing and sequencing, shaping processes which provide momentum and give texture to narrative.

Working from these understandings, we invited learners – preservice teacher students in the first case, English as an Additional Language learners in the second – to explore the ways that technologies could enable forms of self-expression and representation. With the rise of ICT, argues Kress (1995), we are experiencing a "visual turn", whereby the weight of meaning has shifted from print to image. Syntactic demands on print language have lessened as visual content becomes more complex and abstract. Focusing thus on semiotic modes, or creating meaning through signs and symbols, we asked adult students to create their own stories for a peer audience.

This chapter will detail the challenges of each initiative, as well as the ways they achieved and even exceeded teaching intentions. The two studies discussed here reinforce the notion that narrative is central to human experience and thus central to learning, both formal and informal. The second research premise is that digital tools are well positioned to enable learners as creators of their own stories. Digital resources enable not only traditional forms of storytelling (for instance, podcasts of The Moth stories, http://themoth.org/stories), but also ways that specifically digital forms of narrative can be voiced (for example, Inanimate Alice, http://www.inanimatealice.com/episode4/). We will critically reflect upon the employment of digital tools to explore narrative representations of experience, and particularly the role of the teacher/facilitator in shaping the content. From these instances, implications might be drawn for related explorations across similar kinds of educational contexts.

Changing Education Landscapes?

Bill Green (2001), speculating on the implications for subject English in the 21st century, points to "the proliferating phenomenon of techno-textuality" (ibid.: 249). A dimension of this techno-textuality, however, has been the opening up in terms of what can now be authored, not only of new kinds of content, but also of form (Green 2001). Particularly in Web 2.0 environments, multiliterate understandings engage complex relationships among visuals, space and text as well as interpreting a range of symbols in critically and culturally appropriate ways. The shift towards "new literacies" (Lankshear & Knobel 2007) emphasises the creative and participatory elements of meaning-making over the ideological. In turn, such elements have been critiqued by Lanier (2010) as over-celebratory and not enhancing innovation. We further recognise, however, that ideological elements might be subsumed in meaning-making as "natural" or "common sense". We are therefore mindful of Green's (1988) critical dimension of his 3D literacy model, which calls attention to values and assumption implicit in the text.

This chapter first explores the reshaping of semiotic form through digital introductions, expanding to wider debates around technology, representation and communication through story. Our second case involves the sense of self that recent immigrants and refugees are able to construct through their own digital stories, and how their personal narratives might sit in tension with broader current political "meganarratives" (Olsen and Craig, 2009).

In the introduction to this collection, Stocchetti points to the "narrative support" (ibid.: 3) required for institutional power to maintain authority. Schools and universities are no strangers to these processes, as education becomes increasingly codified, standardised and regulated. Such processes often sit in marked contrast to the social structures which govern young people's lives.

Differences within ways that in-school and out-of-school literacies are organised have been usefully analysed by Bernstein (1999). While schooling values vertical, segmentally-structured discourses of knowledge, popular (and digital) ways of knowing to which everyone has potential or actual access can be described as "horizontal". They are "likely to be oral, local, context-dependent and specific, tacit, multi-layered and contradictory across … contexts" (ibid.: 8). Young people take up valued knowledge by word of mouth and there is a rapid turnover of what is required to be a participant within and across a number of cultural contexts. Arguments calling for classrooms to draw more effectively on learners' informal practices and ways of knowing grow increasingly pressing (Lankshear and Bigum, 1999; Gee, 2003; Green, 2011).

Yet, the interplay of power relations in terms of practices and processes lead to what Feenberg (1991) describes as a "scene of struggle" (ibid.: 14). An element of the "struggle" includes an over- emphasis on the technology per se at the expense of pedagogical considerations. Selwyn (2011) argues that enhanced learning often occurs because teachers have designed innovative contexts and scaffolding to encourage new practices. We examine two instances where we, as teachers, have worked at the intersections of digital and curriculum design to discover what might emerge from potentially new forms of storytelling within an institutional context.

In exploring our students' "small stories" of learning, we draw from Bamberg and Georgakopoulou (2008), who argue that "people use small stories to construct a sense of who they are, while big story research analyses the stories as representations of world and identities" (ibid.: 382). We were conscious of shaping versions of experience through the questions we asked and the ways processes of selection positioned the respondents (including ourselves as educator researchers). Moreover, respondents choose what to include, highlight, downplay or omit. This shaping, or interpreting act, constitutes a reflexive methodology through its way of seeing the world, then reflecting on it.

Bamberg and Georgakopoulou (2008) claim that it is in the navigation process between small and big stories that a "sense of self" is rehearsed. It is with this constant interactive movement between versions of the self and local contexts that identities are constructed and reconstructed. Digital storytelling offers particularly generative opportunities for these identity processes as it provides what Illich (1979) terms "convivial tools" for author agency and self-expression.

Using the work of Bamberg and Georgakopoulou to frame the identity work in our digital storytelling projects, we developed two distinct focal points. The first study explores the kinds of technological affordances that open-ended digital introductions as personal story could draw upon. The second project establishes a learning community through new media, and examines how such a community can then digitally support personal stories of risk and displacement, sometimes in juxtaposition to broader political narratives or even silence.

Digital Potentials

Our first instance of digital storytelling is realised through a digital introduction task, offered at tertiary level (though could be introduced in any educational sector). Student participants comprised 23 postgraduates, engaged in a one-year teaching qualification. The university cohort draws from a culturally diverse mix of local applicants, most of whom were in their early to mid-20s and chose English as one of their secondary teaching methods.

Students were asked to create a 3-to-5-minute personal introduction to show their lecturer and peers, then complete a written reflection on representational choices they made and why. No specifications by me were made as to the content or software programmes they could choose, beyond Author recommending that students worked 'at the outer edge' of their digital expertise. This was intended, via the reflection, to invite a reflexive approach, as students learned through and about the technology. Moreover, the task design emerged from a belief that critical understanding, rather than encouraged solely as a theoretical concept, is "better achieved when students have some grasp of how media texts are actually produced" (Durrant 2011: 76).

The theory of multiliteracies (the New London Group, 1996; Cope and Kalantzis, 2000) takes reconceptions about literacies in a technologised, globalised environment and maps them on to more established notions of situated practice, in this case, personal storytelling. Through building a social-semiotic theory of multimodality, Kress (1997) develops the notion of affordances. Crucial to choices individuals make when designing multimodal artefacts are the potential resources available for socially- and culturally-shaped uses of different modes. The rules and norms of cyberspace create a different and distinctively new sense of spatial awareness, involving a "fracturing of space" (Lankshear and Bigum, 1999). We can now shift back and forth between different modes of meaning, creating new design patterns. Space is no longer closed and purpose specific, but 'open, continuous and fluid' (Knobel and Lankshear, 2007: 11).

Kress (2003) calls the ways that we can purposefully mobilise these resources *synaesthesia*, or the remaking of semiotic resources within modes (*transformation*) and across modes (*transduction*). Within each mode exist different systems, or organising logics, which affect the ways that the semiotic elements are integrated, or "braided" (Mitchell, 1994). While multimodality is not new, through rapidly changing technologies, we can, and increasingly do, deploy innovative ways to overlay image, word, gesture, image, sound and space. Three-dimensional space opens prospects for cognitive reshaping of texts, which have now become, Kress (1997) argues, affordances. In this sense, the producer's relationship with the text has become something potentially more generative and creative than previously. The processes which drive this shifting meaning-making create qualitatively new forms from those that have previously existed, pre-internet. Users of formerly static systems have become remakers, or transformers, of representational resources.

We sought to understand how pedagogical design could encourage authors to use digital technologies to represent their personal stories in new ways. If synaesthesia, or shifting back and forth between modes, were evident, how might students conjure and recombine elements from available resources? While students who engage in social media may be experienced "curators" (Potter, 2012) of their own digital lives, we wanted to bring their practices into the formal learning environment.

The Introductions

The 23 preservice teachers' interview data, their reflections and the digital introductions themselves provided a number of valued insights into how digital storytelling might offer expanded learning possibilities. From the collected data, themes were identified and mapped on to those emerging in the literature. As not all students from the cohort contributed to the study, findings are drawn from the 14 students who agreed to participate.

The introduction content ranged from limited, in terms of exploitation of form, to rich and boundary pushing. Exploring the ways students drew on available resources to tell personal stories, we looked particularly at intersections between what was told and how it was told. Predictable content could be represented as digitally interesting, while conceptually innovative material might be formatted in traditional ways. The most striking stories experimented with both content and form.

At the limited end, five presentations used the task as a kind of digital scrapbook, posting photos of friends, family and pets, following a chronology from baby to university student and occasionally supported by a favourite music track. The visual and audio resources in these cases mimicked print resources of self-representation; they tended to be linear in structure, rely more strongly on written text and draw upon known conventions such as photo albums.

However, other students consciously wrestled with the "messiness" of ICT (Bigum, 1995), producing introductions that were conceptually and visually interesting to, at the higher end, spectacular. Their programme range included iMovie, Prezi, Xtranormal, Movie Maker, PowerPoint, Google Earth, Animoto, websites and blogs, suggesting many students took on the teacher directive to extend their expertise. A number of reflections detailed hours spent on learning new software, time willingly expended in pursuit of a programme that would achieve their narrative ends. Music, for example, was often problematic to add to images. Yet, reflections suggest that students read guides, searched YouTube instructions and sought advice in their efforts to have their chosen digital platform achieve the effects they wanted for the intended audience.

In some cases, authors "bent" genre conventions as they played with identity constructions. This was done from a distanced perspective and often using knowing humour. Writers have achieved this with print, so the interest here lay in observing whether, and to what extent, the digital affordances added value to the already sophisticated and reflexive productions.

For example, Amy filmed people talking about her and talking "as" her – at no point did she ever either appear or reveal anything substantive about herself. Employing documentary and vox pop techniques, Tom edited clips of his family and friends discussing him posthumously, with one brother struggling to remember he had even existed. Another introduction engaged an animation programme with computer generated, HAL-type voices, to parody his decision to become a teacher education student. He chose a pre-provided Napoleonic war scenario to request safe passage to the outer Melbourne suburb where he would commence his teacher education diploma.

In terms of "braiding" elements to create new spaces for story, a number of students experimented successfully with technological possibilities. Koh from Singapore constructed an on-screen digital jigsaw puzzle with his name written in the centre piece. Other digital pieces contained hyperlinked identity features (a Google map link to his street, favourite satay recipes, a trailer to a popular television series). Clicking and dragging the irregular pieces to the centre piece completed his jigsaw, which formed a map of his own country.

Liam filmed himself in profile, intermittently speaking. He then stood adjacent to his interactive screen profile and conducted a conversation with himself – a playful, decentred expression of authorial voice.

Google Earth provided a platform for Matt to offer an annotated tour of the history of his relationship and work with a Japanese tent theatre company. He uploaded to Google Earth photographs and notes of events that took place in

Tokyo and Melbourne linked to his ongoing collaboration, "flying" us to Tokyo and pasting theatre photos on relevant points of the map. The blending of literal and figurative modes extended his understanding of communication and representation. No two-dimensional form could replicate the geographical space Matt wanted to overlay as an architectural layer to his photographic images.

The level of "orchestration" (Kress, 2003) in these examples was high, as students borrowed and experimented with combinations to explore identity concepts. However, perhaps fewer than half the students reflected in such depth and detail, or exploited the multimodal affordances of the technology. Some introductions made few connections beyond self-evident statements. David Buckingham (cited in Thomas, 2011: x) asserts that "most of young people's use of digital technology is mundane rather than spectacular: it is characterised not by dramatic manifestations of innovation and creativity, but by relatively routine forms of communication and information retrieval". To encourage new combinations and expression of students' local digital knowledge, then, the role of the teacher becomes significant.

As Selwyn (2011) reminds us, the creativity of Kress's synaesthetic affordances is thus not inevitably implicated in digital technologies. The inventive play with time and space by students described in this study could have been mediated through other technologies, though arguably not as readily. In this curriculum design, there was a central focus on semiotic communication and representational interrelationships, highlighted by guided reflection questions. However, open-ended tasks per se guarantee no more "creativity" than more traditionally mediated invitations. The role of the teacher in expanding and scaffolding possibilities appears pivotal here.

Repositioning Student Expertise

In the second case discussed in this chapter, new media were employed to create engaged English as an Additional Language learning communities. The origin for this multimedia emphasis was a year-long project focusing on the out-of-class literacies of a small group of South Sudanese and Liberian young men. There were students from Myanmar (the predominant country, refugee-wise, in Australia at that time) and a smattering of students from China, India, Macedonia and South Sudan. Using personal stories as the foundation, the aim was to acquire and experiment with new digital approaches in the classroom, challenging students' notions of what "learning English" looks like, as well as teachers' perceptions of their own pedagogical role. Students used culturally relevant websites, a class social network and moviemaking to build the learning community around personal stories. This project also aimed to interrogate the roles that teachers play in shaping students' understandings of their own "resources", or expertise.

In this case, 17 students participated from the highly culturally-diverse western suburbs of Melbourne and were proficient in oral culture. The university project intended to build on existing strengths, moving away from deficit notions of learners and learning. The project therefore drew on student skills, dispositions and out-of-school knowledge typically left at the classroom door. The learners also became teachers in this community, sharing expertise and offering collegial support, with Author instructing them to seek peer advice before consulting the teacher.

Two notable participants in this project were Ugul and Makuac. Ugul was a South Sudanese 18-year-old, who positioned himself as an insider in the rap scene prior to arriving in Australia. A student and HIV/AIDS peer educator, he had experienced being singled out above others as a rapper who was viewed as talented, someone whose skills are "in demand" in his social context. Ugul knew the processes of recording, composing raps, shaping lyrics to appeal to particular audiences (girls and their families). He was able to move between Swahili and English when rapping – with a rationale for rapping in either language – but did not discuss his wide-ranging rapping expertise in his English classes.

Makuac, 24, also from South Sudan, was a leader within his community. Makuac uploaded a number of files to the computer (as he had learnt in our prior lessons). He had filmed (on his phone) clips of people dancing from an Eritrean music website. From here, he developed and edited his one-minute film clip from the five minutes of footage he had already saved. His final story represented powerful forms of cultural identity which included remembering – keeping his culture alive, and maintaining an ongoing connection or relationship with his community and culture. Culture was central to his learning – to his ways of acting and/or being in learning situations. Makuac's digital story was a way of keeping the culture close, in tune with life there, for when he might return. Through such moments, the audience powerfully came to see the centrality of culture, especially in relation to music and movement.

Following this Out of Class Literacies project, a number of additional multi-media projects linked to real-world issues and interests of refugee students were created by Author. In Author's Life-Story project, he engaged culturally diverse asylum-seeker students in telling their own multimedia stories. The students in this instance comprised a range of recent arrivals with varying degrees of English language and digital technology competence. Students in this EAL class created a 2-to-3-minute digital story to teach preservice teachers about refugee/immigrant life. They were instructed how to script and storyboard their narratives, use a title, transitions, write a voiceover and credits. They could use their own photos, understanding how copyright worked with free photos and how to acknowledge music. Students were introduced to elements of design, lighting and sound as well as relevant programs: Flickr and Creative Commons, www.mp3.com, Windows Moviemaker, Audacity, Ning, WMA Converter and Windows Photostory. They were encouraged to create profiles, post comments and respond to others' comments on the class Ning (that allowed for blogging, posting of photos and videos, and providing feedback to each other).

In terms of language and literacy teaching, the students were taught the genre structure for their digital reports; for example, how to introduce their story and develop it (through the various stages of the genre). For one project, they completed an oral presentation to the class and then created a video report on the same topic with the same material. In the process they learned the difference between the formal oral presentation and the video presentation. Students at lower EAL levels were provided with scaffolding in the form of sentence stems (This is my house… This is my… where I… etc.).

Students also extensively reviewed their digital reports, where they had specific things to look for, for example, pronunciation, structure, body stance and so on. They also reviewed each other, and this is where major learning took place as they adjusted their pronunciation, speed of speaking or the structures of their reports in response to peer feedback. They were encouraged to improve their reports because they knew that their projects would be viewed by their peers. Language was thus embedded, along with media skills, as part of motivated, authentic and crafted communication, reflecting contemporary notions of literacy as situated practice.

Experiencing success was a key project goal and students' efforts were constantly scaffolded through modelling and an array of accessible online resources as well as the physical presence of the teacher. In the spirit of distributed expertise, one student learned a feature and then taught others, as needs arose. Each was advised to draw on peer knowledge, learning at the point of need and through trial and error; familiar strategies for learning in digital environments (Anstey and Bull, 2006; Gee, 2003). The stories themselves borrowed intertextual elements from film and documentary, using music, framed shots and transitions to engage the audience and scaffold language development. A number of students described their learning trajectory as dramatic, having come from locations, such as refugee camps, without any form of digital technology.

The engagement of students with limited English language skills in digital storytelling proved a rich and generative experience. Strategic in the learning process was the design of authentic tasks which linked to cultural values, and local audiences, thus providing high levels of motivation for developing and strengthening English skills. Peer collaboration was another strong feature of the story-making process. The narratives provided opportunities (for teachers and students) to evaluate English skills, motivated by producing personal stories in real-world contexts. Using Gee's (1994) 'bootstrapping' metaphor to underline the importance of timely support, high expectations lifted the levels of learning activity and production. We noted a pedagogical tension, however, between explicit teaching and the necessity of distancing ourselves as teachers, to allow more space for students to learn. In this case, Author consciously encouraged learner collaboration and autonomy. While the task was well scaffolded to enable students to learn independently, the challenges for both skill development and self-representation were high.

Key to the digital storytelling pedagogical approach was to maintain a strengths focus via students taking control of their own narrative. Much was learned by all participants about students' socio-cultural contexts, dimensions of difference (gender, ethnicity, socio-economic status, sexuality, belief system, locale), expertise (knowledge, skills, strategies) and attitudes/values. Careful curation (Potter, 2012) was required of students. Like the students in the first instance discussed, they made choices about what to share about themselves and their communities in their narratives. Self-protection and respect for the community at times played out against agency and the freedom to express oneself through digital formats.

These kinds of considerations sit within a broader perspective of power relations. In Australia, asylum seekers are detained offshore and widely characterised by both political leaders and media as "illegal". Immigrants and refugees (who may or not be asylum seekers) frequently face isolation and public disapprobation. Many have experienced torture and trauma. The role of educators in seeking participant narratives thus takes on an ethical and political dimension, moving beyond skill and knowledge building. It can be seen as a role of forging empathic connections, a role that sees story as facilitating, challenging and affirming deeper understanding. The digital stories offered recent arrivals occasion to write enthusiastically about their own lifeworlds and articulate their skills and expertise, encouraging audience participants to learn, borrow and adapt from others. The value of digital stories in this case was manifold, reaching well past more traditional EAL approaches (which might also include narrative). Students learned multimedia skills in order to establish a particular sense of self and understand story as a tool of affirmation and interpretation, for both authors and audience.

Conclusion

Authors of stories indicated that personal learning in relation to attempting something new and potentially confronting included strategies such as trial and error, collaboration, timely and point-of-need instruction. The digital affordances provided a generative space for stories to be "explored, controlled and mapped" (Martinez-Borda and Lacasar, 2014: 185). Animating new challenges enabled personal confidence and reflexivity in relation to narrative framing (Green, 2001).

The digital introductions and stories were designed to explore identity constructions through potentially innovative technological spaces. The mode in this case could 'reformulate' and expand communicative possibilities. Prevailing discourses in education around generational and technological determinism continue to be interrogated in the literature, as contextual influences and power relations influence and limit educational change. Green's (1988) 3D literacy model allowed the creators of personal stories to reflect on the production and reception processes at technical, social and critical levels.

The digital stories described here suggest further ways that new media technologies can enable narrative to play out in cultural storytelling contexts. The authors' stories illuminated disjunctures between the realities of personal experience and limitations of more traditional pedagogies. The digital stories reflect self-aware and resonant identity representation in moving from page to screen. Among a traditionally marginalised group of refugee language learners, they provided important and accessible spaces for recognition and affirmation.

The two instances described here argue, however, that the task design needs to be theoretically sound, the tools "convivial" and the role of the teacher relevant and timely. Selwyn (2008) contends that we need to clarify our digital focus on the "state-of-the-actual" rather than "state-of-the-art", continually asking questions about how digital technologies sit alongside pre-existing cultures and structures of schooling. Bearing these contexts and interrogations in mind, the examples in this small study suggest that the range of programmes and devices for storytelling can be made inviting to learners as effective tools of identity representation.

References

Anstey, M. and Bull, G. (2006). *Teaching & Learning Multiliteracies: Changing Times, Changing Literacies*. Newark, DE: International Reading Association.

Asimov, I. (1951, January 14, 2015). The fun they had. Retrieved from http://visual-memory.co.uk/daniel/funtheyhad.html.

Bamberg, M. and Georgakopoulou, A. (2008). Small stories as a new perspective in narrative and identity analysis. *Text & Talk, 28(3):* 377–396.

Bernstein, B. (1999). Vertical and horizontal discourse: An essay. *British Journal of Sociology of Education 20(2).* 157-73.

Cope, B. and Kalantzis, M. (2000). Multiliteracies: The Beginnings of an Idea. In Cope, B. and Kalantzis, M. (eds.). *Multiliteracies: Literacy Learning and the Design of Social Futures* (pp. 3–8). London: Routledge.

Durrant, C. (2011). The 3D model and media education. In Green, B. and Beavis, C. (eds.). *Literacy in 3D: An integrated perspective in theory and practice* (pp. 76–95). Melbourne: ACER.

Feenberg, A. (1991). *Critical Theory of Technology.* New York: Oxford University Press.

Ferneding, K. (2003). *Questioning Technology: Electronic Technologies and Educational Reform.* New York: Peter Lang.

Gee, J. P. (1994). First language acquisition as a guide for theories of learning and pedagogy. *Linguistics and Education 6:* 331–354.

Gee, J. (2003). *What video games have to teach us about literacy and learning.* New York: Palgrave MacMillan.

Green, B. (2011). Into the fourth dimension? Literacy, pedagogy and the future. In Green, B. and Beavis, C. (eds.). *Literacy in 3D: An integrated perspective in theory and practice* (pp. 174–187). Melbourne: ACER Press.

Green, B. (2001). 'English teaching, 'Literacy' and the Post-Age'. In Durrant, C. and Beavis, C. (eds.). *P(ICT)ures of English: Teachers, learners and technology* (pp. 249–271). Adelaide: Wakefield Press.

Green, Bill (1988). Subject-specific literacy and school learning: A focus on writing. *Australian Journal of Education 32(2):* 156–179.

Hardy, B. (1978). Narrative as a primary act of mind. In Meek, M., Warlow, A. and Barton, G. (eds.). *The Cool Web: The pattern of children's reading* (pp. 12–23). New York: Atheneum.

Illich, I. (1979). *Tools for conviviality* (2nd edn.). London: Fontana.

Knobel, M. and Lankshear, C. (2007, February 16, 2013). *A New Literacies Sampler.* Retrieved from http://everydayliteracies.net/files/NewLiteraciesSampler_2007.pdf.

Kress, G. (2003). *Literacy in the New Media Age.* London: Routledge.

Kress, G. (1997). Visual and verbal modes of representation on electronically mediated communication: the potentials of new forms of text. In Snyder, I. (ed.). *Page to Screen: Taking literacy into the electronic era* (pp. 53–79). St Leonards Sydney: Allen and Unwin.

Lankshear, C. and Bigum, C. (1999). Literacies and new technologies in school settings. *Pedagogy, Culture and Society 7(3):* 445–465.

Lankshear, C. and Knobel, M. (2011). *New Literacies: Everyday practices and social learning* (3rd edn.). Berkshire, England: Open University Press.

Lanier, J. (2010). *You Are Not a Gadget: A Manifesto*, New York: Alfred A. Knopf.

Martinez-Borda, R. and Lacasar, P. (2014). Children and video games: Oral and written narratives. In Stocchetti, M. (ed.). *Media and Education in the digital age: Concepts, assessments and subversions* (pp. 183–201). Frankfurt: Peter Lang.

Mitchell, W. (1994). *Picture Theory.* Chicago: University of Chicago Press.

Olsen, M. and Craig, C. (2009). 'Small' stories and meganarratives: Accountability in balance. *Teachers College Record, 111(2):* 547–572.

Phillips, L. (2000). Storytelling: The seeds of children's creativity. *Australian Journal of Early Childhood, 25(3):* 1–5.

Potter, J. (2012). *Digital media and learner identity: The new curatorship.* New York: Palgrave McMillan.

Selwyn, N. (2011). *Schools and schooling in the digital age: A critical analysis.* London and New York: Routledge.

Selwyn, N. (2008). From state-of-the-art to state-of-the-actual? Introduction to a special issue of *Technology, Pedagogy and Education 12(2)*: 83–87.

The New London Group (1996). A pedagogy of multiliteracies: Designing social futures. *Harvard Education Review 66*: 60–93.

Thomas, M. (ed.) (2011). *Deconstructing digital natives: Young people, technology and the New Literacies.* New York Routledge.

Gloria Gomez-Diago

From Storytelling to Storymaking to Create Academic Contents. Creative Industries Through the Perspective of Students

Abstract The new technologies and specially the possibilities offered by the internet, multiply the capabilities to write and to tell stories, to create them collectively, to redesign them, to cite them, to amplify them, to link them, to comment them, et cetera. Having available a multitude of resources not only for being storytellers but for accessing to diverse information and contents, changes the possibilities and conditions in which storytelling is generated in comparison with before internet and prompts us to focus on the importance of storymaking abilities in the classroom. In a context where storytelling can be performed without spatial or temporal constraints and where algorithms like Narrative Science's natural language generation programme[1] can write original stories by drawing down content from big data sources, the act of writing and of sharing ideas by using words is still essential to participate in the construction of our societies. Written communication is especially important in academic contexts because it is through texts that contents are created. Aimed to improve the abilities and skills of pupils to generate contents, we designed and applied an experience which consisted of using storymaking as a context for learning, by giving students of the last year of the Advertising and Public Relations Degree at the University of Vigo a role in the building of the contents delivered in the course "Advertising and Cultural Industries". Students co-created a collective book named *Cultural/Creative Industries in an Environment in which the Physical and the Virtual Merge* (2016).[2] During the four months

1 "Quill is a natural language generation (Advanced NLG) platform that goes beyond reporting the numbers – it creates perfectly written narratives to convey meaning for any intended audience. While advances in data visualization and data science are helpful, they don't take us the last mile. Data visualizations are often complex, requiring expert-level analysis and explanation. Quill immediately adds value to data by identifying the most relevant information and relaying it through professional, conversational language. The result? Intelligent narratives that efficiently communicate the insights buried in Big Data that people can comprehend, act on and trust." Cfr. https://www.narrativescience.com/quill

2 Cfr. Collective Book: Industrias Culturales/ Creativas en un Entorno en el que lo Físico y lo Virtual se fusionan. Retrieved September 2nd, 2016 from https://sites.google.com/site/publicidadindustriasculturales/home/industrias-culturales-creativas-en-un-entorno-en-el-que-lo-fisico-y-lo-virtual-se-fusionan

of the course, we applied an action research framework[3] similar to the one we developed to identify and to assess the consequences of using privative software in the classroom (Gómez-Diago, 2004), which consisted on collecting impressions in the classroom through direct observation and interaction and in the elaboration of an open question which was asked to the thirty eight students at the end of the course. The outcomes obtained were very positive. Firstly, students could build their knowledge by delving further into the topics in which they were more interested. Secondly, as a result of their work, they could obtain not only explicit or conceptual knowledge but also procedural or tacit knowledge.

From Storytelling to Storymaking. From Story-Receivers to Story-Participants

Storytelling can be performed through different media and with different purposes. Nowadays, thanks to the unlimited possibilities at our disposal for communicating, we can develop, share and co-create storytelling on a multitude of online platforms. Even with the penetration of the internet, according to Internet World Statistics (2016), at 46.1 percent, and without forgetting that in the 21st century, there are countries in which some topics are impossible or very difficult to discuss, the facilities available for storytelling permit citizens to generate and to share ideas collectively. Therefore, it is logical to think that the freedom to engage in storytelling contributes to create more plural and dynamic societies, at least in the sense that before the internet, only few sectors of society, that is, people with a powerful status, could address storytelling to a wide audience.

After Gutenberg invented the print, the possibilities for storytelling – as well as for receiving new ideas – were extended, making the circulation of ideas easier. By using print, Martin Luther spread the ideas of the Bible, which, due to the fact that they were not available in languages other than Latin, had been modified and used by the Catholic Church to abuse the people.

Storytelling evolves with the technologies available and their uses. The telegraph and the telephone were created to allow people to communicate with each other, to enable dialogue. When mass media appeared, they were rapidly adopted as a tool with which governments transmitted their ideas to the audience, the masses, especially during periods of war. The model of communication represented by mass media is understood as transmission, and what is of importance to the transmitters is to get the audience to think what they want or about the

3 Engaging in 'action research,' requires the professional educator to continuously ask, "How can my work be modified to produce better results" (Sagor, 2009: 10).

things they want. These technologies base the construction of communication on the monologue.

The capacity to storytelling is historically not only linked to the development of technologies but to the roles of citizens in society, to the capacity of power. Benkler (2006) differentiates societies in this way based on the facilities for storytelling:

> Among the Reds and the Blues, everyone is busy all day, and no one tells stories except in the evening. In the evening, in both of these societies, everyone gathers in a big tent, and there is one designated storyteller who sits in front of the audience and tells stories. It is not that no one is allowed to tell stories elsewhere. However, in these societies, given the time constraints people face, if anyone were to sit down in the shade in the middle of the day and start to tell a story, no one else would stop to listen. Among the Reds, the storyteller is a hereditary position, and he or she alone decides which stories to tell. Among the Blues, the storyteller is elected every night by simple majority vote. Every member of the community is eligible to offer him- or herself as that night's storyteller, and every member is eligible to vote.

Cyberspace does not eliminate the social differences between citizens but allows users to communicate among themselves and to cooperate through networks of various purposes where they can dialogue and create stories collectively. Some of these networks have as their main purpose to motivate communication between users, but there are also social networks which turn the interests of users into collective actions expressed, for example, through the creation of platforms oriented to share products and services. One such network is Uber,[4] which allows users and car owners to connect; another example is Peerby,[5] which is oriented to allow users to share time and to borrow the things they need from people in their neighbourhood. As we found out in another study, further examples are crowdfunding platforms, which integrate several carefully designed features that generate credibility, trust and engagement in the users, (Gómez-Diago, 2015) allowing creators to obtain funding from the citizens who support their projects with small donations.

Thanks to the internet, people can contribute to storymaking as "story participants". This term refers to the important fact that we cannot only create stories and participate in the building of ideas and concepts collectively, but we have also access to an unlimited range of content and experiences generated in any part of the world, which enables us to discover issues of interest and to specialise on them. This is altering our perspectives and enriching our cultures, which are no longer

4 https://www.uber.com/es-ES/

5 "Need something, but don't want to buy it? Borrow the things you need from neighbor" https://www.peerby.com/

as dependent on our physical environment as they used to be. We can join – and create – networks defined by our interests.

Storytelling in cyberspace can be defined not only through the physical or virtual platforms where it emerges (such as social networks like Facebook, Twitter or Instagram), but also by taking into account the several applications that users assign to this practice. There are a multitude of motivations behind storytelling. In this way, Kang et al. (2014: 2397) identified the benefits of using communication networks to prevent adolescents from being bullied. There are also a multitude of online platforms where users share experiences related to an infinite range of topics, such as medical problems or sports advice.

Storytelling/Storymaking in Research: Studying Social Life and Generating Academic Contents

Davis (2002: 3–19) highlights a resurgence of interest in narrative as a social act and a form of explanation, on storytelling as a social process for investigation, and on the narrative constitution of identity. According to him, the storytelling process is a social transaction which engages people in a communicative relationship. Through identification and co-creation, the storyteller and reader/listener create an affective bond and a sense of solidarity. Davis point outs that narrative can be a focus of research in at least two ways:

(1) As an object of inquiry and explanation, as researchers study how stories are socially produced and function to mediate action and to form identities;
(2) As a method of studying social life. Researchers gather and observe narratives as a window through which other aspects of world can be accessed.

We consider these two approaches in fact rather similar because in both cases the stories are understood as a method of studying social life. This type of investigation is very common in communication research, where there are a multitude of studies, usually underpinned both in the realisation of content analysis and on derivations such as framing analysis, as well as other perspectives such as critical analysis.

According to Mayring (2014: 18), content analysis has a long history; the first efforts to analyse communication in a systematic manner were made centuries ago. Its first definitions place its origin as quantitative research for an objective and systematic description of the manifest content of communication (Berelson, 1952: 18). Moretti et al. (cited in Young and Lee, 2014: 15) understand content analysis as a method to classify written or oral materials in categories with similar meanings. In the early decades of the nineteenth century, it was used as a method for the analysis of news articles. The method was developed in the 1930s because mass media such as radio and newspapers were gaining in importance. Apart from content analysis, researchers also apply critical analysis to document and, in some cases, to denunciate how some topics are socially constructed and represented through mass media. This line of research is, in a broad sense, derived from the perspective of the Frankfurt School,[6] developed among others by Adorno (1903–1969) and Horkheimer (1895–1973). Critical research is defined as the one discipline intended to study the role of mass media in the society.

According to Gerbner (1983: 355) message-making and storytelling capabilities provide the basic humanising and evolutionary process of our species. Telling a story always requires making sense of observations and the interpretation of facts. Used in this sense, storytelling works as an epistemological tool: deriving a philosophical thought or a scientific conclusion is nothing else but storytelling. Heissenbüttel (in Mentzer & Sonnenschein, 2007, p. 62. Cited in Nyffenegger, 2009: 4), and Benmayor, 2008: 189) conceptualise digital storytelling and theorising as an active learning process that engages the cultural assets, experiences and funds of knowledge that students bring to the classroom.

We used storytelling and, specially, storymaking as an environment in which to perform the learning process of students and to combat some of the problems detected by Nyffenegger (2009: 3) and experienced by pupils when writing: (1) they are not aware that writing competence can be achieved by practice and exercise, applying techniques like brainstorming, mind mapping or sketching; (2) they ignore the close ties between reading and writing skills, overlooking what they can learn from reading and how reading can improve their writing; and (3) they do not consider writing as a process with many steps and as a knowledge-generating act. They rather see it as knowledge-telling in a linear process and expect their very first draft to be the final result.

We were also interested in letting students contribute to producing academic work by providing them some guidance. In this way, Kalogeras (2014: 30) explains that storytelling works at the intersection of the emotional and the epistemological aspects of learning, bridging story and theory, intellect and affect. As emotions are reclaimed cognitively, they enable students to write themselves into existing discourses and to contribute personal perspectives to an academic community.

---

6 At the beginning, the Frankfurt School was linked to the University of Frankfurt, but emigrated in 1933 to New York City and was associated with Columbia University for seventeen years (Rogers 1997: XV). The members of the school enjoyed political and economic freedom to conduct their research as they were funded by the millionaire Herman Weil (Rogers 1997: 112)

In research, storytelling or narrative can also be understood as a manner of writing and rewriting and generating academic contents and contexts. Nowadays, social research is mostly based on the presentation of data which does not provide a new perspective or a new idea, but confirms a hypothesis. Gunkel (2015) alerts to the problem of having a social science which solely presents data at a moment when there are algorithms which permit us to obtain them and to present them with ease.

Aimed to motivate the students' capacity to take part in their learning process, and taking advantage of the fact that they have resources available on the internet for studying any topic of their interest, we designed an experience which consisted of creating a collective book whereby pupils could investigate and represent in their chapters the main characteristics and situation of creative industries.

Creating a Collective Book

The task of elaborating this publication allowed us to develop a context in which students could not passively engage with content in class. They built their contents by reading articles and/or books, by watching documentaries and interviews, by listening to podcasts and/or by attending conferences. Students became the architects of their learning process. In this manner, they needed to research, to read, and to immerse themselves into the topics they had chosen to build the chapters which constitute the collective book. Each of the included forty-four texts is a story individually created by a student, who followed the guidelines and the suggestions provided. The texts were revised, edited and grouped into eight parts that include most of the topics discussed in the classroom, and also point to some mainstream issues related to creative industries:

(1) McLuhan's ideas for analysing cultural industries
(2) Intellectual property, creative commons licenses, free software
(3) Culture economy and innovation, new models of funding
(4) Evolution and trends in the creation and consumption of cultural products
(5) Identifying tools and models for creation
(6) Reflecting on the role of journalism
(7) Redefining the music industry
(8) Identifying examples of advertising communication which generate new business models

The forty-four texts refer to almost all the elements involved in the development of creative industries. The diversity of themes and perspectives turns this collective volume into a practical resource for providing specific knowledge of new ways and approaches to the study of creative industries. Thus, the chapters focus on identifying specific tools that could be used by cultural industries, such as software and applications, on providing analytical perspectives regarding how cultural industries face the financial crisis, on identifying the advantages of the internet with regard to the development of a specific cultural industry, on identifying and explaining theoretical approaches such as those developed by Marshall McLuhan.

Establishing Guidelines

On the first day of class, having been introduced to the meanings of cultural industries, the students were asked to write down on a piece of paper the topics in which they were most interested in this area of study. Their ideas referred to five main categories:

(1) graphic design
(2) video games
(3) cinema
(4) journalism
(5) fashion

Afterwards, in order to assess their overall ideas and impressions regarding the state of cultural industries, we conducted an open discussion. In the course of the dialogue with the students, it became evident that the majority of them did not grasp certain concepts of high importance in communication studies, such as free software, open source, crowdfunding, crowdsourcing, or creative commons licenses.

When students reach their senior year of academic study, it is very hard to change the concepts and ideas they were trained to utilise. In this final course, most of the students are tired, and they carry an anxiety generated by the desire to enter the workplace, mixed with the fear of not finding employment in these difficult times.

Most of the pupils were 21 years old. Being conscious of the challenge of motivating a group of students to introduce new concepts into their approach, as well as that of motivating them to read in languages other from Spanish or Galician – an activity that they were not accustomed to – we designed a method oriented to make students the protagonists of the learning process.

Instead of giving them lectures based on understanding communication as a transmission process and intended to have them copy it, the purpose was to motivate them to integrate concepts and ideas into their vocabulary. The aim was to provide the students with an overall approach to how the introduction of the internet has changed the situation of the cultural industries. This was done, for example, by explaining the perspectives of some of the most relevant authorities, analysing examples of new business models, testing virtual applications related to cultural industries and critically analysing reports provided by governmental institutions.

The adoption of new concepts, approaches and ideas by students was the objective of these dialogic sessions. They were allowed and encouraged to participate by commenting on ideas exposed, and by formulating questions.

To motivate students into further reading and immersing themselves into topics of their interest, we created a website where the contents exposed in the classroom were published in chronological order. This website also permitted us to engage three students who could not attend most of the sessions due to work commitments.

The students were asked to write a text of three to five pages' length. Writing gave the students an opportunity to structure their thinking and to identify their areas of interest or a possible lack of knowledge, among other things. Even if students are accustomed to storytelling with their friends and colleagues through social networks, such as Facebook or Twitter, the features of these virtual platforms, focused on the use of short texts, do not motivate students to train the practice of writing about a theme at a length of several pages. And, as stated above, for taking part in the construction of society, writing abilities still are important.

The students had to choose one of the topics presented in class and to develop it further. In order to help them, they were provided with support via website and e-mail individually, helping them to structure their proposals and supplying them with several references to texts and videos related to the subjects developed in class published in journals, blogs, magazines and such.

Some formal and structural guidelines were stated to allow the students to prepare their texts. The formal specifications established a maximum text length of five pages written on one side, as well as the use of Times New Roman font, type size 12 and line spacing 1.5. Moreover, the students were required to include a title, an abstract, some subtitles, a conclusion and a references section, in which they were required to cite at least three sources of different types so as to base their chapters on different types of sources such as raw data, theoretical articles, reports and so forth.

The pupils could focus their efforts on a particular cultural industry, such as the publishing industry, the film industry or the music industry, but they could also concentrate on practices and activities influencing the landscape of cultural industries such as file sharing. Moreover, they were encouraged to link their cultural industry of interest to one of the concepts or practices which are influencing this type of industry, such as network economy, cultural policies, cyberspace, copyright, creative commons, licenses, crowdfunding, crowdsourcing or virtual worlds. They were also encouraged to apply in their chapters the theoretical perspectives provided by authors explained and discussed in class, such as Marshall McLuhan, Yochai Benkler or Manuel Castells.

Finally, we provided the students with resources on specific topics such as new technologies applied to fashion, new ways of managing online communication, virtual museums, online journalism, digital print trends, games industry, virtual worlds, cinema etc. These resources were shared via the website created for the course and via email when the students demanded it or when we perceived that they needed it.

Evaluating the Chapters

We gave the students two weeks to deliver their first document. We corrected any misleading use of terms and made suggestions in order to change the structure of the writing, among other things. As the chapters were freely created, it was possible to evaluate various dimensions, going further than making orthographical corrections.

Most of the students did not use references correctly. Instead of including a reference section, they added a section named bibliography, in which they included sources not cited in their texts. In addition, some students cited sources but did not go further; they did not provide the quotations with a context by developing them, by explaining their agreement or their disagreement. In the course of reading the documents, it became evident that the students had difficulties to cite in a proper way and, more importantly, did not understand the meaning and the importance of the citation. In some cases, they mentioned the author of the citation but had clearly taken the quotation from an author different from the original one, yet leaving this unindicated. The value of the citation was explained.

The majority of the students did not know that they must cite the authors of the images and photos they use to illustrate their works. Instead, they included images without adding any reference to their authors. This was the context for explaining to the students how to interpret, how to use the license of creative commons, and how they can access images, graphics and photos on any topic via advanced search engines. A number of students also used data to illustrate their argument but did not indicate the source of that data.

Regarding the style, some students wrote their chapters from a general point of view, speaking about the economic crisis and its consequences for the cinema industry but failing to point to possible causes or to facts that allow us to recognise the problems facing that industry. At first, some students found it hard to understand the purpose of the chapters. They were asked to choose an issue related to cultural industries, to delve into the topic, and to provide some conclusions.

At the end of the course, practically all students had understood the idea, but in the first versions of their chapters, they used a lot of empty sentences and created false dichotomies such as whether it is better to publish online or offline (printed books are being favoured by communication technologies because of the opportunities afforded by printing-on-demand). Both rhetoric practices, using empty expressions and creating non-existent oppositions to create a polemic, were very common in the first documents generated by the students. This rhetoric has similarities with the one used in popular television programmes, whose discussions are motivated by manichean propositions. In all cases except one, the difference between the students' first and second documents was very big. They had four weeks to improve their work.

Students received many corrections and suggestions for their texts. As some of them asked for more help, time was provided to help them individually within help desk support hours.

When students had corrected their first document, they presented it orally in the classroom to share their work with their classmates, who were asked to write down keywords that, according to them, could help to define the work they were listening to. Furthermore, they were allowed to ask questions or to introduce their ideas once the presentation had finished. Some of the students used videos and slides to support their speech. Others merely read their documents out loud to their classmates.

The process of sharing the documents with classmates enabled the pupils to gain a comparatively broad perspective of the topics covered during the course. There were students who found it easier to speak in public than others did. This activity was also an opportunity to hear the students who participated less during the sessions.

Results: Knowledge Acquired by Students: Conceptual/Explicit and Procedural/Tacit Knowledge

At the end of the course, twenty-eight students took the final exam. In the exam consisting of nineteen questions, the students were asked to explain and to apply certain concepts. In the last task, the students were asked to identify the type of knowledge they had acquired by writing their chapters.

We grouped the knowledge identified by the students in two categories: conceptual and tacit knowledge. Each student is represented by a number. Twenty-seven of twenty-eight students identified at least one type of explicit knowledge acquired by them as a result of their participation in the creation of the book. There was only one student who did not answer this question: the only one whose work barely improved after the corrections. Twenty-six of the twenty-eight students identified some kind of explicit knowledge as the fruit of their work.

Conceptual/Explicit Knowledge Acquired by the Students

Below, we list the explicit knowledge identified by the students as obtained during the creation of the collective book. As we will see, the students recognise different types of knowledge. In this way, student (1) states that she learnt about the role of intellectual property in the cultural sector, student (2) asserts that he learnt about the ideas of Marshall McLuhan, student (3) expresses that she learnt about the situation and importance of cultural industries in China, student (4) discovered new business models for reinventing the discography industry, student (6) deepened her knowledge on the need of cinema industry to refund its business model, student (7) discovered a multitude of online applications related to fashion industry, student (8) investigated the problems faced by scriptwriters who want to sell a script to a producer, student (9) states that he acquired knowledge about the situation of the game industry in Spain, student (10) obtained knowledge about online platforms which allow users to create graphic design, student (11) identified smartphone applications in cinema as knowledge acquired, student (12) learnt about how serious games can be used with different objectives, student (13) reached the conclusion that citizens nowadays have a big responsibility for being manipulated, student (14) obtained knowledge about the situation of publishing industry and about the democratisation of art through forms of expression such as urban knitting, student (16) maintained that he obtained knowledge about how the peer-to-peer practice is shaping the cultural industry, student (17) learnt about the possibilities that the internet generates for music professionals, student (18) acquired knowledge about new forms of editing and publishing, student (19) understood the crowdfunding phenomenon and its applications in the cultural sector, student (20) obtained insights about the new forms of watching television and about the meaning of public domain, student (21) acquired knowledge about the characteristics and applications of virtual worlds, student (22) states that she learnt about the process of starting a fashion company and that she also understood the value of the role of professional bloggers in a sector such as fashion, student (23) learnt about the situation of the gaming industry in Spain, student

(24) acquired knowledge about the origin and evolution of the video games industry, student (25) learnt about cultural and economic indicators which illustrate the relationship between culture and advertising, student (26) expresses that she learnt to situate the role of new technologies in the fashion sector as one reducing the costs of designs and introducing new services such as allowing users to try on clothes in simulated environments. Student (27) identifies as knowledge obtained Marshall McLuhan's concepts such as the global village, as well as an understanding of the most important virtual worlds and the possibilities they open up for communication, commercialisation and research.

*Table 1: Conceptual/explicit knowledge acquired by the students by elaborating their chapters*Abbreviation of student (STU)*

STU	Explicit Knowledge Obtained by the Students
1	"Intellectual property"
2	"Marshall McLuhan's work"
4	"Situation of cultural industry in China"
5	"New business models for the discography industry"
6	"The need to have the cinema industry reinvent its strategy"
7	"The multitude of online applications regarding to fashion"
8	"The problems that scriptwriters face when they want to sell a script"
9	"The situation of the video game industry in Spain"
10	"Online platforms to create graphic design"
11	"Smartphone applications linked to cinema and to culture"
12	"Possibilities of serious games"
13	"The responsibility of citizens for being manipulated"
14	"The situation of the publishing industry and the democratisation of art through forms of expression such as urban knitting"
15	"The identification of new avenues for journalism"
16	"The role of peer-to-peer (P2P) practices in shaping cultural industry"
17	"The possibilities generated by the internet for music professionals"
18	"New forms of editing and publishing"
19	"Crowdfunding phenomenon and its applications"
20	"New forms of watching television. The meaning of public domain"
21	"Characteristics of multiplayer virtual worlds"

S T U	Explicit Knowledge Obtained by the Students
22	"Process of founding a fashion company. I have also changed my mind regarding the work of a blogger. I thought that it had no value, but I now think the contrary"
23	"The situation of game industry"
24	"The origin of video games. What is more clear to me now is that we must speak about users and not about masses"
25	"I found cultural and economic indicators which illustrate the relationship between culture and advertising"
26	"The role of new technologies in the fashion world as tools for reducing the costs of designs and facilitating the daily life by allowing us to try on clothes in simulated environments"
27	"Marshall McLuhan's concepts such as the global village. Virtual worlds and their possibilities as an environment for communication, commercialisation and research"

Most of the students identified another type of knowledge acquired by preparing their chapters, something we refer to as tacit knowledge. This type of knowledge relates to the way-of-doing and it is probably the most difficult one to gain because it needs practice and time. Only ten of the twenty-eight students did not identify tacit knowledge obtained as a result of their work. It should be pointed out that even if the students did not cite this type of knowledge as gained, it does not mean that they did not obtain it.

It must be highlighted that when the students were asked to respond the type of knowledge they had obtained by writing their chapters, they probably associated knowledge with content because the question was asked without further clarification in order to motivate an open answer.

Procedural/Tacit Knowledge Obtained by the Students

Student (2) expresses that she has learnt to apply the ideas of Marshall McLuhan to the actual context, student (3) finds that he has learnt to search information and to elaborate conclusions, student (4) admits that has discovered the need for being informed about what happens in other countries in respect of cultural industries, student (9) finds that he has learnt to express his ideas in a better way, student (13) states that she has learnt to apply the agenda-setting concept to contemporary times, student (15) expresses that he has learnt to investigate and to analyse the information obtained, student (17) affirms that she has become able to search information by using reliable sources of information, to organise items and to focus on a topic, student (18) expresses that he has learnt to research to avoid having misconceptions, student (19) admits that she has learnt to search and compile data in an effective way and to transform data and contents reviewed into something that makes sense, student (20) highlights that he has leant to research and to discover new information about cultural industries, student (21) admits that she has learnt to categorise information obtained to improve the capacity for analysing, student (23) expresses that he has learnt to use references and to write more critically, thus giving a unique perspective to the topic studied, student (24) expresses that she has learnt to use sources written in English and, finally, student (25) states that he has become able to contextualise cultural industries and to describe how they react to socioeconomic variables.

*Table 2: Procedural/tacit knowledge acquired by the students by elaborating their chapters*Abbreviation of student (STU)*

STU	Procedural/Tacit Knowledge Obtained by the Students
1	
2	"To apply the insights of McLuhan to the actual context."
3	"To search information and to elaborate conclusions."
4	"I discovered the need for being informed about what happens in other countries."
9	"To express my ideas."
13	"To apply the agenda-setting concept to contemporary times."
15	"To investigate and to analyse the information obtained."
17	"To search information by using reliable sources of information, to organise my time, and to focus on and immerse myself in a topic. Furthermore, I have learnt how heart-warming it is doing my own research. It makes you feel that four years of study have been worthwhile."
18	"To avoid creating false ideas and to research."
19	"To search and to compile data in an effective way. To transform the data and the contents obtained into something of my own that makes sense."
20	"To research and to discover new information about cultural industries."
21	"To categorise information obtained, to improve my capacity for analysing."
23	"To use the references and to write more critically, thus giving my perspective to the topic."
24	"To use sources written in English."
25	"To contextualise cultural industries and to describe how they react to socioeconomic variables."

Conclusions

Storytelling is one, if not the most, important activity giving form to society. Actions are motivated, accepted or punished by storytelling. The widespread use of the internet makes it possible that more citizens contribute to the practice of storytelling, being part of a collective storymaking, whereby users cocreate, share documents and build social networks. Nowadays we have at our disposal an infinite number of devices, virtual environments and technologies allowing us to be storytellers in different ways by using a myriad of communicative resources such as texts, images, sounds, videos, etc.

In the context of education, it is mainstream to cultivate the capacity of students to generate contents to have them engaged as active participants in the construction of their learning process. The experience shared in this chapter allowed the students to learn with greater immersion than pedagogical strategies based on the memorisation do. As a consequence of the students taking responsibility and interacting meaningfully, they acquired a deeper understanding of the issues involved in the subject. Understanding storytelling as a context for interaction allowed us to develop the curricula in an active manner, by having into account the individual and collective interests and needs of students, and experimenting, therefore the transformative capabilities of this approach.

References

Benkler, Y. (2006, October 7). Three Storytelling Societies. Retrieved from storyfieldconference.com/SFC-Benkler-StorySocieties.html.

Berelson, B. (1952). *Content analysis in communication research*. New York: Free Press.

Benmayor, R. (2008). Digital Storytelling as a Signature Pedagogy for the New Humanities. *Arts & Humanities in Higher Education 7(2)*: 188–204.

Davis, J. E. (2002). Narrative and Social Movements: The Power of Stories. In Davis, J. E. (ed.). *Stories of Change: Narrative and Social Movements*. State University of New York Press, pp. 3–30

Gerbner, G. (1983). The Importance of Being Critical – In One's Own Fashion. *Journal of Communication 33(3)*: 355–362.

Internet World Stats (2016). Retrieved from http://www.internetworldstats.com/stats.htm. Last accessed 29, August 2016.

Gómez-Diago, G. (2014). Emancipative Technology in Formal Education: the case for "Free and Open Source Software (FOSS)". In Stocchetti, M. (ed.). *Media and education in the digital age. Concepts, Assessments, Subversions* (pp. 341–357). Frankfurt am Main: Peter Lang.

Gómez-Diago, G. (2015). Communication in Crowdfunding Online Platforms. In Zagalo, N. and Branco, P. (eds.). *Creativity in the Digital Age* (pp. 171–190). London, Heidelberg, New York, Dordrecht: Springer-Verlag.

Gunkel, D. (June 19, 2015). Man vs. Machine. Northern Illinois University. Retrieved from http://www.niutoday.info/2015/06/19/man-vs-machine/.

Kalogeras, S. (2014). *New Era of Media Convergence in Higher Education*. Hampshire: Palgrave Macmillan.

Kang, S., Chung, Y., Chung, W. (2014). The Role of Communication Storytelling Networks in Bullying: A Comparison Between U.S. and Korean Adolescents. *International Journal of Communication* 8: 2396–2419.

Mayring, P. (2014). Qualitative Content Analysis: Theoretical Foundation, Basic Procedures and Software Solution. Retrieved from http://www.psychopen.eu/fileadmin/user_upload/books/mayring/ssoar-2014-mayring-Qualitative_content_analysis_theoretical_foundation.pdf.

Nyffenegger, F. K. (2009). Stories for Academia. How storytelling may improve academic writing. Paper submitted to ELIA Teachers' Academy 2009 in Sofia.

Rogers, E. M. (1994). *A History of Communication Study. A Biographical Approach*. New York: The Free Press.

Sagor, R. (2009) Collaborative Action Research and School Improvement: We Can't Have One Without the Other. *Journal of Curriculum and Instruction 3:* 7–14.

Susana Tosca, Anne Katrine Nørgaard Isholdt &
Niklas Tarp-Petzke

Social Media Storytelling as a Method for Teaching Literature

Abstract This paper investigates how a social medium (Facebook in this case) can be a platform for a novel way of teaching literature focusing on social roleplaying of the literary characters. We call this new form "social media storytelling". Our project transmedially recreates the world of an original work of literature, a Danish medieval ballad. We describe our experiment, contextualise our findings and argue for the potentials of such a dialogic form.

Introduction

In a blend of design and action research, we developed a teaching resource that made use of social media to teach *Folkeviser* (old Danish ballads of medieval origin) to high school students. The essence of the project was to create a transmedial storytelling platform inside of Facebook where students had to play the roles of the different main characters of a selected ballad. In this paper, we present and evaluate our project from an educational perspective, as well as address the more general questions:

- What is social media storytelling?
- What are the affordances of a social network as a storytelling platform?
- How are stories appropriated and re-enacted by the students?
- What are the opportunities and challenges inherent to this format in relation to education?
- Are there any successful guidelines for the transmedial migration of stories (in our case from text to Facebook)?

Facebook and *Folkeviser*

Our project joins two very different objects. On one side, we have the social network of Facebook, populated by millions of people who voluntarily share information about their lives in order to connect to others. Facebook has an extraordinary presence in the Danish society (in 2014, 95 percent of the 16- to 89-year-old Danes had a Facebook profile).[1] There have been attempts to incorporate Facebook and other social networks as teaching and learning resources,[2] mostly as a social forum in which to expand the classroom digitally.[3] Other projects have embraced the possibility of using Facebook profiles for cultural dissemination purposes.[4] But to date, no projects exist that use Facebook as a scene to transmedially recreate the universe of a literary work as we have done.

On the other side, we have the Danish *Folkeviser*, a series of ballads of medieval origin (starting in the 1200s) that survived in oral tradition until they were written down (mostly in the 18th century). Their verses tell stories about knights, battles, magical encounters or unhappy love affairs, and were sung as accompaniment to ring-dances (Fibiger and Lütken, 2012: 64–65). Although originally an entertainment product of the nobility, *Folkeviser* grew increasingly to be perceived as popular songs. As such, they are considered repositories of ancient wisdom, crucial to understanding the development of the Danish national character and modern culture.[5] *Folkeviser* are notoriously difficult to teach because of their archaic form and language and their remote worldview.

The goal of our project was to use the familiar social network as a bridge to connect with the unfamiliar old verse. We decided to combine a digital edition of a selected song with a set of activities where 9th grade children (15-year-olds) would produce digital content.

---

1 As published in the annual report on Danish society media use released by Statistics Denmark, the central authority on Danish statistics (Retrieved from http://www.dst.dk/pukora/epub/upload/18686/itbef.pdf, September 1st 2016)

2 Such as in Cape Town (South Africa) (Retrieved from http://www.tandfonline.com/doi/abs/10.1080/02500160903250648, September 1st 2016)

3 For example, see http://www.ednfoundation.org/wp-content/uploads/Facebookguide foreducators.pdf

4 Such as the profile of an 18th century girl that the Danish National Museum made to promote an exhibition: Retrieved from http://www.formidlingsnet.dk/flirt-filosofi-og-facebook, September 1st, 2016

5 As stated in the introduction to *Folkeviser* in the literature canon of the Danish ministry of education: Retrieved from http://pub.uvm.dk/2004/kanon/kap06.html, September 1st, 2016

Fig 1. A Folkevise digital edition

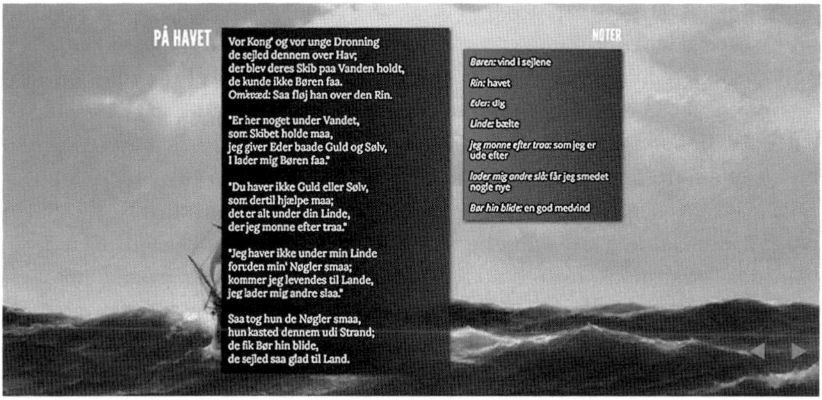

Theoretical Background

Epistemologically, our project is constructivist in nature, as our premise is that children have to be active in order to learn, engaging in what Freire (2007) has described as a process of inquiry, interpretation and creation. Children contextualise new knowledge according to their own experience, particularly when engaged in production of some kind. More specifically, we align ourselves with scholars like David Buckingham and Allan Martin, who have proposed the idea that digital literacy has different levels (Lankshear and Knoebel, 2008), where the lower levels refer to basic operating skills, and the upper levels are about producing and transforming.

We define **social media storytelling**[6] as the targeted use of social media as a storytelling platform where participants interpret a fictive role, here in the context of a teaching resource. In our project, children perform fictional characters within the environment of a social medium, which is usually built around writing statements of what one is thinking/doing, joining groups and events, or sharing pictures, locations, videos and other material. We were inspired by Sarah Schmelling's humorous book *Ophelia Joined the Group Maidens Who Don't Float: Classic Lit Signs on to Facebook (2009)*. Schmelling (transmedially) transforms well-known literary classics into Facebook streams where the story is retold through character

6 We are aware that the term has been used by Bryan Alexander in one of the chapters of his book *The New Digital Storytelling*, but he just considers storytelling through podcasts and video and the user interaction that occurs (2011, pp. 77–90.

statements that behave as real people and use all the social media conventions of sharing material, inviting others to events, etc. The mood is highly parodic, but the transmediation of the stories reveals a deep knowledge of themes, structure and symbolic importance.

It is relevant to note that in this project, storytelling equals fictional storytelling[7] and is not about mediating stories of the true selves of the participants, as in the approach known as "digital storytelling" advocated by Lambert (2006), Lundby (2008) and others. In this respect, it might seem counterintuitive to use social media as a platform, since they are built so that real people share information about their real lives. In fact, Facebook's terms of service state that users must use their real name when creating an account.[8] We decided to transgress this as we wanted to exploit the interaction dynamics our subjects had acquired by using Facebook in their real lives. Could these in any way help to boost their understanding of literary fiction in the spirit of Sarah Schmelling? To minimise the ethical breach, the fictional accounts existed in a closed circle as they were only friends with each other, and we deactivated them after the experiment had ended.

We will now briefly introduce two other concepts that have been at the core of our theoretical framing.

In a learning context, **creative digital production** can be understood as an activity where children are encouraged to produce their own material (text, image, sound, etc.) in response to a problem/question, which is framed in such an open way that it allows for different resolution strategies not given in advance. Creativity is not about reinventing the wheel every time or arguing that these children are geniuses, but rather about giving them a relevant framework to recombine ideas and complex concepts "into a new structure, with its own unity, but showing the influence of both" (Boden, 1990: 130). In this way, it is close to the idea of problem solving in an unconventional manner, as proposed by Maier as long ago as 1931. Thus, productive practices reinforce processes of learning as they get children to make personal syntheses by putting their experience of the world and the context matter of school together in new meaningful combinations.

The last of our defining concepts is that of **transmediality**, an idea that is present in several disciplines: literature, film and media studies, computer games and even economics (see e.g. Jenkins, 2003; Dena, 2009; Bechman Pedersen, 2009; Evans, 2011). Most work on the subject focuses on industry practices or consumption

7 As it does, for example, in the work of Marie Laure Ryan (2004, 2014)

8 Facebook Terms of Service, retrieved March 6th, 2015: https://www.facebook.com/legal/terms

patterns (Jenkins, 2003), and some on the storytelling potential of mixing different media (Jenkins, 2003; Klastrup and Tosca, 2004, 2011, 2014).

In the case of our project, the transmedial perspective is useful because we are transporting a world (the *Folkevise*) from one medium (oral/written) into another (digital/social network). It is not merely a question of adaptation, because adaptation is mostly about transporting content. We are also interested in how each medium renders meaning in different ways. We are "re-coding" the static world of the *Folkevise* into a dynamic source for analysis and social media performance.

Transmedial worlds are about getting audiences involved and encouraging text production beyond the original text. "Most often transmedia narratives include key story information over a variety of platforms, each used for what it does best; multiple entry points into the storyworld; and the opportunity for collective action rather than passive consumption" (Gambarato, 2012: 84). In our project, we are drawing on a transmedial world that is so strong that school children will be motivated to expand it through personal creativity and common roleplay, as supported by the social network of Facebook. Others have tried to apply transmedial storytelling to a learning context (like Pence, 2011; Lacasa, 2010; Wakefield, Mills and Warren., 2013; Wankel and Blessinger, 2013), mostly arguing that it can develop a nuanced understanding of the affordances, strengths and languages of the different media platforms, that is, focusing on metareflection and communication.

Methodology

Our project is a blend of action and design methods that we can call "Design Based Action Research" (Magnussen and Sørensen, 2011). We had a set of theoretical hypotheses that led to the design of a teaching resource to be tested in an intervention, which is typical design research (Wang and Hannafin 2005). We also incorporated the teacher's perspective in various ways: by having a teacher as a part of the design team, and by explicitly working to incorporate the official guidelines from the Danish Ministry of Education pertaining to the teaching of literature at this level.[9] That is, in accordance with the participatory action research perspective, we want to bring about change (Kemmis and McTaggart, 2000: 273) from within the praxis we are studying.

9 Retrieved from http://uvm.dk/Service/Publikationer/Publikationer/Folkeskolen/2009/Faelles-Maal-2009-Dansk/Undervisningsvejledning-for-faget-dansk/Sprog-litteratur-og-kommunikation, March 6th, 2016

The research consisted of four phases: a research and documentation phase, an implementation phase (including prototype design, test and improvement), an intervention phase and an analysis phase.

The **research and documentation phase** involved the team extensively investigating the *Folkeviser* as literary form, as well as locating the different teaching materials that have been developed over the years. These materials were mostly traditional literary "activity packs" where children are introduced to the world of the *Folkeviser*, then presented with some of the central texts with modernised language and then asked to analyse or answer questions about the texts. Some alternative materials exist,[10] but most resources are classically formed: studies of themes, characters and symbols meant mostly as reading aids for children.

In our **implementation phase**, we produced a website[11] to gather all the materials: information about *Folkeviser*, a description of the teaching materials and guidelines to using them, the educational goals of the project, and the annotated edition of the chosen *Folkevise* that would be used in connection with Facebook. This website was mostly conceived as a resource for teachers. In this phase, we did a test run of the learning resource at the IT University of Copenhagen, during which five test subjects tried out the prototype and were interviewed for feedback at the end. As a result of this test, we made some changes to the final design in order to improve the flow of the activities.

Our **intervention phase** was carried out at the school of *Osted fri -og efterskole* on the 3rd of March 2014. The participants were 17 students from ninth grade (15-year-olds) and their teacher. The intervention ran for 80 minutes, during which time the students went through the digital edition of the *Folkevise* and interacted with each other on Facebook. The six roles were played in groups of three students, so we could observe the in-group communication regarding both the meaning of the verses and which action to take on Facebook at each turn. Our role at the intervention was to observe and to take notes. Besides informally talking to the students during the intervention, the following day we also held a 40-minute debrief and evaluation session with the students and the teacher, in which we together discussed the process and the learning that had occurred.

After the completed intervention, we began the **analysis phase,** during which we conducted a design reflection (what worked and what did not in our learning material and the pace of the activities) and an analysis of both the content

---

10 Such as Rather Homemade Productions film om Ebbe Skammelsen, retrieved from https://www.youtube.com/watch?v=-QujVaDO8A0, March 6th, 2016

11 Project's website: http://www.itu.dk/~nita/folkeviser/

produced (all the Facebook pages and their activity) and the process that the students had been through.

Our Learning Resource

Our learning resource is made of several related parts:

- a digital edition of the *Folkevise* Germand Gladensvend
- a set of six characters which are to be played by the students and their Facebook accounts
- a series of eight Facebook tasks for each of the six characters to complete in between reading the passages of the *Folkevise*
- an information package for teachers and students[12]

The *Folkevise*: Germand Gladensvend

This is one of the so-called magical *Folkeviser* that deal with the supernatural. The story of Germand Gladensvend has a classic narrative arch with an introduction to the characters and the conflict, a complication of the plot and a climax, in which the story is resolved and the fate of the characters sealed. We have cut it in eight sequences that are presented to the students one by one. They click on the screen to go from one sequence to the next. In between sequences, they receive prompts to interact in Facebook. Here are the sequences of the story:

Strophe	Plot
1–5:	The King and the Queen are at sea and get in trouble with an evil Gam (a sort of monstrous bird, not unlike a griffin). They are forced to make a deal with it to save their lives: they will give the monster "what lies under the belt" of the Queen (she thinks it is her keys, but the monster knows she is pregnant).
6–8:	The Queen realises that she is pregnant and that the Gam has cheated her. She gives birth to a son who is baptised immediately and called Germand Gladensvend (which means "happy boy" as a sort of protection against evil).
9–12:	Germand grows up in hiding and learns about his fate.
12–16:	The Gam reappears when Germand is a teenager and asks for him, but the Queen denies having had a son.
17–19:	Germand is now 15 and in love with the English princess, whom he wants to marry against the wishes of his family.

12 ibid.

20–24: Germand flies to England (dressed in his mother's magical bird costume), and on his way meets the Gam but convinces him to wait for his due payment until he is back from England. The Gam marks him by drinking half his blood and taking one of his eyes, to be sure he can find him again.

25–29: Germand arrives in England and meets the English maids; but all are afraid of him because of his terrible appearance. Only the princess, Sølverlad, takes care of him. She curses Germand's mother, whom she deems responsible for his travails, but he defends his mother: it is just fate.

30–33: Germand flies back home, but on his way he meets the Gam and with him, his terrible destiny. Sølverlad follows him and kills all the birds she finds on her way (trying to get to the Gam) but fails. She never finds Germand, only his right hand.

The six characters

We created six characters for the students to roleplay:

- The Queen (Ragnhild Mathilde)
- The Gam (also called "the troll")
- Germand Gladensvend (the Danish prince)
- Sølverlad (the English princess)
- A blogger (Bettina Blokker)
- A journalist (Meta Fugl)

Each had a character-sheet with their profile information to log into the Facebook account. The first four characters are the protagonists of the *Folkevise*, and the other two are additional characters with a mission to witness and report in genres well known to the students.

Fig 2. One of the characters

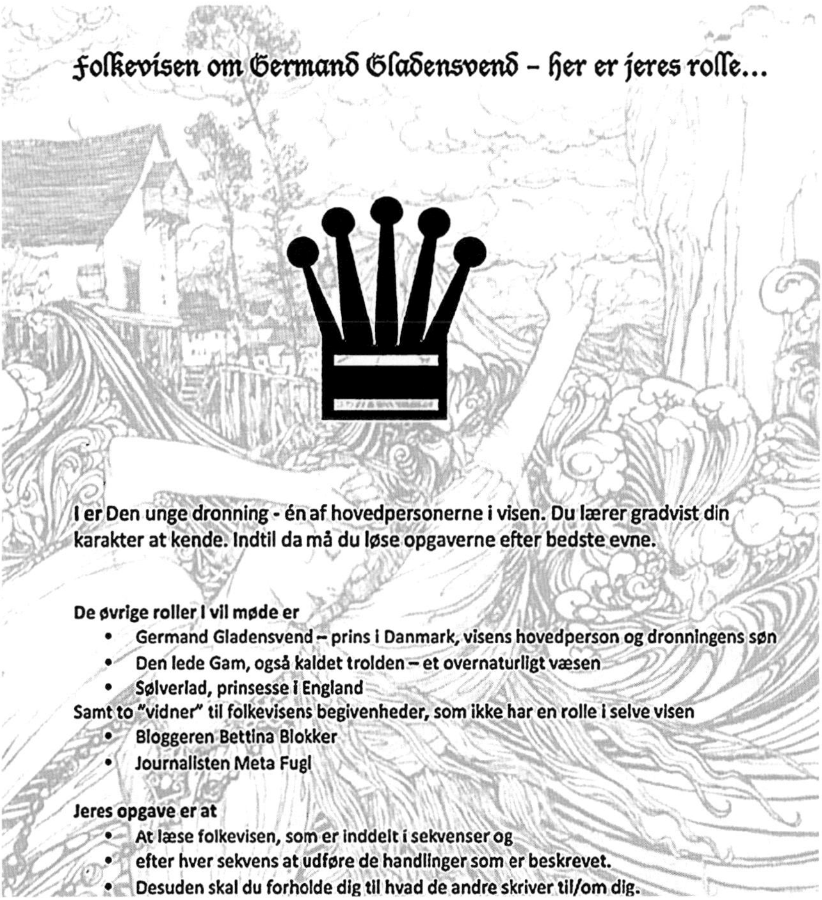

The Facebook tasks

When reading the digital edition of Germand Gladensvend, each of the eight sequences of the story is followed by a prompt specific to each character concerning a task they have to complete on Facebook; that is, there are 48 different tasks (eight for each of the six characters).

The tasks make use of the most common Facebook features, such as setting profile pictures, writing status updates, liking, sending messages and notifications, and creating events. Moreover, each task fulfils a function (F) related to literary analysis and the competences the students have to develop at this level:

F1: make a synthesis of the story
F2: analyse or hypothesise
F3: explain a word or concept
F4: create something new
F5: deepen personal relations

There is no space here to present all 48 tasks in detail, but as an example, these are the Queen's tasks, with an indication as to their literary analysis function, F:

- After 1–5: You are very confused about what has happened on the ship. Write a status update: what are you thinking most deeply? (F5)
- After 6–8: Write on the Gam's wall what you think about him and create a life event on your timeline. (F5)
- After 9–12: Join the Facebook group "Big thinkers" and answer the question. (F2)
- After 12–16: You don't know what to do. Ask for help – maybe someone knows how to fool the Gam. (F5)
- After 17–19: Post five rules of conduct on your son's wall to guide him in his life. (F2)
- After 20–24: You miss your son. Use Bitstrip to make a short comic strip about your situation. (F4)
- After 25–29: You have heard about Sølverlad's accusations. Explain your version of the story! (F5)
- After 30–33: Create a life event on your timeline. (F1)

Fig 3. A task

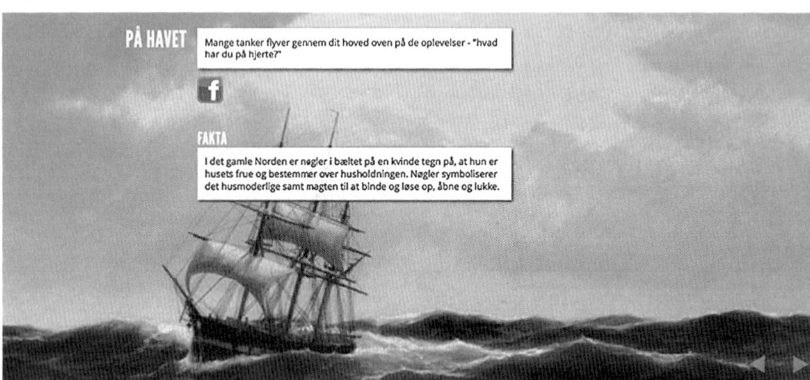

To conclude this section, we want to consider the affordances of a social network as a storytelling platform. Facebook makes our inner life visible (who are our friends and relations, what are we thinking now, what do we like and not like) and our dealings with the world explicit (where are we at what point, doing what and with whom). In this respect, Facebook is a machine to perform and situate the self in relation to a network.

On the other hand, The *Folkeviser* are old texts about a long-lost world we no longer understand. The inner lives of the characters are not described or expressed: we do not know what they think or why they did what they did. We believe that Facebook can be the ideal vehicle for the students to explore that old world, as well as the inner life of the mythical characters. Our learning resource will in this way be based on "creativity and stimulate(s) true reflection and action upon reality" (Freire, 1985: 84), allowing students to negotiate and rebuild the ethos, topos and mythos of the transmedial world of the *Folkeviser*.

Analysis of the Intervention

Our intervention is both product oriented (the reading of the *Folkevise* + Facebook interaction) and process oriented (group work and evaluation), so our analysis uses data from both sources. We begin with a general introduction to the student and teacher activity, technical issues and flow, and then delve into the two transmedial storytelling topics introduced in the previous section: how students engage in world-building activities and expressive and poetic activities.

Unfolding of the intervention

The intervention took place in 80 intense minutes, during which the students interacted with the digital edition of Germand Gladensvend and worked with their characters on Facebook. The 17 students were divided into five groups of three (and one group of two). There was an extremely high level of activity,[13] where 85 percent of the students were constantly at work, talking, writing and laughing about the tasks. On the few occasions when a student did something else (like look at their mobile phones), the others would ask them to focus again. The first strophe and activity took longer, as students had to get used to the form and what was expected of them. All groups worked independently throughout, except for one that needed a lot of help from the teacher. The groups organised themselves spontaneously in a similar way: one person read the verses aloud, one posted on

13 The teacher confirmed that the activity level was much higher than it usually is in literature analysis activities.

Facebook, and the third assisted them. The collaboration flowed easily, with good humour, as in this exchange:

A: "I think you have to write that [...]"
B: "what was that?"
C: "hey, I have another idea [proposes something else]"
B: "is that what we want to say? that is what YOU want to say [writes]"
A: "wait! we'll find an old word for that!"

There was no break for any of the groups, even though their production volumes varied significantly. Some of the groups struggled more to find meaningful answers to the Facebook prompts, while others were quicker and filled the remaining time with extra interactions with the content posted by others in Facebook. In this way, the activity allows for some differentiation in the classroom.

The teacher had participated in modelling the Facebook activities by giving us some educational constraints, mostly related to the importance of students working with the original text and analysing the plot (related to the "F" analysis functions detailed above), but she had not been sure she had understood how the activity would flow. However, as soon as we got started, she was up to date and supported the process very effectively, focusing on comprehension of the *Folkevise* and its characters and pushing the students to think for themselves.

The students had their own computers with them, and there were no technical problems of note. The website with all the materials worked perfectly, and all students knew Facebook well. They even used functions we had not planned for, such as the chat and hashtags, took pictures of themselves or played music from the Middle Ages in the background. In this way, they incorporated elements of their daily media use into the activity in a natural way.

Apart from the online "conversation" in which the fictive characters engaged, the groups also talked to each other aloud in the classroom. They were extremely interested in who played which character and in pointing others to their production: "Hey, check out our profile picture!" "Come on, Germand! Answer our interview!" There was a lot of laughter, some shouting and a relaxed atmosphere.

Fig 4. The class

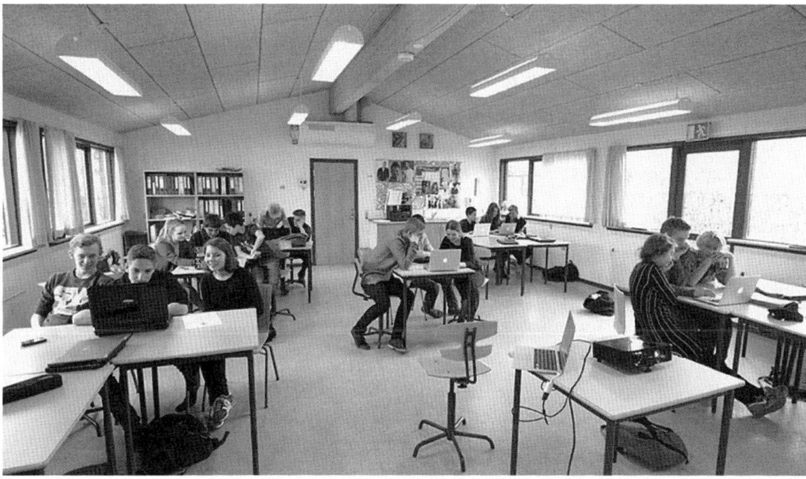

We followed the student Facebook production on-site, as we also had access to their profiles while they were posting. Most groups completed the activities required of them and seemed to understand the text of the *Folkevise* in a satisfactory way. However, we detected a lot of "noise" in between the answers, with students engaging in playful banter, often of a sexual nature. Some of this noise was unproductive from a learning perspective, but on other occasions it proved an interesting way of re-interpreting the content of the *Folkevise*. They relished exaggerating the qualities of the characters, turning them into monstrous or funny figures (a bit like the parodies in Schmelling's book we introduced above), even when completing the activities as required. As an example, here is the answer to the Queen's fifth prompt ("Post five rules of conduct on your son's wall to guide him in his life"), written before Germand leaves her to pursue his happiness in England:

My Dearest Son You shall follow these 5 rules:

1. *You shall go to bed at 7*
2. *You shall treat your beautiful maiden well*
3. *Fly but be careful. Beware the evil Gam*
4. *Never look for danger yourself*
5. *You shall never fuck Sølverlad Rex*

The contrast provided by the crude fifth rule is a kind of playful appropriation that can earn the other students' approval. Humour allows for a duplicity whereby the students are both satisfying the teacher's requirements and distancing themselves from the texts with typical teenage subversion. But actually, even subversion supports creative learning, since this kind of joke adds an extra interpretive layer which requires that the receiver has understood the context of the *Folkevise* in order to find it funny. The fifth line quite aptly condenses the implicit fears of the *Folkevise* mother, even though they have been "translated" into vulgar teenage vernacular.

Engagement in world-building activities

As described above, much of the production activity of the students (and the accompanying discussion) was centred on understanding and expanding the world of the *Folkevise*. This is the predominant student activity in the whole intervention because of the very framing of our learning resource in sequences, which have to be understood before moving on to the next "turn". Three of the five literary analysis functions that informed our shaping of the Facebook prompts were conceived to make the students dig deeper into the world of the *Folkevise* (make a synthesis, analyse/hypothesise, and explain). Here we present some examples of how these functions translated into Facebook actions.

All groups were very engaged in explaining and talking about what they just had read in order to be sure they understood the plot and what was going on:

A: "who talked to the Queen?"
B: "The Gam"
A: "who is the Gam?"
B: "the one who takes her child"

The same kind of explaining/synthesising intention can be traced in many of the posts:

Fig 5. "The other day I walked past the Queen's apartments and I saw a fine diary. I had to read it. This is what it said: The other day I was sailing and we lost the wind. The horrible Gam came and said he wanted my firstborn in exchange for our safe journey to land"

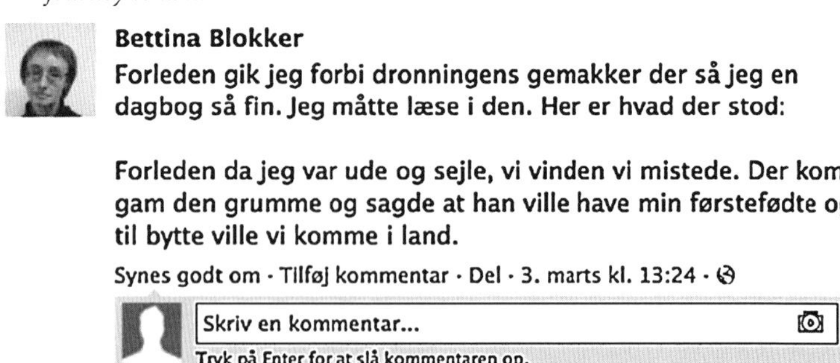

And what is a Gam, indeed? There was a lively exchange about mythical creatures and artefacts (the bird costume, the maiden's bower). Sometimes, the negotiation about meaning leads to humorous interpretations. For example, in the case of the maiden's bower (*jomfrubur* in Danish), the students play with the double meaning of *bur*, which can mean both a room (archaic use) or a cage (modern use)

Fig 6. "We have been informed by a reliable source that the so-called jomfrubur is actually a brothel. Shame on you, Germand Gladensvend"

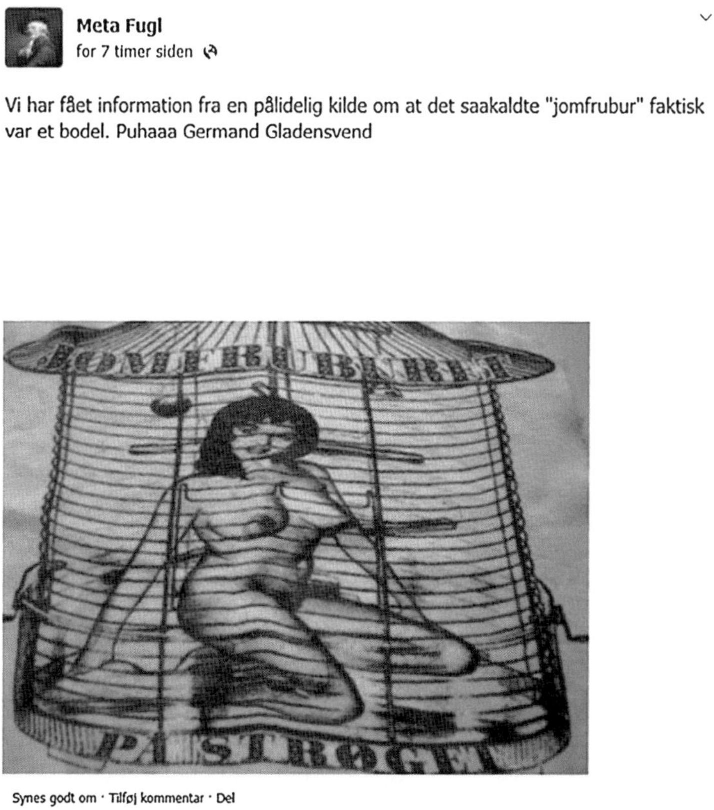

Other examples of fleshing the world out include offering hypotheses as to the different occurrences in the story. The students try to explain how things fit together, not only internally in the story but also, remarkably, in relation to our own world, such as here:

Fig 7. "I think that Ragnhild Mathilde (the Queen) is not at sea. I think this is all about the oppression of women, since men are only interested in 'boobs and noobs'. Here is a quote from the song that proves this 'everything under your belt, is what I am interested in'. This means that the only thing people pay attention to in a woman is her looks, and not what she says #FEMINISM"

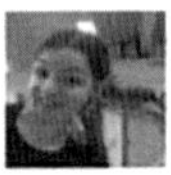

Sølverlad Rex
Jeg tror at Ragnhild Mathilde, ikke er på havet. Jeg tror at det handler om kvindeundertrykkelse, siden de kun ser på boobs – i noobs.
Her er et citat fra sangen der beviser det: det er alt under din Linde,
der jeg monne efter traa. Det betyder altså at det eneste folk ligger mærke til er hvordan kvinden ser ud, og ikke hvad de siger!!! #FEMINISM
Synes godt om · Tilføj kommentar · Del · 3. marts kl. 13:23 ·

Maybe the members of this group are not completely right in their interpretation, but they are nonetheless questioning the female roles in the old story, in which a woman is often defined by her sexual or reproductive status, and her actions are reactive and not proactive, except for Sølverlad's final revenge on the birds. The old world collides with our contemporary world in a way that provokes the students to start a discussion.

Apart from all this interpretive work, the students also engaged in world-building by incorporating images and music, and some even by using archaic language or rhyming their contributions, a creative impulse that is related to the next section.

Engagement in expressive and poetic activities

Two of the five literary analysis functions behind our Facebook prompts were intended to make the students express themselves (create something new, deepen personal relations), extending the transmedial world of the *Folkevise* in new ways. Our prompts specifically wanted the students to work with the inner life of the characters, something that is not explicit in the text of the *Folkevise*, and many posted status updates about how they felt about the different events of the story: "I can't take this anymore", "so sad", "don't let your son fly over the sea, I don't know how you can call yourself a mother and my soon mother in-law". Such utterances took place both on Facebook and in the classroom as the groups kept talking to each other throughout. The expressions of sentiment were somewhat exaggerated (often peppered with profanity), but the students made an effort to adapt them to the situation in the *Folkevise*.

Another way to get other people to talk about their inner life in our contemporary media is to interview them, like here:

Fig 8. "IT'S INTERVIEW TIME BITCH! How come you were baptised so quickly? SP33DY! Do you believe in jebus? Who is the guy in the boat? Aren't you a bit ugly? Who christened you? SwegPriest? Please answer"

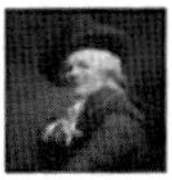

Meta Fugl ▹ Germand Gladensvend
IT'S INTERVIEW TIME BITCH!
Hvordan kan det lige være at du blev døbt så hurtigt? SP33DY!
Tror du på jebus?
Hvem er ham i badet?
Er du ikke lidt grim?
Hvem døbte dig? SwegPræst?
Svar plz

The group performing Germand Gladensvend efficiently answers all the questions with humour and poise. They are at all times conscious of being "the hero" of the story and often remind the others of their status. At one point, the hero expresses defeat, and the group playing the character of the blogger (Bettina) cheer him up with a homemade verse:

Gladensvend lev op til dit navn
selv om din kone ikke er sikkert i havn
Selv om der er moder savn
så kommer din kamp til gavn
Vær du en glad svend og lev i nuet min kære ven

"*Gladensvend live up to your name* ['happy boy'] / *even though your wife is not safe at sea / even though you miss your mother / your fight won't be in vain / be a happy boy and live in the present, my friend*". This is by no means the only instance of students writing in verse, a remarkable feat if we remember that they are allotted only eight minutes per sequence.

The students also find alternative ways of expression tied to the affordances of Facebook. For example, after the Gam has drunk the prince's blood, he adds a life event to his timeline about "becoming a vampire":

Fig 9. Gam's life event

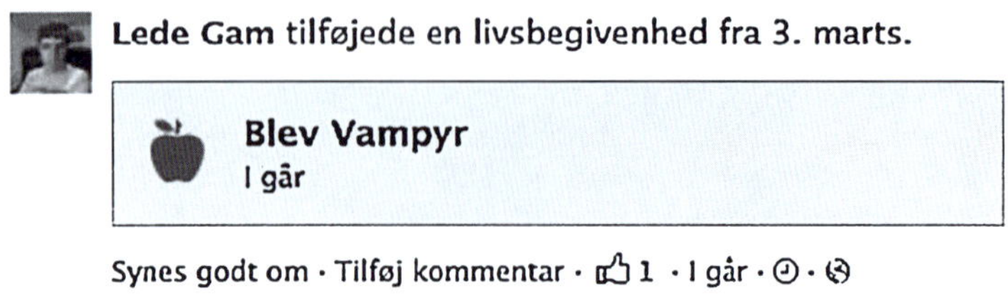

The same kind of humorous exploitation of Facebook features can be found in the following example. After having created a group called "the big thinkers", the journalist Meta creates a poll where all the characters have to answer whether they think that Germand should marry Sølverlad. The result is *javist din kvist*, a humorous way of saying yes.

Fig 10. The poll

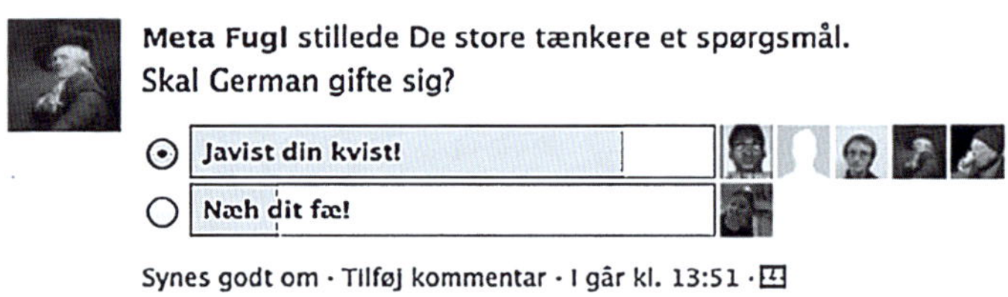

The expressive activity of the participants occurs both at the level of text and that of visual imagery, and on several occasions, the students employ multimodal expression to reinforce a particular message. In the following screenshot, Germand Gladensvend expresses his loss in the following way:

Fig 11. "I lost my eye today. I lost my beloved today. I said farewell to life today"

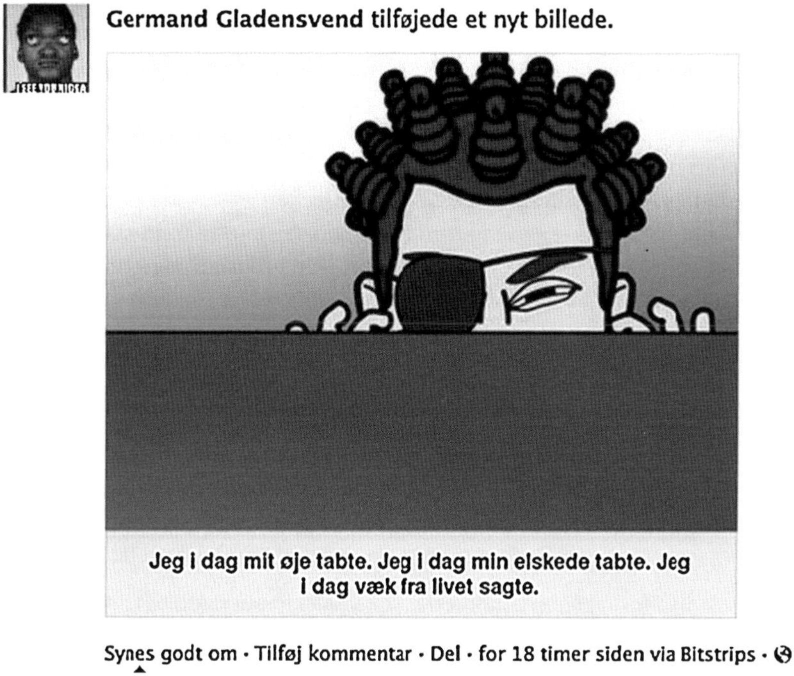

In all, the students act creatively in the form as well as the content of their participation on Facebook. Many of their contributions have sexual undertones, but it is also arguable that sexuality is one of the main topics of the *Folkevise* itself: there is a love story between Germand and Sølverlad, oedipal undercurrents in his relationship with the possessive mother, and a very strong Gam, who intrudes violently into the lives of mortals and takes what he wants (the students often sexualise him as having a big penis).

One group ask themselves as they work: "Is this something we know for sure or something we think?" This is a good question that reflects on the students' own learning process. How much of the way they interpret the old texts is plausible deduction and how much is fabulation? *Folkeviser* are often about transgression and the dangers of changing life state or messing with the unknown. In the classroom we visited, transgression is certainly less dangerous as it is limited to sexually explicit language on Facebook.

Debrief session

The final part of the intervention was the debrief session that we held with the class on the day after the students had worked with Germand Gladensvend. The teacher asked them to summarise the plot of the *Folkevise* in groups and to work with the characters. While one group presented, another group had to ask them a question that made them go deeper into one of their arguments. The discussion was very good, with students engaging in complex hypothesis-making and argumentation. The teacher told us that they are otherwise never so engaged with this kind of activity and that they worked at a higher level than usual.

The groups were confronted with their exaggerated erotic interpretations and had to defend their own playful content production by finding good arguments. For example, a group was accused of over-interpretation after having insinuated on Facebook that Germand and his mother had an incestuous relationship. They defended themselves by going back to the text and finding the passages which demonstrate that Germand has an unhealthy maternal bond and that she is overprotective and does not want him to be free from her influence. All groups displayed a heightened sense of ownership (and pride) over their own productions.

Finally, students and teacher evaluated the whole activity together and were very positive about both the format and the learning that had occurred.

Discussion: Content Versus Process

At the beginning of this paper, we asked how stories are appropriated and re-enacted by students in social storytelling of this kind. We hope that the previous section has clearly shown that students are able to put the *Folkevise* into perspective from their standpoint as 21st century teenagers in a creative way.

We have to note, though, that the content produced on Facebook cannot alone stand as proof of learning and needs to be put in context. Firstly, the process by which the groups agree and produce the content has a learning value in itself, as meanings are decoded, appropriated and acted upon. Secondly, the debrief session on the following day is as important for learning and reflection as the Facebook session itself. The teacher pointed to the Facebook activities that were more productive in relation to the *Folkevise* and gave the groups a way to reflect upon their content production. The common discussion made learning visible by providing a safe space for reflection.

The dichotomy content vs. process also has two dimensions that were more important than we had anticipated. The first was a time dimension, because it took a couple of rounds to create a meaningful world (enough content) on Facebook so that the actions of the characters had weight and motivated further interaction. It is difficult to start on an empty social network, especially because the transmedial world of the *Folkevise* is also unknown at the beginning and only takes shape slowly.

The second is the social dimension, as the students were very attentive to each other's production and opinion, both on Facebook and in the classroom. The social community of the class is a motivating factor, but it can also disturb the process as the personal relationships between the students (and their roles, such as that of the class clown) are carried onto the digital platform. Content was evaluated against a backdrop of existing relationships, which can be expressed more freely than in traditional teaching activities.

Conclusion: Opportunities and Challenges

We dare to conclude that social media storytelling can facilitate the kind of learning advocated by Freire, but that the creative digital productions need to be contextualised before and after the interactive sessions. It is extremely important to evaluate the productions in a debrief session in order to reflect on the learning process.

From a transmedial perspective and in relation to teaching literature, we can say that social media are a good vehicle for:

- expressing the inner life of characters, even if it is done parodically
- filling in details about the fictional world
- relating fiction to the everyday media practices of the students
- acting upon content (both literary and peer produced); not being just a passive receiver

Of course, experimenting with a new form poses some challenges, as Teske and Horstman report in relation to their implementation of transmedia storytelling in an English literature class school setting. The students can resist, putting the learning experience at risk, or get confused by the new genre affordances and their own role, since it goes beyond that of a traditional passive audience (Teske and Horstman, 2012: 7). We believe that this risk can be mitigated by producing comprehensive guidelines and a well-planned process description, so that both teachers and students have the necessary contextual information. The second risk is that of trivialisation, as shown by some of the examples above, where the advantages of social media (the quick response, the "likes" and short abrupt declarations) sometimes produce utterances that twist the original characters into vulgar caricatures. We must admit that the student-produced Facebook texts cannot stand alone, and that the learning process is not completed until the teacher picks up those texts and engages students in a conversation in order to qualify them academically, as was done in the debriefing session after our intervention. It was interesting that subversion happened mostly at the language level (swear words) and that the students did what was asked of them and showed both great understanding of the meaning of the work and ability to synthesise. The teacher's guidance is key to validate the literary value of the controversial utterances, so that a dialogue about "why did you write this in this way?" motivates the students to concentrate on the topic and be more talkative and show more literary involvement than they usually do in a classic text analysis session, according to our teacher.

The biggest challenge to our format are the restrictions imposed by Facebook's terms of service, as we do not wish to encourage illegal use. Facebook does not allow fictional accounts, and this of course includes accounts that, as here, are "played" by a group of people. We argue that the collective roleplaying of one character is important to make students reflect together on their interpretation and synthesis processes. We have considered creating our own platform to support social media storytelling, but then the students would not be able to transfer their use experience in the same productive way we have experienced. This might however be the only way forward, since Facebook does not seem to be keen on opening the door to fictional uses of their platform.

References

Alexander, B. (2011). *The New Digital Storytelling. Creating Narratives with new Media*. Santa Barbara: Praeger.

Bechman Pedersen, A. (2009). *Crossmedia: Innovationsnetværk for traditionelle medieorganisationer.* PhD Thesis. Aarhus University, Denmark.

Boden, M. (1990). *The Creative Mind: Myths and Mechanism*. London: Routledge.

Dena, C. (2009). *Transmedia Practice: Theorising the Practice of Expressing a Fictional World across Distinct Media and Environments.* PhD Thesis. University of Sydney, Australia.

Evans, E. (2011). *Transmedia Television – Audiences, New Media and Daily Life.* New York: Routledge.

Fibiger, J and Lütken, G. (2012). *Litteraturens veje*. Copenhagen: Systime.

Freire, P. (2007). *Pedagogy of the oppressed*. New York: Continuum.

Gambarato, R. R. (2012). How to Analyze Transmedia Narratives? In Joesaar, A. (ed.). *Baltic Film and Media School Screen Studies.* Tallinn: Tallinn University Press.

Jenkins, H. (2003). Transmedia Storytelling. *Technology Review.* (15th January, 2003)

Kemmis, S. and McTaggart, R. (2000). Participatory action research. In Denzin, N. K. and Lincoln, Y. S. (eds.). *Handbook of qualitative research.* London: Sage. (pp. 271–330)

Klastrup, L. and Tosca, S. (2014). A Game of Thrones: Transmedial Worlds, Fandom, and Social Gaming. In Ryan, M. and Thon, J. (eds.). *Storyworlds across Media.* University of Nebraska Press. pp. 295–314

Klastrup, L. and Tosca, S. (2011). When Fans Become Players: LOTRO in a transmedial world. In Krzywinska, T. and Parsler, J. (eds.?). *Ring Bearers: The Lord of the Rings Online as intertextual narrative.* Manchester: Manchester University Press. pp. 46–69

Klastrup, L & Tosca, S. (2004). Transmedial worlds – rethinking cyberworld design. CW '04 *Proceedings International Conference on Cyberworlds 2004.* Tokyo. pp. 409–416.

Lacasa, P. (2010). Children Transmedia and Virtual Experiences Inside and Outside the Classrooms. In Wong *et al.* (eds.). *Proceedings of the 18th International Conference on Computers in Education.* Asia-Pacific Society for Computers in Education, pp. 663–667.

Lambert, J. (2006). *Digital Storytelling: capturing lives, creating community.* Berkeley: Digital Diner Press.

Lankshear, C. and Knoebel, M. (2008). *Digital Literacies: Concepts, Policies and Practices.* New York: Peter Lang.

Lundby, K. (2008). *Digital Storytelling, mediatized stories: self-representations.* New York: Peter Lang.

Magnussen, R. and Sørensen, B. H. (2011). Design-based action research. In Egenfeldt-Nielsen, S., Meyer, B. and Sørensen, B. H. (eds.): *Serious games in education: a global perspective.* Aarhus: Aarhus University Press, pp. 47–58.

Maier, N. R. F. (1931). Reasoning in humans: II. The solution of a problem and its appearance in consciousness. *Journal of Comparative Psychology 12(2):* 181–194.

Pence, H. E. (2011). Teaching with Transmedia. *Journal of Educational Technology Systems* 40(2): 131–140.

Ryan, M. (2004). *Narrative across Media: The Languages of Storytelling.* Lincoln: University of Nebraska Press.

Ryan, M. and Thon, J. (2014). *Storyworlds across Media: Toward a Media-Conscious Narratology.* Lincoln: University of Nebraska Press.

Schmelling, S. (2009). *Ophelia Joined the Group Maidens Who Don't Float: Classic Lit Signs on to Facebook*. New York: Penguin.

Teske, P. and Horstman, T. (2012). "Transmedia in the classroom: breaking the fourth wall". In *Proceeding of the 16th International Academic MindTrek Conference* (MindTrek '12) (pp. 5–9). ACM, New York

Wang, F. and Hannafin, M. J. (2005). Design-based research and technology-enhanced learning environments. *Educational Technology Research and Development 53(4)*, pp. 5–23.

Wakefield, J., Mills, L. and Warren, S. (2013). Learning and Teaching as Communicative Actions: New Ways of Learning – Transmedia. In Herrington, J., Couros, A. and Irvine, V. (eds.). *Proceedings of EdMedia: World Conference on Educational Media and Technology 2013* (pp. 1609–1614). Association for the Advancement of Computing in Education (AACE).

Wankel, C. and Blessinger, P. (eds.). (2013). *Increasing Student Engagement and Retention in e-learning Environments: Web 2.0 and Blended Learning Technologies* (Vol. 6). Emerald Group Publishing.

Index